# WILD WOMEN

# WILD WOMEN

Seekers, Protagonists *and* Goddesses *in* Sacred Indian Poetry

# ARUNDHATHI SUBRAMANIAM

EBURY
PRESS

An imprint of Penguin Random House

EBURY PRESS

USA | Canada | UK | Ireland | Australia
New Zealand | India | South Africa | China | Singapore

Ebury Press is part of the Penguin Random House group of companies
whose addresses can be found at global.penguinrandomhouse.com

Published by Penguin Random House India Pvt. Ltd
4th Floor, Capital Tower 1, MG Road,
Gurugram 122 002, Haryana, India

First published in Ebury Press by Penguin Random House India 2024

ISBN 9780143464907

Typeset in Garamond by MAP Systems, Bengaluru, India
Printed at Replika Press Pvt. Ltd, India

www.penguin.co.in

# Contents

# Preface

**'Can you peel the Nothingness, the Nakedness that covers and veils?'**
[Akka Mahadevi]

I once read of a Zen teacher who delivered a talk about little-known women in the Buddhist tradition. At the end of it, a young woman in the audience was in tears. She wept for a long time afterwards.

Reading the anecdote, I recalled an experience of my own: the rush of something indefinable when I uttered the thirty-three names of Devi at a goddess temple. Something unmistakable occurred that day. There was a surge of power, an exultation. And I know it had to do with the power of naming, of acknowledgement. This was not a moment of ideological victory. It was more of an energetic upsurge—the stirring of something long relegated to the shadows suddenly recovered in a shock of remembrance.

This book probably had its earliest beginnings in that discovery.

There are many reasons to assemble a volume of sacred poetry by and about women in India. But the core motivation for me was the stirring of groundwater that I sensed when those names of the sacred feminine were uttered.

It is possible to read this book as a litany—ragtag perhaps, and far from comprehensive. But a litany nonetheless. An invocation of diverse women. Women mystics and seekers; women who are channelled; women who are worshipped; women who are part of our DNA as friends, fellow-questors, foremothers, reference points, goddesses. A roaring legacy of wild women.

Yet, if there is one thing that poetry reminds us of, it is to beware of conclusions. These poems invite us to the mysteries of identity. They invite us to wear the body—playfully, inventively, consciously. They invite us to revel in the masquerade—the party where everyone knows that masks aren't meant to be taken seriously, that bodies are always worn provisionally and that no mirror is ultimately needed to know oneself. 'This body you're wearing to the party, this body will end as ash,' says Lal Ded. No face, however exquisite, will outlive the party.

The many faces of the Wild Woman—seeker, protagonist, goddess—aren't meant to be frozen. They are identities to be lightly worn, ecstatically discarded. They point us to the truth of our lives—as hyphens between body and spirit, shivering rope bridges between the known and the unknown, mask and ash.

Collectively, the poems add up to one great cry. A cry that is a howl, a dirge, a prayer, a complaint, a love-song and an anthem. And yet, in their own way, which is the guile of poetry, they offer us a wavering manual. A manual on how to walk that windswept path between faith and improvisation, veil and nakedness, identity and erasure.

Welcome to Wild Women—women whose language is (and how could it be otherwise?) poetry.

# Introduction

There was a time when I believed all writing on the spiritual spelt solemnity. That was a long time ago when I believed that spirituality itself was a kind of transcendent turnip-hood.

Much has changed since. I am more aware of the crackling aliveness of inner journeys and, at times, of turnips, too!

I am aware that the spiritual quest is always about *both*—sensuality and sublimity, the body and the beyond, matter and more. The ratios vary. But the journey of the spiritual traveller is always fuelled by appetite—an appetite for a more profound experience of life itself. Not surprisingly, the finest sacred poems bristle with both greed and passion, rage and wonder, grief and joy.

This book started out as an anthology of poems by women mystics of the Indian subcontinent. Then it grew into something more, but that's a story for later. The mystics and seekers still comprise the first and largest section of this book.

These are women who left behind poems about inner journeys. Women who refused to be bullied by the sentinels of culture and faith. Women who surrendered not to external authority but to the diktats of the spirit. Women long sanitized by the grand narratives of religion. Women flattened into vacuous calendar art. Women trivialized by those who view the pursuit of the divine as the resort of the bovine.

In a world riven by the dogmas of religion and rationality, many have fallen through the cracks.

It feels like it is time to tune in again. To hear them 're-fanged'. To hear them in all their brazenness, their heartbreak, their temerity. To honour them with the simple act of attention.

The names Mirabai (or Meerabai, Meera), Akka Mahadevi and Andal are familiar to many. But how do we reconcile the antiseptic stereotype of Meera with the damp abandon of much of her verse? How do we match the much-deified Andal with the feral energy of her lines? Listening to the honeyed renditions of so many devotional songs, I cannot help but wonder how we lost that vital link to the poems themselves—poems that ask why on earth menstrual blood should be considered impure, or that blithely command the gods to wash the devotee's hair or do the dishes!

It is time to reclaim the edge in these voices. To smell the danger again. Not just for their sake but for ours too.

These are poems for all those who seek a less lopsided legacy of spirit. For those who know that exclusionary perspectives are damaging to both perpetrator and recipient. For those who recognize the value of road maps and lanterns in the dark, who know what it is like to lie on cold bathroom floors or to smell the 3 a.m. desolation of the pillow. These poems remind us that we are not alone—in our terrors, our longings, our meltdowns. They remind us that the precarious path of the spirit has been walked in a variety of ways. That the cry for meaning has rent the night skies many times before.

Some of those cries were by women. Women who improvised new trails, sang new songs and built their own bridges across abysses—cultural and spiritual. And by women who remind us of what it means to be human.

The spiritual chronicles of India mention several female wayfarers. Some names are well-known; others are much less so. But we invariably hear of them as docile followers or obsequious servitors. They are seldom invoked as pioneers, spiritual warriors, founding mothers. We do not hear of them as part of a continuum that we can invoke with pride. There is joy in ancestry, a delight in staking one's claim to a shared family story. In that sense, this is also a book about lineage. About a reclamation of a forgotten or somewhat-erased mentorship, of sorority. A tribute to female spiritual bloodlines.

Above all, this book is about poems. It is an invitation to read these women not just for what they say but for *how* they say it.

The best poems do not resort to the language of certitude. Instead, they tell us there is a way to ride a life of uncertainty. But only when we confront it first-hand. The finest poems melt down barriers between the holy and the unholy, the pure and the impure. You don't need to be a believer to hear them or an insider to be moved by them. You don't need to be a poet to smell their authenticity.

I have long been uncomfortable with the assumptions of gender neutrality on spiritual journeys. I have longed to read about women with hungers and hormones. Not about ethereal spirits and anaemic renunciates but *real* women. These poems are about women with both bodies *and* spiritual quests, appetites and deeper aspirations. They don't allow one to cancel the other out.

Translation makes them available to us. While we may long to hear some of them in their source languages—where they were often sung—this book is a celebration of translation rather than an apology for its inadequacies. A translation is a window. A window to poems that might otherwise remain confined within narrow literary bastions. It allows us to look out at new landscapes and inhale the scent of new neighbourhoods. It also allows us to venture further, if we are so inclined, and seek out these poems in their original avatars, where they still live, green and wetly alive.

A poem is a pellet of verbal energy. It is language compressed under conditions of such heat and pressure that its chemistry is altered. It can singe. It can detonate. It can combust.

A poem can offer us respite from too much meaning. In a world that sees noise as news and opinion as identity, this is more necessary than we imagine. When bruised with silence, language pulsates with a life deeper than shiny verbal cleverness. That is the sorcery of poetry.

These poems do not preach; instead, they are an invitation to experience. They offer a deep dive into a longing that lies far beneath our busy daytime consciousness. This is the human voice, charred with emptiness. This is song, riddled with gaps. This is poetry as power—the power of conscious utterance and the raging power of all that must be left unsaid.

*

**'Alone, I crossed the Field of Emptiness.'**
[Lal Ded]

The approach to this book is not encyclopaedic.

It would be impossible to document every woman mystic of the subcontinent. Nor is that the intention. At the same time, the fifty-six women poets featured in this book are diverse. They range from early Buddhist nuns to tantric adepts, from Vaishnava and Shaiva devotees to Sufi and Vedantin explorers of the sacred beyond name and form. They represent multiple languages, social, sectarian and regional contexts, spiritual constitutions, and individual temperaments.

Listening to them together is not to ignore their uniqueness. It is instead a homage to the many facets of the existential quest. A homage to a soundtrack of joy, irreverence and freedom—qualities often doctored or erased by patriarchal narratives and religious orthodoxies to this day.

What do these women have in common?

Primarily, a commitment to exploring those age-old uncertainties around living and dying—the meaning of a life suspended between an unpredictable earth and an inscrutable sky. There are conflicts, of course, between the worlds they inherit and the inner worlds they inhabit. Some of the finest poetry is born of that collision. But that doesn't blind them to the contradictions. Nor does it stop them from asking for more.

These women simply don't settle.

Irrespective of how they choose to live, whether as monastics, mendicants or homemakers, they don't settle for received knowledge. They refuse to spout scriptural piety. They refuse to spout windy metaphysics. They speak—each one of them—of *experience*.

While they draw on the symbols of their cultural traditions, their poetry turns our gaze, time and again, from doctrine to interiority, from scholarship to blazing nowness. Many speak of precisely that moment—the startled 'oh' with which the inheritor turns improviser. Several of the early Buddhist nuns speak of that inner homecoming. 'Like the flame's unbinding/ was the liberation/ of awareness,' says the nun Patachara, whose awakening occurs as she simply pulls up the candlewick in her room.

'Brighter than a million suns it was . . . / All suffering vanished in a glance,' says Dayabai, the eighteenth-century mystic of Delhi. She adds, 'Here, at this mysterious depth/ I find myself entirely at home.' The Tamil poet Avudai Akkal speaks of it too: 'like the full moon, brimming intoxicated/ I emptied into a radiant, infinite sky.' In that moment of ecstatic spillage, their anchorage is not cultural but existential.

We know little about these lives. Poised between folklore and hagiography, these stories are honeycombed with gaps. Most seem to be catapulted into spiritual journeys at an early age. Afterwards, there are frequent periods of ordeal, followed by spiritual initiation. Then comes the poetic efflorescence, although these phases are not linear. Finally, there is the stage of acknowledged sainthood, at which point these lives vanish into fluffy clouds of miracle, often accompanied by extraordinary exits from the body.

If one is hungry for hard facts, these legends can be unsatisfying. Yet, there is a certain poetic justice in the way so many of them dissolve into the embrace of their beloved gods. This is particularly true of those who spurned relationships with mortal men, such as Andal, Akka and Meera. Vanishing into a tempest (Muktabai), being transported by divine elephant trunk to Mount Kailasa (Avvaiyar) or fading into a lingering echo in the Kashmir Valley (Habba Khatun) could also be viewed as denouements with an inherent aesthetic logic.

The life choices of these poets are diverse. The inner journey calls for self-reclamation but not always for the absence of a relationship. Some, like Meera, Akka, Lal Ded and Rupa Bhavani, opt out of marriages and choose to walk the world as solitary mendicants. Others, like the early Buddhist nuns, are committed to being a light unto themselves but are grateful for the sanctuary of a monastic community. Bhadda Kapilani, the nun, tells us that she and her husband made a joint decision to become truth-seekers after several happy years of married life.

Several women poets, however, remain within the familial fold. Sometimes, this entails a painful negotiation with orthodoxy, as Bahinabai tells us. But they are also able, at times, to successfully transform their husbands and families. A hardened bandit abducts the poet Toral but later becomes her ardent devotee and spiritual partner. Gangasati is ready to renounce her body with her husband but realizes the importance of nurturing a spiritual ethos within her family. She stays on to impart counsel to her daughter-in-law. Thirty-three Kannada poets in the Vachana literary tradition married men who were fellow poets and seekers. Gangambike and Neelambike are at the forefront of their mystic–reformer husband's movements to uphold social equality and gender freedom. Still others, like the Vajrayana Buddhist adept

Lakshminkara and the Punjabi courtesan–mystic Peero, fostered deep transformative intimacies outside marriage.

The intention of this book is celebratory but not triumphalist. The aim is not to underplay the social incomprehension and hostility with which several of these poets had to contend. At the same time, these are not poems of bleak victimhood. A spiritual initiation empowers Avudai Akkal, a brahmin widow, to transform her life from pain to auspiciousness. She sings of it again and again. Centuries before her, Avvaiyar and Karaikkal Ammaiyar opted for a radical overhaul of identity. (One chooses to become an old woman, we are told, and another a demonic ghost.) Dalit poets Kalavve and Soyarabai indict the horrors of caste inequality. However, they become interrogators rather than mute sufferers. Punnika, the slave girl, whose voice speaks to us from over twenty-five centuries ago, asks savagely caustic questions of a brahmin that retain their bite even today.

There is pain in several stories. It is a reminder of the camouflage to which unconventional women have resorted in order to survive. But there is also the power of self-transformation. These poems can be trenchant in their critique and moving in their lament. Their dominant spirit, however, is one of jubilation, freedom, self-discovery. That makes them a symbolic triumph over cultural myopia and rigidity.

Ingenuity was essential. The female seeker needed to be something of a spiritual guerrilla to be in the world, and yet, not of it. The women here were clearly canny pirates of the cultural high seas. 'Wisest to play the fool,' says Lal Ded. 'Be discreet, if you get my drift,/ hide it well, hide it deep,' says Gangasati. 'So what if they call you bad, or good? . . . They mistook your body for you/ and reproached you . . .' says Tarigonda Venkamamba.

Lakshminkara, Muktabai and Lal Ded sometimes turn to an elliptical language—*sandhyabhasha*—to speak of what counts in utterances intelligible only to the ears of initiates. 'The zoom ant/ swallowed the sun/ . . . a pregnant fly/ delivered a kite,' says Muktabai. Lakshminkara instructs her disciple in a similar coded twilight language: 'A mouse chases a cat!/ An elephant flees from a crazy donkey! . . . If you're stunned, adept,/ Drop your doubts!'

The innate paradoxes of the mystical experience probably inspired this language of obliquity. However, as these women grew in self-possession, they were also aware of the sense of keeping their radiance under wraps. There were the perils of social hostility and exile. But there were also the subtle jealousies of an unconscious world. Additionally, there were the distractions of unwanted attention that several spiritual travellers have known the wisdom of shunning.

Many speak of male spiritual guides. The early Buddhist nuns speak of the luminous presence of the Buddha. Akka Mahadevi walks the world alone, but her mettle is put to the test by a senior male mystic, Allama Prabhu. Bahinabai receives her initiation from Tukaram, although it is an unusual connection between a brahmin woman and a low-caste guru. From Sahajo to Liral and Avudai Akkal, the verse is suffused with gratitude to male mentors. As Liral says, 'After much effort, I have met my beloved saint./ The earth and sky roll, as he parts the veils of the Self.'

At the same time, several women are aware of being spiritual transformers in their own right. Muktabai seems to have converted an accomplished male yogi, Changdev, which suggests that she was fully capable of offering spiritual initiation herself. Tarigonda Venkamamba refuses to bow before a male religious pontiff and awes an orthodox establishment with her intellectual brilliance and self-assurance. Liral and Gangasati prove to be game-changers not just in their families but in their communities as well. Janabai speaks of her indebtedness to her employer, the poet Namdev, but her work sings of a happily irreverent relationship with her male god, Vitthala. At least in poetry, deity and devotee are equal partners in crime!

Jiradei and Lakshminkara are shadowy figures in the Vajrayana tradition but seem to be advanced tantric practitioners capable of initiating several into the path. In the 1860s, the saint Sri Ramakrishna Paramahansa had a female tantric mentor, Bhairavi Brahmani, who was a formidable expert on sixty-four tantras. Such accounts point to the presence of a number of female adepts who have either remained unknown over the ages or were relegated to footnotes in larger narratives. Information about them is meagre, but their persistent background presence remains heartening.

While their vocabularies are often traditional, these women embody a dazzling spirit of autonomy. Like inspired practitioners of any discipline, they seldom toe sectarian lines and scriptural rule books. Instead, they undercut rigid ideas of obedience in inventive ways. Their poems seem to know that art and spiritual practice are born of that fragile tension between discipline and rebellion.

'I have not bowed, I never will/ The one who listens/ Is resplendent, within me/ That is worship, that's what I do,' avers Rupa Bhavani. Nagalambike rejoices over her discovery of a new, invented family: 'With the guru as my parents,/ the linga as my husband,/ wandering mendicants as my in-laws . . . / I shall follow the dictates of my conscience.'

Meera's poems are steeped in devotion to an absent lover, but such an illicit love also makes her a boldly unconventional wife: 'rana/ I won't live/ within/ your walls/ i've cast/ my veil aside.' Bahina honours the role of the guru but knows that even this figure cannot be used as a crutch: 'Even your friend–philosopher–guide/ will disappear in the invisible.'

An indebtedness towards gods and mentors pervades these songs. And yet, they understand the mysterious dance of surrender and sovereignty that is the life of the spirit. The poet Peero sings: 'The qazi, the brahmin pandit/goad me to read the

Kalma, the Purana./They seek in the written script,/my ferryman Lord/who stands outside/and beyond all this . . . / How will they lead/ who themselves are lost?'

                                      *

**'My lover is casteless,
beyond the binaries of Hindu–Turk,
beyond gender . . .'**
[Peero]

The poets in this book are too diverse to be accommodated within any single philosophical rubric. Their affiliations range from the Buddhist to the Vedantic, the Sufi to the Bhakti, the tantric to the yogic, the Shaiva to the Vaishnava. Temperamentally, some are more contemplative, while others are in more exuberant modes. Some invoke a deity; others speak of an unnamable sacredness.

Two thousand five hundred years ago, Mahaprajapati Gautami, the Buddha's foster mother, tried valiantly to persuade the Buddha to admit women into the clergy. He declined. Only when his closest disciple, the gentle Ananda, pressed the point on three occasions did he agree. The result of that joint perseverance is that remarkable work, the *Therigatha*. The nuns in this text acknowledge their mentor and the support of the female community. But we also hear the giddy euphoria of those who have become architects of their own lives. As Mutta writes, 'So freed! So thoroughly freed am I—/ . . . from mortar, pestle/ and crooked old husband.' Vasitthi, a woman once considered insane, writes: 'Applying myself to the Teacher's words,/ I realized the state of auspicious bliss./All griefs have been cut off,/abandoned . . .'

As they document the bottlenecks and breakthroughs of this inner journey, the later women continue to redefine the figure of the female seeker in a variety of ways. Some are more meditative; some scholarly; some on tantric paths of rapid self-transformation; and still others, like the eighteenth-century courtesan–poets,

Muddupalani and Mah Laqa Bai Chanda, approach the spiritual realm with a distinctly worldly air.

Those who speak of a divinity with a name and form might seem less accessible to some readers. Yet, the finest 'deity' poems do not necessarily endorse a narrow sectarianism. For those on yogic and tantric paths, the deity is a mirror of an unfolding inner journey. For the devotee, on the other hand, the deity is a glorious instrument to dismantle oneself, an invitation to dissolve in love. This is seen as a swifter and far more pleasurable alternative to grim penance or the slow path of incremental self-improvement.

Many combine their spiritual practice with a life of devotion. Several would define their primary path as one of *bhakti*. Indeed, if there is a word that needs to be urgently reclaimed from all manner of jingoism, surely it is bhakti. The time is ripe to rescue the word from secular contempt *and* religious self-righteousness.

True bhakti does not spell allegiance to the status quo. It is not about replacing a secular authority with a sacred one, a despot with a deity. Quite the reverse. The gods and gurus of this poetry aren't humourless dictators. Bhakti is emphatically not sycophancy. It is not trite faith. It is not the absence of a spine. It is not the absence of dissent. Although it may not have overturned social structures in any enduring way, the Bhakti literature of the subcontinent offers us a powerful inheritance of surprises.

The word emerges from the Sanskrit verb *bhaj*, which meant 'to distribute'; later, this connoted 'to partake', 'to enjoy'; and still later, it came to mean 'to adore' or 'to honour'. It came, in short, to mean devotion. There is nothing culturally or historically unique about this. One might argue that human beings have known devotion since the beginning of time. Yet, bhakti—as a scorching subjective experience, viewed as the supreme path to the sacred—had a very distinct moment of origin. While it was invoked by Upanishadic literature and the Gita, it acquired, in the hands of certain regional poet–lovers, a new identity altogether.

xxii          Introduction

Beginning in the southernmost part of India between the sixth and eighth centuries with Tamil hymns to Shiva and Vishnu, this searing heart-centred spirituality rapidly made its way across the subcontinent. It infected seekers everywhere with its cry for meaning, and its refusal to outsource its existential questions to an elite language, caste or clergy. Damp and delirious, these direct addresses to the divine could only be composed in demotic tongues and by those who knew this chronic homesickness first-hand. By the eighteenth century, the entire land experienced something of this appetite for a personal encounter with the sacred.

Whether addressed to a formless divine or a local deity, bhakti was not just devotion. It was a crazy, spirited, at times argumentative, at times erotic, decidedly nonconformist relationship with the sacred.

What many of the women in this book bring to their verse is the interior landscape of the heart as a space of self-transformation. Avvaiyar concludes that the grandest address is where the divine chooses to reside: 'the heart of the devotee'. Lal Ded acknowledges the heart as a locus of alchemy: 'I roasted my heart in passion's fire/ and found Shankara.'

The heart here is the bridge between binaries. It is the transformer, the integrator. It is the still small voice from the core that reminds us we are both—flesh *and* spirit, earth *and* sky. It refuses to sunder freedom from form. It refuses to hack the sensual from the sacred. We are not one or the other, these poems tell us; we are *both*. They confront the reader with the magnificent dual inheritance of being human.

What's more, they tell us that there isn't much difference between the two. Matter is imbued by spirit, form by emptiness, the mundane by the miraculous. Within this brittle body, declares Liral, are 'the moon, the sun, and a million stars . . . / . . . the lock, the key and the locksmith.'

The path of the heart is at times discredited as a soft option. It is seen as a path of neurotic excess and greasy sentimentality. Yet, what we hear in these songs isn't prissy obedience but open-throated longing. 'I've cast my veil aside/ . . . left/my mother's home/ . . . now I dance/ like a madwoman,' cries Meera. Janabai threatens her beloved god in similar terms: 'Bareheaded, I shall walk through the market . . . I have come now to wreck your home.' Toral is unambiguous: 'Bhakti is a dagger's edge.' So is Akka Mahadevi: 'O brothers, why do you talk/ to this woman,/ hair loose,/ face withered,/ body shrunk? . . . / she has lain down/ with the Lord . . . / and has lost caste.' Lal Ded's poem is a warrior cry: 'Chaining him in my heart's dark cellar,/ I stripped off his skin with the whip of Om.'

Such longing is not born of an infantile need for a divine paterfamilias. Nor is it the resort of those who lack the intellect to craft their own destinies. This is the way of the razor's edge. The path of those who have nothing left to protect or prove. This is one of the most courageous journeys back home.

It is also a spell that is needed to counter the other spell—the hypnosis of the everyday world, the pragmatism of mass consciousness. What the heart path offers these poets is the fuel to sustain a journey that appears to go against common wisdom and, indeed, every shred of common sense. This journey of 'falling upward', of 'sailing upstream', is for those who trust that there are no places alien to the heart's geography. Bhakti, says Janabai, is a spell that holds even her god in its thrall.

There were, of course, the inevitable feuds and tensions. Yet, devotion had a way of spilling over doctrinal borders. With their insistence on an unmediated relationship with the divine, the bhakti movements were irrigated by a number of tributaries. In turn, they irrigated them. Many bhakti currents swelled in reaction to the growing influence of the Sharana movements, the orthodoxies of brahminism and Islam, and the rising rigidity of caste. But whenever the experiential overshadowed the ecclesiastical, whenever poetry trumped punditry, whenever the devotee overcame the doorkeeper, we hear the non-exclusionary resonance of the heart path again.

While this book does not seek to offer a token representation of every faith and wisdom tradition, there is no denying that the spirituality of the land was energized by multiple swirling cross-currents. The Buddhist insight of holding emptiness and compassion in dynamic equipoise; the Jaina principle of conscious non-violence; the Tantric insistence on the body as a site of wisdom; the Yogic path of self-transformation; the Advaitin insight that there is no 'other', in the first place; the Sufi love of the divine as a journey of exquisite ego-annihilation; the Christian notion of the personal creator and ideal of selfless service; the Sikh emphasis on an immersive remembrance of the divine name—all these contributed to the riverine heart journey of this subcontinent, in very singular ways. These traditions were enriched, in turn, by the upsurge of the many varied Bhakti movements.

Devotion often seems like an inadequate word to describe this longing without limits. Bhakti was radical because it was not the preserve of experts. Instead, it belonged, as it still does, to a fellowship of vagabonds, lovers, moongazers. Those who have lost their certificates, their citizenship cards—everything but their ragged longing for more. Theirs is not the hauteur of the pundit, but the humanity of the heartbroken.

To the mind accustomed to division, bhakti can be disconcerting. For those who believe that the paths of heart and head, bhakti and *jnana*, are unrelated, these poems remind us that they are anatomically inseparable. There is evidence of a searching intelligence here. There is also much skill and self-assurance. Dayabai speaks of devotion to her guru. But this empowers her to become an acrobat on her life journey: 'Behold her art:/ Watch her leap and fall and leap once again,/ Capering from moment to moment/ Across the vaults of the sky.' Lal Ded speaks of walking the tightrope of consciousness with agility: 'Alone, I crossed the Field of Emptiness,/ . . . I stumbled on my own secret there/ and flowered, a lotus rising from the marsh.'

The inner journey, the poems tell us, puts every part of the self at risk. That includes the ruptured heart, the battle-scarred body and the garrulous mind. There is no way to turn inward, these poems suggest, without being, at some point, gobsmacked and even, at times, terrified.

Dayabai tells us the journey home takes a near-lunatic willingness to place one's head on the block. 'The ancient battle with the enemy within' calls for 'weapons of wisdom', she avers. Lakshminkara would agree: 'Lay your head on a block of butter and chop—/ Break the blade of the axe!' There is indeed no spiritual journey worth its name, they suggest, from which you return with your user name and password intact. You are unmade. You are hacked. And still, you want more.

At the same time, the woman is no meek supplicant. Instead, she is an improviser, sassy enough to make up the rules as she goes along. She is often imperious in her demand for attention from a distracted god. She seeks this god, sometimes invents him, dismantles him, longs for him, rages at him, lusts for him, consumes him or is consumed by him. The possibilities are endless. In several poems, the poet is not content to merely worship but seeks to consume, even *embody*, the divine.

The one 'on Shiva's path', says Rupa Bhavani, 'becomes Shiva Himself.'

\*

**'I eat god'**
[Janabai]

The paradoxes are many. While patriarchy posed its very real provocations, the female role in the inner realms of art and spirituality has also been viewed as a special privilege. In the tantric traditions, the female presence is vital and, as some texts suggest, perhaps the only path to spiritual awakening. Lakshminkara declares: 'One must never disparage women/ of any class/ for each is the Goddess of Knowing/ made manifest in the phenomenal world.'

On the path of devotion, too, the primacy of the female seeker is acknowledged. But the logic is somewhat different. Its fundamental premise is intimacy with the divine. And wherever intimacy, rather than rule and ritual, reigns supreme, women poets seem to have a place of privilege.

Besides, as Bhakti scholar A.K. Ramanujan points out, women seekers were already emblematic of a conscious 'powerlessness'—a spiritual ideal. 'Before God, all men are women,' he writes, 'but no female saint, however, she may defy male-oriented "relational" attitudes, takes on a male persona. It is as if, being already female, she has no need to change anything to turn toward God . . . She is already where she needs to be . . .'

And yet, the women here are powerful alchemists, not mere inheritors of biological femininity.

The most compelling poems are those that turn passivity into receptivity. In the Vaishnava world view, the devotee who seeks union with the divine is, by definition, female. As Meera is said to have sardonically retorted to the scholar Jiva Gosain, who refused to meet her because she was a woman, 'Ah, really, and you are a man? I was not aware that there was a male in Vrindavan other than Krishna!' Scholar Vijaya Ramaswamy writes of a similar trope in the poetry of the Virashaiva spiritual movement of the twelfth century: 'A striking feature . . . is the oft-repeated aphorism, "*Sharane Sati, Linga Pati*", meaning the . . . spiritual aspirant is the eternal bride and Shiva the eternal bridegroom.'

The aspiration here is obviously not biological womanhood but something else. Accessing life's deeper mysteries clearly calls for a very different set of skills from those affirmed by the outer

world. Attunement and alignment are the watchwords here rather
than assertion and attainment. We are drawn into a delicate dance
of vigilance and relaxation, of clarity and mystery, of action and
inaction—something that could perhaps be viewed as the wisdom
of the womb. As one travels into the subterranean realms of the
self, success lies in a dynamic readiness, a vibrant stillness. There
is an ability to hold space rather than invade it. There is also a
willingness to be less oppositional, less suspicious of plurality and
significantly less territorial. The Biblical image of 'the lilies of
the field' and the Taoist image of the 'watercourse way' come to
mind here.

This then could be seen as the way of many of these women—a
view of the sacred as not merely transcendent but deeply immanent,
woven into the very fabric of creation. Self-realization is not grimly
acquired or achieved but rather received with ease and naturalness.
The seeker is not a conqueror but a collaborator with an innately
intelligent life process.

Not surprisingly, a vital ingredient in this poetry is the physical.
The body sweeps into this verse with élan—with all its wisdom,
vulnerability and capacity for daily aggravation and wonder. The
spiritual, we are reminded, lies not just in meditation but in a life
muddied by the mundane. Working, eating, drinking, sleeping and
praying—all these activities, humdrum and holy, are invoked in
the same breath. 'Jana sweeps with a broom/ The Lord loads
up the garbage/carries it in a basket on His head,' says Janabai,
jauntily casual. In these poems, the body is not a barrier but the
very sanctum of the sacred.

And so a new breeze blows into sacred verse, accompanied by
a wider appetite for ambiguity and inspired contradiction. There
is an ability to embrace the soiled and the unsoiled, the domestic
and the divine. It empowers the devotee to articulate a new kind
of love. The prostitute devotee, Sule Sankavva, addresses her
beloved god as Nirlajjeshwara, 'One Without Shame'. This is not

a poem about self-purification in order to become worthy of an immaculate god. It is about seeing the divine as a compassionate fellow-traveller—one who is willing to get grimy and polluted but is no less sublime for that reason.

When the divine is without shame, how can there be room for human guilt? By inviting us to journey into every gritty crevice of the heart, Sule Sankavva and so many others remind us that every demon, and indeed every deity, is simply our own face looking out at ourselves. Devotion, or the power of one-pointed attention, they suggest, can transform the density of pain, rage, fear and doubt into radiant clarity.

When Janabai's timid god comes asking for food, she turns mother and provider. And she is delighted when he 'belches his love all over' her. It is he who attains 'bliss' that day. Her deity is now her powerless infant. She is free to nurture him, feed him, scold him, reform him. At other times, when Janabai tired of her duties as a domestic servant, the roles are reversed. Her god turns mother, briskly bustling around the kitchen, putting away the dishes, even washing her hair. In this love, there is no giver or taker. Both served and servitor are equal partners in the business of living.

There are other poets who also choose to personify the divine as a mother. 'And now/to enslave me/you materialize/as Mother,' says Avvaiyar, the old woman poet, in her address to her deity. Kanhopatra, the sex worker devotee, says likewise: 'Mother Krishna in my innermost core,/ From your unseeing eyes, let mercy flow.' (Perhaps not surprisingly, for a woman surrounded by ravening male figures, trust was possible only when the divine was viewed in a maternal role.) Lal Ded declares that unchecked thoughts can 'grow into monsters', but infuses her counsel with a touch of motherly wisdom: 'take heart, most of the time/ they're like children crying for milk.'

As the poet begins to accept the sacredness of embodiment, she begins to question hierarchy. 'If menstrual blood makes me impure,/ Tell me who was not born of that blood,' demands Soyarabai, the fourteenth-century Dalit poet. Avudai Akkal, the brahmin widow poet, punctures ideas of defilement in verse after verse. In one, she defines menstruation as a celebration of female bonding and spiritual awakening. In another poem about *teettu* (ritual impurity), she writes, 'All scriptures, all castes, all divisions, all stations/And all holy men are teettu:/Do they know this . . .?' About *ecchil* (the idea that one can be polluted by another's saliva by sharing the same container of food or water), she proclaims, 'The first sound is ecchil, the first form is ecchil,/ The four Vedas of the Brahmins are echhil.' This is as joyously indecorous as sacred poetry ever gets!

Interestingly, even when the landscape is domestic, the poems lose none of their edge. It is not a cosy hearth to which the women invite us. It is a place of peril, a smithy of surprises. Something bubbles dangerously in these cauldrons, and it's not just the food!

As the self becomes a site of experimentation, the kitchen turns into a sacred laboratory. The idiom grows menacing, even violent. 'I eat god/I drink god I sleep/on god,' says Jana. 'I pestled my heart in love's mortar,/ roasted it and ate it up,' says Lal Ded. 'Take these husbands who die, decay, and feed them to your kitchen fires,' sings Akka.

When the body's hungers are acknowledged, the fire of sexual desire rises as well. Metaphors of sexual longing and union grow profuse. 'I am in love/ Who cares what happens next?' exults Meera. 'I have Maya for mother-in-law/the world for father-in-law/three brothers-in-law, like tigers . . . / I will/ . . . go cuckold my husband with Hara, my Lord,' declares Akka Mahadevi. 'You entered/filled me/pulled out sharp/ your rapacity/emptied me/eat me into plenitude,' says Andal.

The courtesan poets also bring in a singular note of candour. There is the Buddhist courtesan-turned-nun Amrapali's unflinching view of her naked, ageing body and Muddupalani's lively engagement with the sexual politics of Radha and Krishna's romance. The engagement with the physical is sometimes critical, sometimes voluptuous. Amrapali speaks of its limitations, but Muddupalani speaks of its succulent possibilities. The body is no longer a mere envelope of meat and bone. Instead, it seems to turn into a sacred door, a mysterious gateway to the beyond.

And so, by addressing a new kind of divinity, these poems seem to breathe him into being. When the seeker acknowledges her body, the gods inch closer as well. They grow more empirical, more embodied, more eager to please. No longer lost in doctrinal nicety, they often wear regional names, preferences and personalities. They are no longer impressed by ceremonial wizardry. They aren't seduced by intellectual bicep-flexing. These gods respond to authenticity.

What's more, the relationship is no longer prim or politically correct. This is not a patronizing god who obliges his devotee with the occasional *darshan*. This is a god willing to be besmirched by love. A god who is happy to be viewed as a spouse, lover, mother, child or friend. A god with a lively curiosity about family politics. A god who understands those days when husbands are unreasonable and mothers-in-law vexatious. And so we have Janabai's astonishing conversation with her god: 'god my darling/ do me a favour and kill my mother-in-law./i will feel lonely when she is gone/but you will be a good god won't you/and kill my father-in-law.'

And when the same god obligingly gathers and throws away his devotee's trash, she informs us nonchalantly: 'So much under the spell of bhakti is He/ He now performs the lowliest of tasks.'

After years of communicating through intermediaries, this is a responsive god—whimsical and exasperating at times but deeply lovable. Even the women who praise a formless divine seem to believe that a cry from the heart is all it takes to be heeded. There is nothing remote about this notion of the sacred. It exudes a distinctly 'local scent of infinity'.

A simple logic underlies this approach: devotion bridges a divide that never was.

'And when I found You hiding inside me,/ I ran wild, playing now me, now You,' says Lal Ded, reminding us that the charade of separation can be played by choice rather than ignorance. They call him 'sky-dwelling' and 'earth-dwelling', says Karaikkal Ammaiyar, but she knows better: 'Inside my heart, he dwells./ So say I.'

This is where the many diverse women in this book converge. 'Wherever the lost ones meet,/ a carnival begins,' says Peero. And it is to this carnival that these poets invite us. To sacred intimacy's deepest mystery: an embrace that knows no separation; a love that is neither a dialogue nor a soliloquy.

Where divine possession is, quite simply, freedom.

# A Note on Selections

I embarked on this book five years ago. Some eighteen months into my reading, I believed (in what now seems like a case of staggering naïveté) that I had clinched my table of contents. I had no clue then how utterly unprepared I was for the siege of the coming years.

For a siege is exactly what it was. Suddenly, women started emerging from everywhere. They blinked up, kitten-eyed, from the footnotes of familiar books. They parachuted, uninvited, into conversations. They toppled off forgotten shelves. The elegantly curated list I began with was nothing short of laughable. I had no choice but to start over.

Was the ambush pleasurable? Once I decided to abandon deadlines, yes. I must confess, however, that there were at least three occasions when I contemplated abandoning the project entirely. It seemed too unwieldy, too interminable.

But what of those women—those amazing, infuriatingly ubiquitous women? While I often put this project on the back-burner, I could never bring myself to forsake it. Not entirely.

The omissions were unavoidable. This book was never envisioned as a roster of every seeker who has ever walked the Indian subcontinent or every goddess who has ever graced the sacred imagination. From the start, it set out to be a thali—an explosion of flavours and textures on a single plate—rather than a multi-course meal.

As a lover of poetry, I looked for poems that surprised me—either by a swivel in tone, a startling metaphor or a canny turn of phrase. Poems that sliced through preconceptions and plunged me into strange places. Or poems that came alive as speech acts—pulsating and compelling. On some occasions, I opted for the most familiar poem, a popular favourite. On other occasions, I opted for one that worked best in translation. The poets here served up their share of surprises. They kept me hooked even as the shape of the project lost its initial svelte silhouette.

There were many ways to organize this material. I experimented with several. I worked with tone, then with regional category, then with sectarian affiliation. None of them seemed to fit. I then decided to return to my original impulse: *naming*. The essential impetus behind this project was to invoke the *names* of women. To turn cameos into protagonists. To invite backstage workers into the spotlight. And so, the names of poets and goddesses take precedence over all else.

The first two sections are straightforward lists: the names of poets, accompanied by brief prefatory notes and poems. Here, I allowed both the poets and their poems to guide me. On occasion, I decided to represent a poet with several translations, and on other occasions, when the right poem was difficult to locate, by a single one. The attempt has been to offer readers a *taste* of a poet's work and orientation. The hope is that at least some readers might be inclined to embark on a more immersive reading of their own. The third section is a happily muddled mix of poets and divinities, inviting readers to pay homage, if they are so inclined, to a fascinating pantheon of major and minor goddesses, evoked in diverse literary styles, from the folk to the classical and the modern.

The sequence of poems by each poet in the book does not indicate original order. The poems are drawn from multiple anthologies and sources. Collectively, they aim to offer a seamless and uninterrupted reading experience, and hope to motivate the reader to turn to the bibliography for more reading material on the poets who excite them.

A considerable part of this book comprises new translations. Many of the translators are poets. That is because the literary criterion was vital to this project. Each one approaches the business of translation differently. Some translations are scholarly; others are freer and more intuitive. A few of the translations are by musicians, a few by academics, and still others by spiritual practitioners. This mosaic of differences was integral to the design.

Extensive email exchanges accompanied some of these translations. There were long letters about strategy. And there were longer letters still about the appropriateness of a single word—the kind that delights those who live in the laboratories of language. Did the translators always feel an affinity for these poets' spiritual allegiances? Not necessarily. But they were respectful of differences, and I believe their work navigates contextual gaps with sensitivity and agility.

This book is not merely an anthology of poems but of *sacred* poems, even if the notion of the 'sacred' is variously defined. As an omnivorous reader myself, I am not squeamish about what is often dismissed as 'esoterica'. I did not want my introductions to be sanitized of the insights of legend, or at times, of arcane literature, for I knew that these often point to a truth deeper than historical fact. Since these poets lived lives profoundly wedded to mystery, that mystery is an integral part of this project.

There was much deliberation over choices. But it was when I decided to trust the process that the book took shape with a certain inevitability. At times, I allowed wildcard entries to take over my life. At times, I determinedly closed my file and said, 'No more,' leaving a back door open for someone to gatecrash the party! And at times, I simply allowed the project to simmer and cook in its own juices.

Are all the poets in here truly 'wild'? What of those who seem to abide by doctrinal orthodoxies? What of those who choose camouflage over open rebellion?

All of them, I believe, belong here. Primarily because they never fall silent. Most of them probably doubted, in their darkest moments, if anyone—even the divine—was really listening. And still, their voices add to a chorus that is more—so much more—than the sum of its parts.

British poet Carole Satyamurti writes, 'One quiet woman is much like another./ Two quiet women can take on the world and his brother.'

This much is certain. The women in here can take on the world and his brother.

And then some.

**Arundhathi Subramaniam**
3 July 2023

# PART ONE

*'I Have Not Bowed, I Never Will'*
—Rupa Bhavani

# Mystics, Seekers, Devotees

# Vac

## [Before 1000 BCE]

Happily, among the earliest works of sacred literature of the subcontinent is the song of a woman awakening to the ultimate truth.

Was this song composed by a female mystic? Or is Vac a goddess, a personification of the power of speech? Even as these questions are contested, the poem endures. And it haunts. Perhaps it was authored by a male poet, as some believe. But the fact that it is attributed to a woman who speaks in the first-person singular is significant. The fact that it presents a woman in a blaze of power and glory is even more significant. It is why it marks the beginning of this book.

The 'Devisuktam' can be seen as a song by a goddess revelling in her own magnificence. But it can also be seen as a poem by a very specific female sage named Vac or Vagambhrni (the daughter of the sage, Ambhrna), who is, in fact, clearly mentioned as its author. The Vedas are viewed as eternal wisdom revealed by those in such a state of oneness with the ultimate truth that the 'seer' and the 'seen' could often not be separated. If this is the song of a historically particular woman, she does seem like a somewhat immodest one! And yet, the overriding tone of this poem is not mere self-regard. Here is the joy of one whose experience has exploded from fragmentation into wholeness: 'Beyond the sky, beyond this earth, so great have I become.'

Vac is both a mystic *and* a goddess. She is both a woman *and* the conscious core of the cosmos, that limitless womb from which heaven, earth, god and mortal, indeed the very 'Father on his head', emerge. The result is one of the oldest and grandest paeans to nonduality in the history of the world.

~

I move with the Rudras and the Vasus; I, with the Ādityas
and the AllGods
I bear Mitra and Varuṇa both; I, Indra and Agni; and I,
both the Aśvins

I bear the full-beaten Soma; I, Tvaṣṭr, Pūṣaṇ, and Bhaga
I place wealth for the offerer of oblations, the good
ritualist, the pressing sacrificer

I am the sovereign, the gatherer of treasures, the knower,
the first among those worthy of sacrifice
Me, the gods have placed variously; I have many places;
cause many to enter

By me, he eats food, whoever sees, breathes, hears
what is said
Unthinking, they abide in me; listen, you who will be
listened to, I tell you a thing to be believed

I do say this myself; pleasing to gods and men
Whomever I love, I make mighty; a knower, a seer, a sage

I bend the bow for Rudra; for the arrow to slay
Brahman's foes
For the people, I make war; heaven and earth, I have filled

I birth the Father on his head; my womb, in the waters,
in the sea
From there I spread across the worlds; I brush my brow
on the sky

I, like the wind, blow; enfold all the worlds
Beyond the sky, beyond this earth, so great have I become

*[translated by Kanya Kanchana]*

# Early Buddhist Nuns

## [Sixth to Fourth Century BCE]

The *Therigatha* is a collection of seventy-three poems in which the senior nuns of the early Buddhist period document their journeys to liberation. Candid, rich in personality and human quirkiness, these poems are characterized by an intensely personal tone. The *theris* (nuns) do not erase or sanctify their backstories. Instead, they speak of very real struggles and breakdowns, reminding us that the path to self-reclamation has often been ordinary, unheroic and deeply human.

The text encompasses a spectrum of voices—a heartbroken mother who has lost her children, a former courtesan surveying an ageing body, a housewife liberated from the drudgery of domesticity, a psychologically disturbed woman, among others. These are women who speak as individuals, not as scripturally-doctored stereotypes, and their poems make the gap of 2000 years seem irrelevant.

While the authors of many poems are identified, others remain anonymous. Since the poets are renunciates, they speak of the extinction of desire and sensuality. This is in interesting contrast to the later Buddhist women mystics in the Vajrayana tradition, whose work is more celebratory of the body. However, the thrum of freedom pulses through these poems and the euphoria is unmistakable.

The poems were orally transmitted in Magadhi for a few centuries before being compiled in Pali in the first century BCE. Collectively, they constitute the earliest anthology of women's poetry. This is also the earliest known anthology of female spiritual experience in the world.

## Anonymous

The nun in this poem is unnamed. What is striking is its verbal frugality
and freshness of metaphor. The nun's robe is self-made. All borrowed
feathers have been cast off. Passions can no longer be kindled by external
sources. In this hard-earned state of composure, the nun subsides into a
deep state of slumber. The relief and sense of homecoming are palpable.

~

Sleep, little theri, sleep comfortably,
wrapped in the robe that you've made,
for your passion is stilled —
           like a pot of pickled greens
              boiled dry.

*[translated by Thanissaro Bhikkhu]*


## Punnika

Punnika was a slave girl from Shravasti whose life was spent carrying out
domestic chores. One day, while fetching water, she heard a sermon by
the Buddha. He spoke of how a true disciple's words could be likened
to 'the roar of a lion', fearless and incisive. Such words could confidently
refute false doctrine whenever it was encountered, he said. This had a
deep impact on the young woman.

One morning, she went out to collect water when she encountered
a Brahmin performing his ablutions and ritually purifying himself
with water. Reminded of the Buddha's 'lion's roar', she was seized by
a new boldness and asked the Brahmin some razor-sharp questions
about purity, impurity and the meaning of karma (kamma in Pali).
This seems to have chastened and transformed the man. Later, freed
by her master, who was also impressed by her newfound clarity and
confidence, Punnika went to the Buddha and asked to be ordained.
Her story is a reminder of the way in which the emancipatory potential
of the Dharma (Dhamma, in Pali), that spiritual teaching of radical

equality, could galvanize the humblest sections of society. The robust
rationality of her questions and her spirit of self-determination are
striking. In this verse, we see Punnika, the slave, turn lion-woman.

~

[Punnika:]

I'm a water-carrier, cold,
always going down to the water
from fear of my mistresses' beatings,
harassed by their anger and words.
But you, Brahman,
          what do you fear
that you're always going down to the water
with shivering limbs, feeling great cold?

[The Brahman:]

Punnika, surely you know.
You're asking one doing skillful kamma
and warding off evil.
Whoever, young or old, does evil kamma
is, through water ablution,
from evil kamma set free.

[Punnika:]

Who taught you this
— the ignorant to the ignorant —
'One, through water ablution,
is from evil kamma set free?'
In that case, they'd all go to heaven:
          all the frogs, turtles,
          serpents, crocodiles,
          and anything else that lives in the water.

Sheep-butchers, pork-butchers,
fishermen, trappers,
thieves, executioners,
and any other evil doers,
would, through water ablution,
be from evil kamma set free.

If these rivers could carry off
the evil kamma you've done in the past,
they'd carry off your merit as well,
and then you'd be
      completely left out.
Whatever it is that you fear,
that you're always going down to the water,
      don't do it.
Don't let the cold hurt your skin.

[The Brahman:]

I've been following the miserable path, good lady,
and now you've brought me
      back to the noble . . .

*[translated by Thanissaro Bhikkhu]*

## Mutta

Mutta was born in Kosala into a poor family. She married when she came of age, but the domestic life held no attractions for her. New winds of freedom were blowing through the land; the power and promise of the Buddha's teachings were in the air. Mutta knew she could no longer live the married life. She persuaded her husband to consent to her renunciation. She left her home and was ordained as a nun. After a life of meditation, she was enlightened. This verse reveals the elation of a woman unshackled from domesticity and the compulsions of *samsara*.

~

So freed! So thoroughly freed am I!—
from three crooked things set free:
    from mortar, pestle,
    and crooked old husband.
Having uprooted the craving
that leads to becoming,
I'm set free from aging and death.

*[translated by Thanissaro Bhikkhu]*

## Ubbiri

Ubbiri lived in Shravasti and belonged to an affluent household. Her beauty drew the attention of the king of Kosala, and the two subsequently married. A few years later, she gave birth to a young girl, whom she named Jiva. The parents were overjoyed. However, soon after this, the little girl died, and Ubbiri could not recover from the loss. Inconsolable, she wandered around the cremation grounds.

Hearing of the new spiritual teacher in town, she paid homage to the Buddha. But her heart remained heavy. As she stood forlorn by the river Achiravati, the Buddha is said to have appeared to her in his subtle body and asked her why she wept. Ubbiri replied that she could not recover from the loss of her daughter. The Buddha said, 'Burnt in this cemetery are some 84,000 of your daughters. For which of these do you weep?'

The question pierced Ubbiri's heart. It helped pluck out 'the dart of sorrow' that had been embedded since her bereavement. 'It was hard to see while it was stuck in my heart,' she says. Now, she began to 'see' again. And so, a spiritual journey began. After years of meditation and immersion in the Dharma, Ubbiri was self-realized.

~

*[Ubbiri recalls the Buddha's words:]*

"Jīva, my daughter",
you cry in the woods.
Come to your senses, Ubbiri.
     Eighty-four thousand,
     all named Jīva
have been burned in that charnel ground.
For which of them do you grieve?'

Pulling out
     —completely out—
the arrow so hard to see,
embedded in my heart,
he expelled from me
     —overcome with grief—
the grief
over my daughter.

Today—with arrow removed,
     without hunger, entirely
     unbound—
to the Buddha, Dhamma, and Saṅgha I go,
     for refuge to
     the Sage.

*[translated by Thanissaro Bhikkhu]*

## Bhadda Kapilani

A leading disciple of Gautama Buddha, Bhadda Kapilani was the
wife of yet another major disciple, Mahakassapa. He became, in fact,
the leader of the Buddhist Order after the Buddha's time. Born into

a wealthy family, the young woman was reluctant to marry since her inclinations were ascetic from an early age. However, her marriage was arranged against her wishes. Fortunately, her husband shared the same inclinations. They lived happily for many years.

But after the death of his parents, they were entrusted with the management of his family estate. They now grew aware of the violence and discontent built into the householder–landowner life. They consulted each other and arrived at the same decision. They shaved each other's heads, donned yellow robes, released their servants and left home. Not wanting to be seen any longer in their social roles as a couple, they decided to part ways. Bhadda took the road to the right, which led to Shravasti. Here she encountered the Buddha at the Jetavana monastery. Five years later, when the community of nuns was established, she was ordained and had a profound spiritual awakening soon afterwards. The Buddha acknowledged that her ability to remember past lives was exceptional.

This poem is fascinating for several reasons. First, for those who interpret the spiritual path as the resort of losers, this is important testimony: here is a woman who opted for the spiritual path after a reasonably happy life rather than as a result of unfortunate circumstance. Second, it indicates that the decision to go forth into mendicancy was a joint decision made by two mature consenting adults. We are offered a new template of spouses as equal spiritual partners. Also, when she speaks of the 'true Brahmin', Bhadda is drawing attention to caste status as a matter of achievement, not ascription—an important distinction to which the path of the Buddha invited its adherents. Finally, when Bhadda speaks of her husband's spiritual accomplishments in the first two verses, it is not merely out of spousal pride but with a view to establishing her own spiritual credentials. If Mahakassapa was a great adept, she seems to say (in a declaration akin to Punnika's lion roar), so too am I.

~

He is the Buddha's son and heir—
    Kassapa of the tranquil, collected mind,
who recalls his previous lifetimes,
    who has pierced the mysteries of heaven and hell.

All rebirths annihilated,
    master of the highest knowledge,
he has attained the threefold wisdom,
    and this makes him a true Brahmin.

In the same way, Bhadda Kapilani has mastered
    the threefold wisdom and vanquished death.
Wearing this body as her last apparel,
    she has vanquished Mara and his host.

Having seen the world's dangers firsthand,
    we went forth as truth-seekers,
and now taintless, quenched, passions cooled,
    we are free, we are free.

*[based on renditions by Caroline Rhys-Davids, by Hellmuth Hecker and Sister Khema]*

## Patachara

Like Ubbiri, the life of Patachara, one of the leading nuns in the early Buddhist monastic order, represents a journey from profound loss to self-retrieval. Her story is one of the most memorable in the Pali canon.

Born to doting parents in a wealthy merchant family in Shravasti, Patachara was considered the most beautiful girl in town. The young woman flouted convention by falling in love with a domestic servant. The two eloped and lived happily in a remote forest hamlet. However, in a devastating turn of events, on a return journey to her parents' home, she lost her husband to a snakebite. A storm broke out, and the grief-stricken single mother lost both her children as well: one was snatched away by a hawk, and the second was swept away by a river current. Shattered by these losses, Patachara made her way to her parents' home only to find that her childhood house had collapsed during the storm and all its inhabitants had been killed. Overnight, Patachara had lost her husband, children, parents and brother. Destitute, naked and half-crazed with grief, she wandered the countryside. She was ostracized and reviled as mad until she stumbled into an assembly at the Jetavana monastery one day.

A luminous being stood before her. He regarded her with a glance she was never to forget and said simply, 'Regain your mindfulness, sister.' Patachara came to her senses instantly and sat down before the Buddha. 'Not in children is there refuge, not in father or in kin; for one attacked by the End-Maker, there is no refuge in relatives. One who understands this quickly turns to the path to nirvana,' said the Enlightened One. As he concluded these lines, Patachara became what the Buddhist literature calls a 'stream entrant'. Later, Patachara became one of the most respected figures in the monastic order. She was known to be diligent in enforcing monastic discipline—another interesting paradox, given her earlier life of psychological disorder.

This verse is a reminder of just how undramatic a spiritual awakening can be. There is no momentous revelation. Just observing the way water flows as she washes her feet is enough for Patachara. She enters her cell, pulls up the wick of her lamp and relaxes into a state of grace. Gently, without fuss, like so many before and after her, Patachara is free.

~

[*I thought:*]
'Plowing the field with plows,
sowing the ground with seed,
supporting their wives and children,
young men gather up wealth.

So why is it that I,
        consummate in virtue,
        a doer of the teacher's bidding,
don't gain unbinding?
I'm not lazy or proud.'
Washing my feet, I noticed
        the
        water.

And in watching it flow from high
            to
            low,
    my heart was composed
    like a fine thoroughbred steed.

Then taking a lamp, I entered the hut,
        checked the bedding,
        sat down on the bed.

And taking a pin, I pulled out the wick:
    Like the flame's unbinding
    was the liberation
        of awareness.

*[translated by Thanissaro Bhikkhu]*


## Vasitthi

Vasitthi was a well-born woman in the city of Vaishali (in the modern-day state of Bihar) and married a man from a distinguished family. The two lived happily. However, she lost her son at an early age. Heartbroken, she wandered the streets until she came to Mithila. There she saw the Buddha walking down the street, a figure of startling equanimity. Like Patachara, she regained her senses and asked to be ordained. The Buddha instructed a senior nun to ordain and admit her into the order. After years of contemplation, she was self-realized.

~

Overwhelmed with grief for my son—
        naked, demented,
        my hair dishevelled
        my mind deranged—
    I went about here and there,
    living along the side of the road,

in cemeteries and heaps of trash,
        for three full years,
afflicted with hunger and thirst.

Then I saw
the One Well-Gone,
gone to the city of Mithilā:
        tamer of those untamed,
        Self-Awakened,
        with nothing to fear
        from anything, anywhere.

Regaining my mind,
paying him homage,
    I sat myself down.
He, Gautama, from sympathy
taught me the Dhamma.
Hearing his Dhamma,
I went forth into homelessness.
Applying myself to the Teacher's words,
I realized the state of auspicious bliss.

All griefs have been cut off,
        abandoned,
            brought to this end,
for I've comprehended
the grounds from which griefs
come into play.

*[translated by Thanissaro Bhikkhu]*

## Ambapali

The tale of Amrapali (Ambapali in Pali), the beautiful courtesan of
Vaishali, represents what has often been seen as a classic narrative

from sexuality to samadhi, from the epicurean life to the existential quest. Discovered at the foot of a mango tree in a royal garden as an infant, Amrapali grew into a woman so lovely and accomplished that many princes and noblemen vied for her affections. A series of life events turned Amrapali into a court dancer and courtesan. Her talents and beauty drew many to Vaishali and she became a wealthy and powerful woman. According to some accounts, the king of the hostile neighbouring kingdom of Magadha, Bimbisara, fell in love with her, and the two had a son named Vimala Kondanna.

She encountered the Buddha later in her eventful life and was moved by his teachings. The Buddha himself spent time in her mango grove and accepted her invitation to dine with him (suggesting his own non-judgmental attitude towards the socially stigmatized). He gratefully accepted her generous offer of her entire property, including her gardens, which became the site of a monastery and the venue of several important sermons. Soon after this, Amrapali relinquished her position as courtesan and became an active champion of the Buddhist order, dedicating her life to the service of the destitute. Her son grew up and turned to monkhood. It is said that when she once heard her own son preach, she decided to be ordained as well.

In this extraordinary poem on ageing, the nun surveys the ruins of her own body and acknowledges the truth of her master's gospel of impermanence. The poem can be read both as a cautionary tale about youthful feminine vanity *and* as a supremely elegant 'boast' by a woman who has clearly enjoyed a lifetime of sensual plenitude! (Perhaps a life of abundance, consciously enjoyed, often makes for a genuinely happy renunciation in later years?)

The sophisticated poetics of the work point to Amrapali's cultural refinement. As it recounts a journey from youth to decrepitude, starting from the head and journeying anatomically south, it is so vivid that it becomes an invitation to perceive a deeper beauty. The female body is regarded with a mix of dispassion and awe. How did the proud citadel of the body turn into this crumbling house, this home of 'many pains'? There is regret, but also a note of wonder at the beauty and fragility of the life journey.

~

Black was my hair
—the colour of bees—
and curled at the tips;
    with age, it looked like coarse hemp.
The Truth-speaker's word
        doesn't change.
Fragrant, like a perfumed basket
filled with flowers: my coiffure.
    With age it smelled musty,
    like animal fur.
The Truth-speaker's word
        doesn't change.

Thick and lush, like a well-tended grove,
made splendid, the tips elaborate
with comb and pin.
    With age, it grew thin
    and bald here and there.
The Truth-speaker's word
        doesn't change.

Adorned with gold and delicate pins,
it was splendid, ornamented with braids.
    Now, with age,
    that head has gone bald.
The Truth-speaker's word
        doesn't change.

Curved, as if well-drawn by an artist,
my brows were once splendid.
    With age, they droop down in folds.

The Truth-speaker's word
     doesn't change.

Radiant, brilliant like jewels,
my eyes: elongated, black—deep black.
    With age, they're no longer splendid.
The Truth-speaker's word
     doesn't change.

Like a delicate peak, my nose
was splendid in the prime of my youth.
    With age, it's like a long pepper.
The Truth-speaker's word
     doesn't change.

Like bracelets—well-fashioned, well-finished—
my ears were once splendid.
    With age, they droop down in folds.
The Truth-speaker's word
     doesn't change.

Like plantain buds in their colour,
my teeth were once splendid.
    With age, they're broken and yellowed.
The Truth-speaker's word
     doesn't change.

Like that of a cuckoo in the dense jungle,
flitting through deep forest thickets:
sweet was the tone of my voice.
    With age, it cracks here and there.
The Truth-speaker's word
     doesn't change.

Smooth—like a conch shell well-polished—
my neck was once splendid.
    With age, it's broken down, bent.
The Truth-speaker's word
        doesn't change.

Like rounded door-bars—both of them—
my arms were once splendid.
    With age, they're like dried up pāṭalī trees.
The Truth-speaker's word
        doesn't change.

Adorned with gold and delicate rings,
my hands were once splendid.
    With age, they're like onions and tubers.
The Truth-speaker's word
        doesn't change.

Swelling, round, firm, and high,
both my breasts were once splendid.
    In the drought of old age, they dangle
    like empty old water bags.
The Truth-speaker's word
        doesn't change.

Like a sheet of gold, well-burnished,
my body was splendid.
    Now it's covered with very fine wrinkles.
The Truth-speaker's word
        doesn't change.

Smooth in their lines, like an elephant's trunk,
both my thighs were once splendid.
    With age, they're like knotted bamboo.

The Truth-speaker's word
      doesn't change.

Adorned with gold and delicate anklets,
my calves were once splendid.
      With age, they're like sesame sticks.
The Truth-speaker's word
      doesn't change.

As if they were stuffed with soft cotton,
both my feet were once splendid.
      With age, they're shriveled and cracked.
The Truth-speaker's word
      doesn't change.

Such was this physical heap,
now: decrepit, the home of pains, many pains.
      A house with its plaster all fallen off.
The Truth-speaker's word
      doesn't change.

*[translated by Thanissaro Bhikkhu]*

# Karaikkal Ammaiyar

## [Sixth Century CE]

An unforgettable figure, Karaikkal Ammaiyar endures in the image of the ecstatically ghoulish 'upside-down' woman poet—one that has prompted many seekers to wonder if their ostensibly civilized lives are truly right-side up! She is one of three women amongst the sixty-three celebrated devotees of Shiva (the Nayanmar) in Tamil literature, and the only poet amongst the three.

She was born into a wealthy merchant family in Karaikkal, a maritime city in south India. Named Punitavati at birth, she developed a deep devotion for Shiva at an early age. When it was time for her to be married, her alliance was arranged with an affluent trader named Paramadattan.

Legend has it that one day Paramadattan sent home two mangoes and asked for them to be served to him at mealtime. Before he returned from work, a mendicant came to Punitavati's door and asked for alms. She had nothing to offer him but one of the mangoes. At midday, when Paramadattan returned for lunch, his wife served him the other mango. He relished it and asked for the other. Distressed, Punitavati prayed for help. Shiva seemed to respond to her prayer, for a mango miraculously fell into her open hand. She served it to her husband. It was so succulent that the husband grew suspicious. He asked where it was from. Punitavati told him the truth. Incredulous and scornful, Paramadattan challenged her to produce another. She prayed, and yet another mango fell into her open palm. As soon as she handed it to her husband, however, it vanished.

Paramadattan was converted in an instant from disbelief to awe. However, such a wife could clearly never be an equal, much less a subordinate. Paramadattan claimed he had to leave for urgent work and hastily moved out of their household. In time, he married another (presumably less intimidating) woman. It was clearly easier to propitiate Punitavati as a goddess than live with her as a spouse.

Branded 'divine', Punitavati decided she had had enough of familial life. She prayed to Shiva to grant her a different form, to stave off the unwanted attention of other men, and perhaps more in keeping with the self she had kept under wraps. He complied. The anxious-to-please wife now turned into a wild figure—fiery, skeletal, wraith-like. She became Karaikkal Ammaiyar—the revered woman of Karaikkal, an outlaw questor embraced by an outlaw divinity.

When Shiva asked her to visit him in his remote mountain fastness, Mount Kailash, she undertook the pilgrimage, walking all the way on her hands rather than her feet! When he bade her visit him yet again at a temple at Thiruvalangadu, she did so once more on her hands, and what's more, composed poems along the way. In her incandescent work that extols devotion as the key to liberation, Ammaiyar describes herself as a demon companion to Shiva. There are no decorative traces of bridal mysticism here whatsoever.

The upside-down ghostly form of Karaikkal Ammaiyar is an abiding image. It embodies the many paradoxes and inversions of the spiritual journey. It also indicts the tensions in the life of the female sacred traveller, nudging us to think (despite changing gender roles) of the pervasive dogmas around female youth, beauty and achievement even today. What is 'deviant'? What is 'normal'? And which of the two is freer?

The questions linger on.

~

Breasts withered,
veins bulging,
sunken eyes, white teeth,
hollow belly, hair reddened,
two teeth extending;
with high shins and bony ankles:
a female ghoul stays

     howling,
in this dry wilderness.

Matted locks
swinging in all eight directions,
his limbs cool, dancing in the fire,
     our father,
his place this is: holy Alangkatu.

*

After having taken birth and practised language,
then everything was love, and
I came close to your beautiful red feet.

Lord of the Sky-dwellers,
    with the throat that glistens,
    as if suffused with ink-black,
when indeed, will you end
my suffering?

*

Then too,
without seeing the sacred form,
I became subjected.

Now also,
I do not see the sacred form.

*At all times,
of what form is he, your Lord?*
—to those who ask thus,
what shall I say?

What is it like—your form?

*

Is it out of longing
or
because you don't have
any other dwelling

that you don't part from the
Daughter of the Mountain,
you, with the beautiful,
cloud-like bull?

Or is it
because she fears parting
from you, and being
separate?

You tell us.

                              *


*Sky-dwelling, he is*, there are those who say.
                    Let them.
*Earth-dwelling, he is, the King of Gods,*
that too, they say.
                    Let them.
In-dwelling in knowledge,
in whose throat, from before, poison's
dark lustre spreads,

inside my heart, he dwells.

So say I.

                              *


It is I
who has penance.

It is I
whose heart is a good heart.

It is I
who has contemplated
cutting off the bonds of birth.

It is I who has—

to that Lord with the eye in his forehead,
ash-covered, and
draped in the skin of a tusker—

become a servant.

                                    *

One thing alone,
        I dwelt on.

One thing alone,
                I steadfastly determined.

One thing alone,
                I shut in my heart's interior.

One thing alone—
(see!)
        the Ganga-bearing, crescent-wearing,
        shining-haired one,
        in whose beautiful hand,
        is leaping flame

—to him,
        to become servanted.

*[translated by Kala Krishnan]*

# Vidya

## [Seventh to Ninth Century CE]

While the poet Jayadeva is credited with bringing the Radha-Krishna theme to its magnificent fruition in the twelfth century, what remains relatively unknown is that a woman poet ushered Radha into Sanskrit verse some centuries before that. That woman was Vidya or Vijja.

A fourteenth-century anthology, Sharngadhara's *Paddhati*, describes her as one of four major women poets: 'Shilabhattarika, Vijja, Marula and Morika are poetesses of renown with great poetic genius and erudition. Those who have command over all branches of learning, having participated in dialogues with other scholars and having defeated them in debates, are regarded as sound scholars and experts.'

Little is known about Vidya, although it is believed she was from the southern state of Karnataka. Eloquent, aurally rich and finely-crafted, her poems centred on themes of love, sensuality, beauty, nature and the seasons. In her poem about Radha, she infuses the trope of sacred love with her own reflections on ageing and mortality. What becomes of those blue flowers on which Krishna and Radha made love? Do they wither, or remain as alive as the evergreen romance of the world's greatest lovers in the poetic imagination?

While not much is known about her, it is clear is that Vidya was a woman of remarkable self-assurance. Her declaration that the goddess of learning, Saraswati, could only described as fair-skinned by someone unacquainted with Vidya's own dark complexion and

talents, suggests that she possessed both brilliance and chutzpah in
no small measure.

~

And what of those
arbours of vines
that grow where the river
drops away from Kalinda Mountain?
They conspired in the love
games of herding girls
and watched over the veiled
affairs of Radha.
Now that the days
are gone when I cut their
tendrils, and laid them
down for couches of love,
I wonder if they've
grown brittle and if
their splendid blue flowers
have dried up.

*

Not knowing me,
Vidya,
dark as a blue lotus petal,
the critic Dandin
declared our goddess of verse-craft and learning
      entirely white.

*

Green interlaced tendrils
twist over the current,
white sands bank the river
      where a soft breeze lifts

water hens pipe—they pipe brightly—
and the mangrove thickets
        who made them?

Murala River
tell me how these groves came to be—
where sheltered we give to our lovers
all that's desired
happily, always, freely

in the translucent stream
        of it all.

                         *


The heavens
        with clouds
the land with fast running water

the horizon with lightning jags,
torrents of rain

        Milky kuṭaja petals
stroke the forests
creeks churn through the foothills—

Why expose a lone woman
to such pageant

        o season of rain

the torment
the sweet bitter need to be
        touched.

*[translated by Andrew Schelling]*

# Avvaiyar

## [Eighth Century CE]

She is part of folk memory. We have always known her—this grandmother poet of our past. Avvaiyar (literally, 'respectable woman') has been a significant figure in the Tamil literary canon for what seems like forever. Yet, there seem to have been several Avvaiyars in history. One lived around the third-century BCE, a poet of distinction in the Sangam era. Another lived in the twelfth century during the rule of the Chola dynasty. Her work of pithy homespun wisdom is intoned by Tamil speakers to this day.

Some centuries before her, however, was the mystic Avvaiyar, who authored what is one of the foremost esoteric Tamil literary texts. Suffused with references to tantra and kundalini yoga, the *Vinayaka Agaval* is a complex work. This is not just a devotional poem addressed to a local deity. It is instead a roadmap by a self-assured mystic.

But now, from history to legend. A long time ago, a child was abandoned by her parents and raised by wandering minstrels. Deeply interested in spirituality and literature, she had no time for the many suitors drawn to her beauty rather than her eventful inner life. She prayed to her chosen deity, the elephant-headed embodiment of wisdom, Vinayaka, to relieve her of the burden of youth and beauty.

Her god answered her prayer. Her skin turned dry and wrinkly, her hair whitened and her bones stiffened. She was now free to wander far and wide through the Tamil countryside, undisturbed by male attention. (It is interesting that social pressure prompted both Karaikkal Ammaiyar and Avvaiyar to opt for the relative physical invisibility conferred by

29

ghost- and old-age status.) She led a simple life, committed to the practice of yoga. As her wisdom ripened, she became the author of varied literary and philosophical works that reflected the profundity of her insight.

One day, weary from her travels, she decided to rest in a temple, where she was reprimanded by a scandalized priest. Her feet, he pointed out, were directed at the idol in the sanctum. Show me the direction in which the divine does not exist, was Avvaiyar's courteous rejoinder. The self-righteous man had met his match. He slunk away, chastened.

Seamlessly weaving the legends of the varied Avvaiyars into a single one, a famous Tamil film on her also includes a story of her encounter with the boy god Murugan. A poem inspired by the encounter is also included in this selection. (This verse is most likely drawn from the work of the twelfth-century Avvaiyar, who was known for her devotion to Murugan.)

One day, when Avvaiyar was immersed in her spiritual practices, she had a vision of the contemporary Tamil poet, Sundarar, proceeding on a white elephant to Kailasa, the abode of Shiva. With him was his faithful comrade on a white horse. Yearning to join them on their final journey, Avvaiyar began to hurry through her daily practices. But her beloved Vinayaka instructed her to take her time with her meditation. 'You will still be in Kailasa ahead of your two friends,' he assured her.

Hearing these words, Avvaiyar's meditation deepened. The result was the celebrated rhapsody, *Vinayaka Agaval*, that is sung in praise of Vinayaka to this day. At the end of her song and her practice, Vinayaka gently lifted her with his massive trunk and delivered her to her destination. She reached Kailasa before her friends—a spiritual version of the hare-and-tortoise fable that tells us the path of the patient seeker is never unrewarded. (Perhaps there is a subtext here for female seekers as well. For it is telling that Avvaiyar reached her spiritual destination before a famous male poet!)

Included here are two verse extracts from the *Vinayaka Agaval*. This is much more than a rapturous *darshan*, or auspicious glimpse, of the divine. A poet's grasp of diction and image is accompanied by an understanding of the occult physiology of chakras. The typical praise poem to a male god is destabilized by the fact Vinayaka is

addressed as 'mother', inserting a goddess metaphor into the picture.
We see Avvaiyar here as both visionary poet and yogic adept. As for
Vinayaka, he is not mere deity but deliverer. This is not the cheery
rotund god—a staple feature in every Indian living room. This is
Vinayaka, the guru.

~

. . . And now
  to enslave me,

you materialize
  as Mother,

you cleave
  right through

the hypnosis
  of death and rebirth,

to illumine
  those five

perfect
  syllables,

you suffuse
  my heart,

personify
  as teacher,

set sacred feet
  on this earth

to reveal the essential nature
  of things,

ensuring that I am never
   disheartened, you surge

forward in joy and grace,
   hack

right through my delusions
   with the sabre

of your elephant tusk
   and then, tenderly

feed
   my hungry ears

the teaching,
   that nourishes,

but never ever
   satiates . . .

                              *

. . . In the source
   where darkness and light mate

you drench me
   in the grace of ecstasy

pour into my ears
   your limitless

rapture,
   banish distress, reveal

the sacred road
   to freedom,

and disclose amidst the mind's
    cacophony

the perennial Shiva,
    unveiling

within me his eternal
    presence—

the atom within
    the atom,

the beyond that lies
    beyond

the beyond—
    all within this succulent

sugarcane stalk,
    consecrating me as one

of your true devotees, garbed
    in your very own form,

smeared
    in your very own sacred ash,

as you unfurl
    the essence,

the unique essence
    of those five syllables,

infusing me
    with an awareness

of the deepest
    truth.

Vinayaka,
   living wisdom incarnate,

I melt,
   I melt

at your fragrant feet.

                                      *

Lord of the lance,
who asks me what is greatness,

I say to you: great is this world, but
                greater still
Brahma who fashioned it,

         and greater still
the dark lord Vishnu
that sleeps in the mythic sea
of milk waves, from whose navel
the creator emerged,

         and greater still
the diminutive sage Agastya
who consumed this vast ocean,

         and greater still
the earthen urn
from which the ancient
sage was birthed

         and greater still
the Earth
in which the urn
is but a grain of sand

and greater still
the primordial serpent
that bears
the Earth on its hood

and greater still
the Goddess
around whose finger
the serpent is a mere
ring of coils

and greater still
the Supreme Lord
who offered her half
his body

and greater still,
the hearts
of the devotees
in which the Supreme Lord resides.

Lord of the lance,

the heart of the devotee—

*that*
is greatness.

**[translated by Arundhathi Subramaniam]**

# Lakshminkara

## [Eighth Century CE]

A sophisticated practitioner on the Tantric path, Lakshminkara was a teacher, author and proponent of the Vajrayana tradition of tantric Buddhism.

She was the sister of the king Indrabhuti, who ruled over the kingdom of Sambhala in the land of Oddiyana or Uddayana (a medieval centre of Vajrayana Buddhism, reputed for its unique sisterhood of priestesses; believed to be either in the modern-day Indian state of Odisha or the Swat district of Pakistan). Thus, she was clearly born into a family of privilege and was the heir to a good education and a life of comfort. She seems to have been initiated into Vajrayana at an early age. Later, she was betrothed to prince Jalandhara, the son of a ruler in Lankapuri, or Sri Lanka. However, on seeing her future husband return from a hunting expedition, his robes soiled with blood, the young woman was disturbed.

Lakshminkara decided to take charge of her life. She gave away the jewellery and silks from her considerable dowry, ripped off her clothes, smeared ash on her body, threw objects at people who approached her and proceeded to talk so incoherently that she was deemed insane by those around her—a strategy often adopted by spiritual adepts to keep unwanted social intrusion at bay.

Lakshminkara retreated to cremation grounds and caves, where she lived off the scraps of food thrown for dogs and intensified her spiritual practices. After seven years of seclusion, she attained self-realization. Over time, she drew numerous male and female disciples. The first of these was a sweeper of the palace toilets who served her faithfully. Her former fiancé also seems to have approached her for guidance. But in a delicious tale of poetic justice, she assigned the prince's spiritual education to the low-caste palace sweeper.

Lakshminkara's treatise, *Advayasiddhi*, speaks of the importance of paying homage to all women, seeing them as embodiments of divinity. Even while she dismisses exoteric practices of fasting, pilgrimage and ritual, she exhorts the worship of women—a striking feature in a text otherwise devoted to nondual realization. In her words: 'One must never disparage women/ of any class/ for each is the Goddess of Knowing/ made manifest in the phenomenal world.'

Lakshminkara was a virtuoso in the tantric arts. She seems to have introduced spiritual practices around the female deity, the Severed-Headed Vajrayogini (whose blood was seen to nourish both herself and her disciples).

In a song to her female disciples, Mekhala and Kanakhala, her crazy, riddling utterances–a part of a vaster sacred literary tradition of *sandhyabhasha*, or 'twilight language'—cut right through conventional ideas of causality. They become a direct pointer to a dimension beyond the ken of the logical mind.

~

Lay your head on a block of butter and chop—
Break the blade of the axe!
The woodcutter laughs!
A frog swallows an elephant!

It's amazing, Mekhala,
Do not doubt,
If it confounds you, adept,
Drop concepts now!

My teacher didn't tell me,
I didn't understand--
Flowers blossomed in the sky!

It's marvellous, Mekhala,
Have no doubt!
If you're incredulous, adept,
Drop your doubts!

A barren woman gives birth!
A chair dances!
Because cotton is expensive,
The naked weep!

. . . . . .

Amazing! An elephant sits on a throne
Held up by two bees!
Incredible! The sightless lead,
The mute speak!

. . . . . . .

Amazing! A mouse chases a cat!
An elephant flees from a crazy donkey!

It's marvellous, Mekhala,
Do not doubt!
If you're stunned, adept,
Drop your doubts!

Amazing! A hungry monkey eats rocks!
Wonderful! The experience of the mind –
Who can express it?

*[translated by Miranda Shaw]*

# Andal

## [Ninth Century CE]

She is mystic, poet, lover and goddess, all rolled into one. If Meera is the best-known devotional woman poet of north India, it is Andal for the deep south. Andal predates Meera by six centuries, making her one of the most arresting early female voices in Indian devotional literature. The only woman among the twelve Alvar saint poets (of the Vaishnava tradition), Andal is celebrated as the teenage girl who preferred marriage with a god over a mortal man. Voluptuous, smouldering and darkly erotic, her poetry blurs the divide between the romantic and the spiritual, making it easy to see why her work is such a cherished legacy of Tamil literature.

In the town of Srivilliputur, Periyalvar, a great Vishnu devotee, found an infant inside his temple garden. Regarding her as a goddess-child, he raised her himself. Andal (or Kothai, as she was named) grew up into an ardent devotee of Krishna, the widely-loved avatar of Vishnu.

Periyalvar was given to stringing a flower garland and offering it in worship daily at his shrine. One day, Andal wore the garland herself before making the offering. This was considered a scandalous breach of ritual propriety. When he discovered one of her hairs in the garland, Periyalvar rebuked his daughter severely. However, Vishnu appeared in his dream that night and insisted on accepting only the garland worn by Andal. It was clear that the divine preferred love over ceremonial bureaucracy! According to legend, Periyalvar led the young virgin bride, Andal, to the temple in Srirangam, where she was united with the deity— in a thunderclap consummation that was both conjugal and mystical.

Arguments rage around Andal. Was she the female pseudonym of Periyalvar? Was she a mystic? A goddess? What remains uncontested is the literary merit of Andal's work. The *Tiruppavai* and the *Nachiyar Tirumozhi* are considered to be her creations, their verses recited by devotees to this very day. While canonical accounts of her story present her as the unsullied bride of the divine, they cannot suppress the savage passion of her utterances. Conversely, those who are sometimes tempted to view her as a feminist icon cannot overlook the spiritual surrender that suffuses her work. Andal is, perhaps inconveniently, *both*—bold lover and faithful devotee, flesh-and-blood woman and spirit. She refuses to be frozen into simply one or the other. She demands that we acknowledge the complexity of her identity.

~

I melt. I fray. But he does not care
if I live or die.
If that stealthy thief, that duplicitous Govardhana
should even glance at me
I shall pluck these useless breasts of mine
from their roots
I will fling them at his chest
and staunch the fire scorching me.

\*

What is the purpose of future penance
if in this life, I cannot serve my Govinda
in small familiar ways and end the anguish
of my swollen and tender breasts?
Let him enfold me to his perfect chest
Or, let him stand before me,
face me and bid me farewell.
I will accept even that.

*[translated by Archana Venkatesan]*

\*

# The Song to Kamadeva, God of love

Draw the bow at me, loosening braids of reason
until I am an untied string without a knot,

united as wave and postulate. Concluded.
Three times a day I will worship at your feet

with fragrant blossoms of moonflowers,
my heart ablaze, from fiery tips of arrows

woven from efflorescence to spell his name,
Govinda, a musk essence of transcendence.

Aim the arrow at him and let it fly, to pierce
him until I might enter that succulent light.

Around his face, the cosmos revolves, glinting
starlight from his spear, the lion-cub of Yasoda
fierce yet lotus-eyed, dark-hued yet resplendent
with the joy of all creation.

Let the world consider the rituals of our vows,
sing the songs we sing, smell the jasmine strung
into a garland to praise the one who steals ghee
from my mouth as blessing.

Rub the kohl from my eyes, scour the flower-scent
from my body, show me as I am to him, an elemental
offering not good, not bad, but simply present.
Show him as he is to me.

In flooded fields of red paddy, carp leap into flight
that doesn't last, yet won't subside, and spotted
beetles graze our eyelashes as we splash our song
heavenward for liberation.

*[translated by Ravi Shankar]*

*

. . . Streets You shall enter I purify
and decorate—as I do myself.

With twigs that shall not split but surge
aflame I pledge my fidelity. I offer

garlands untouched by bees while hungering
for him who ripped the throat of the demon

bird. God of Love, I plead: aim
my flower body into his.

*

auspicious, incandescent, virginal
am I
accept this

fire me
into the dark one who
will rend

my body's
secret gullet
as he enters me

*

. . .

With soft soot smeared finger I invoke you, First
Principle. You've no excuse not to perform: I offer

all You need of Spring's intoxicants: perfumed
breezes, flowers, drunken bees humming

as string on your bow. From girlhood
I've longed to offer him the fruit of my breasts

now love ripened. Play your part: deliver
me. Make him clasp my offering.

*

You delude others
don't delude
Yourself

I'm rare
resolved in my love
single me out for him

or beware
defeat me
and You defeat Yourself

*

my form remains
a girl's
my musk lost

you entered
filled me
pulled out sharp

your rapacity
emptied me
eat me into plenitude

*

your darkness
chars
my being

my body's fruit
slashed open
acid scrubbed by separation

i'm sacrifice
wrap my cindered mystery
in your musk

\*

bloated with love
sliced
i beg the truth

hold nothing back
no promises for future births
nor for this one's uselessness

answer:
let it end now

\*

*Uncover me.* Why should I wear modesty when the world knows of my barefaced love? If you wish to be dazzled anew by me there's only one cure: I must see the lord of illusion.

He appeared as a dwarf but covered worlds; *he's seeded and grows bursting boundaries.* Why clothe me in convention? Let rapture
recapture me.

*I flame towards trembling stars.* Take me quick to the magician of Ayarpati.

*

invisible god of love
with white on wet umber
with rings of serene shimmer

i encircle you with prayer
as my body blazes:
fire me

at him who's cosmic flame
scorch desire: douse
me in his pouring grace

*[translated by Priya Sarukkai Chabria]*

# Akka Mahadevi

## [Twelfth Century CE]

Akka Mahadevi looms, mysterious and unforgettable, in the subcontinent's spiritual history. Lyrical and ascetic, her emotional vulnerability and spiritual independence make her a unique figure, and it is easy to see why she is an iconic presence in Kannada literature. She certainly ranks among the great sacred poets of the world.

She appears to have been initiated into the Shaiva path by an unknown guru at the age of ten. The local deity in the Shiva temple in her village was Chenna Mallikarjuna. It was this form of Shiva with whom Akka forged an intimate relationship. His name was to weave its way into all her poetry. While accounts vary, Mahadevi seems to have been wooed by a local king or chieftain, Kaushika. Whether she married him is uncertain. She eventually spurned his advances, and chose to walk her path alone, casting off all clothing and all cultural restraint; a naked mendicant, resplendently attired in 'the light of morning'. She became the figure that has continued to walk through the imaginations of generations of seekers.

Her wanderings took her to Kalyana, the spiritual epicentre of the Sharana movement of the time. Here, she found community in the company of poet-saints such as Allama Prabhu and Basavanna. However, she resumed her journey as a wandering ascetic, and her trail seems to eventually melt into the mountains of Srisailam. Here she dissolved into legend, united at last with Shiva, her beloved lord, of whom she sang with such passion and pain.

Akka's 400-odd *vachanas,* or poetic utterances, constitute a remarkable legacy of directness and nuanced delicacy, enacting psychological states of separation and union, carnality and transcendence, legitimate and illicit love, defiance and surrender. There is the pain of being trapped—in body, culture and chronology—and an ache to transcend oppressive roles and frozen identities. As she peels these away, Akka seeks the hidden truth with a deepening feverishness. 'Give me a clue, O lord white as jasmine,' she implores, 'to your hiding places.'

At times, samsara and the sacred seem irreconcilable. There is no way to heal the divide. Their appetites are opposed, their demands insatiable. Akka employs the conventions of Indian love poetry to speak of this divide. The seeker must be cunning and clandestine, she says; there is no other way to deal with the upside-downness of things. There is no other way to reconcile husband and lover, to unite Maya, the mother-in-law, with the uncensored longings of the body, to make peace with body and spirit.

At the same time, there is an ability to hold contradictions in equipoise. For Akka's Lord can be both a legitimate husband and a forbidden lover all at once. She can yearn 'to be with him/ yet not with him'. And the body can be a site of lust and greed, a 'fence of pride' and a 'mask of envy'. But when unstained, it can also become a site of glory, an embodiment of the 'Nothing, the Nakedness/ that covers and veils' itself.

The tone is direct, the torment searing and the desire for union wetly sensual. There is a scathing dismissal of mortal men: flesh-and-blood husbands are imperiously consigned to the kitchen fires. There is a formidable sense of agency, too. The love of Chenna Mallikarjuna invoked here may be unlicenced, but Akka will not be deterred. She will not rest until she has found her elusive mate, pinned him down, become one with him.

Fevered and radiant, Akka Mahadevi's poems continue to scorch and illuminate.

~

Better than meeting
and mating all the time
is the pleasure of mating once
after being far apart.

When he's away
I cannot wait
to get a glimpse of Him.

Friend, when will I have it
both ways,
be with Him
yet not with Him,
my lord white as jasmine?

                    *

Not one, not two, not three or four,
but through eighty-four hundred thousand vaginas
have I come,
          I have come
through unlikely worlds,
                    guzzled on
pleasure and on pain.
                    Whatever be
all previous lives,
          show me mercy
this one day,
          O lord
          white as jasmine.

                    *

He bartered my heart,
    looted my flesh,
    claimed as tribute
    my pleasure,
    took over
    all of me.

I'm the woman of love
for my lord, white as jasmine.

*

Till you've earned
knowledge of good and evil

It is
lust's body,
site of rage,
ambush of greed,
house of passion,
fence of pride,
mask of envy.

Till you know and lose this knowing
you've no way
of knowing
my lord white as jasmine.

*

You can confiscate
money in hand;
can you confiscate
the body's glory?

Or peel away every strip
you wear,
but can you peel
the Nothing, the Nakedness
that covers and veils?

To the shameless girl
wearing the White Jasmine Lord's
light of morning,
you fool,
where's the need for cover and jewel?

*

O brothers, why do you talk
    to this woman,
    hair loose,
    face withered,
    body shrunk?

O fathers, why do you bother
    with this woman?
    She has no strength of limb,
    has lost the world,
    lost power of will,
    turned devotee,

she has lain down
with the Lord, white as jasmine,
and has lost caste.

*

People,
male and female,
blush when a cloth covering their shame
comes loose.
                When the lord of lives
lives drowned without a face
in the world, how can you be modest?

When all the world is the eye of the lord,
onlooking everywhere, what can you
cover and conceal?

*

I have Maya for mother-in-law;
    the world for father-in-law;

three brothers-in-law, like tigers;

and the husband's thoughts
are full of laughing women;
   no god, this man.

And I cannot cross the sister-in-law.

But I will
give this wench the slip
and go cuckold my husband with Hara, my Lord,

   My mind is my maid:
   by her kindness, I join
   my Lord
      my utterly beautiful Lord
      from the mountain peaks,
      my lord white as jasmine,
and I will make Him
my good husband.

              *

I love the Handsome One:
  he has no death
  decay nor form
  no place or side
  no end nor birthmarks.
  I love him O mother. Listen.

I love the Beautiful One
  with no bond nor fear
  no clan no land
  no landmarks
  for his beauty.

So my lord, white as jasmine, is my husband.

Take these husbands who die,
   decay, and feed them
   to your kitchen fires!

*[translated by A.K. Ramanujan]*

                    *

Hear me if you will; spurn me, if you won't;
I cannot but sing your praises, Ayya.

See me if you will; shun me, if you won't;
I cannot but delight in you, Ayya.

Cherish me if you will; detest me, if you won't;
I cannot but embrace you, Ayya.

Love me if you will; loathe me, if you won't;
I cannot but adore you, Ayya.

Chenna Mallikarjunayya,
Applauding you, celebrating you,
I shall dance in ecstasy, Ayya.[1]

                    *

Gazing at him,
I closed my eyes

Listening to him,
I dissolved, forgot myself

Listen, the bed laid out for me
was no use

---

[1] Ayya: a respectful mode of address to a man

Not knowing how to make love
to my lord Chenna Mallikarjuna,

I lost myself, Avva.

                    *

He laid siege to my heart!
He devoured my body whole!
He feasted on every pleasure in every corner!
He came—came to live inside my being!
I'm Chenna Mallikarjuna's beloved,
I am, Avva!

                    *

Other men,
they are like thorns,
hiding under a plane leaf.
I cannot touch them,
I cannot go anywhere near them,
I can neither trust them nor confide in them, Avva.
Because they have thorns in their chests,
I can embrace none of them—

none but my lord Chenna Mallikarjuna!

                    *

Hunger, wait a moment.
Thirst, wait a moment.
Sleep, wait a moment.
Lust, wait a moment.
Anger, wait a moment.
Passion, wait a moment.
Greed, wait a moment.
Arrogance, wait a moment.

Envy, wait a moment.
Every moving and non-moving thing,
I beseech you, wait a moment.
I am your supplicant,
carrying an urgent missive
from my lord Chenna Mallikarjuna.

*

The despairing heart has turned turtle,
The gentle breeze has turned to fire,
Moonlight has turned hot, my friend.

I am agitated like a tax collector
doing the rounds in town.

My dear, go call him,
put some sense into him,
bring him to me, now.

Chenna Mallikarjuna is vexed with me
now that we are apart.

*

Melting,
    like moist soil,
slipping
    like dry sand,
pining
    in my dream,
I turned distraught.

Whirling,
    like kiln-fire,
I seethed,
not a friend in sight.

Chenna Mallikarjuna,
grant me

a body that cannot be seen by seeking,
a bliss that cannot be had by coupling.

*[translated by Vanamala Viswanatha]*

# Sule Sankavva

## [Twelfth Century CE]

A prostitute by profession, Sule Sankavva was a Kannada poet whose work seamlessly combines the gritty reality of her work with her love of Shiva. Interestingly, she chooses to address Shiva as Nirlajjeshwara (literally, 'Shameless God'). This is not some puritanical godhead; instead, he is an unorthodox and amoral interlocutor. She confides in him about her conflicts, and has absolutely no doubt that he will understand. The poem offers an insight into what the figure of Shiva represented to this poet and to the spiritual imagination of the subcontinent—a wildly inclusive divinity that refuses to discriminate between human ideas of the sacred and the profane.

~

Having accepted my fee from one man,
I shall not accept it from another.
Should I do that, they will
make me stand naked
and kill me, Sir.

Should I knowingly mingle
with someone who is not loyal and true,
they will cut off my hands, ears and nose
with a red-hot sword, Sir.

I am going to do no such thing, I know.
I swear on you,
O Shameless Lord!

*[translated by Ahalya Ballal]*

# Molige Mahadevi

## [Twelfth Century CE]

The poetic utterances of thirty-three women associated with the spiritual efflorescence of the Sharana movement in Karnataka have endured. Many of these women poets were married to men who were their spiritual partners as well as poets in their own right.

Molige Mahadevi and her husband, Mahadeva, renounced a life of privilege in Kashmir to migrate south to Kalyana. This was the locus of the great spiritual community, established by the poet–reformer and visionary Basavanna. The Sharana movement fostered by him was a vibrant initiative that offered sanctuary to many. It boasted of the famous 'experience pavilion' (Anubhava Mantapa), a crucible for mystics, philosophers, spiritual seekers and poets. The focus here was on inner experience rather than doctrine or ritual, and on subjective insight rather than scriptural dogma.

Not surprisingly, the movement drew like-minded spiritual travellers from across the land. Molige Mahadevi and her husband earned their livelihood here, collecting and selling firewood. Around seventy of her poems have survived and reveal a spirit of self-assurance and a profound understanding of the spiritual journey.

~

When you give me shelter,
you become formless.

Giving up the investigation of forms
you become powerless, unattached.
Giving up the company of your power
you become free from worry.
Giving up the sense of quantity
that aims at looking into the heart
shed the guise of deceit and humbug
you have put on.
To examine the hearts of other devotees
become free of all passions
endowed with all virtues
full like the ocean of wisdom,
Just once, open for me the temple of your awareness.
You will see the affinity between
my feet and your temple.
No more humbug in this:
O beloved of my lord, Mallikarjuna
of twofold purity.

*[translated by H.S. Shivaprakash]*

*

Why lose precious gold
by collecting petty coins?
Why shake a full pitcher
and make it fall?

When you possess
the symbolic sacred form
bequeathed by the guru,
why enter narrow lanes in confusion,
oblivious to the proximity
of the true form?

You drop a jewel
standing in one place
and search for it elsewhere.
How can you find it again?

You doubt whether you have
seen the Absolute sacred form
within yourself.

Just seek your truth
in the beloved of my lord,
the twice pristine Mallikarjuna.

*

Whatever the seed sown,
roots grow into the earth,
branches head out into the sky.
Union is within, action is without.
As long as duality exists,
there's struggle in devotion.
O beloved of my lord,
the twice pristine Mallikarjuna,
as long as beads exist,
the act of stringing is inevitable.

*

The light born
along the path of vastness
illuminates stone, metal and bronze.
O self-existent sacred form
at the base of my palm,
why doesn't your light
reveal to my eyes the path?

Is it my inertia
or is it your innate nature?
Is it your mischief that plays tricks?
Is it because you are not within me?
Is the separation simply because
I am not as virtuous as you?
O beloved of my lord,
the twice-pristine Mallikarjuna,

become one with me.

*[translated by Ahalya Ballal]*

# Lingamma

## [Twelfth Century CE]

Lingamma's work suggests a woman of no mean spiritual accomplishment. In one poem, she asks rhetorically, 'For one who has transcended the body/ is there any more to learn?' In another, she says, 'The devotee who has overcome the three—/ seeing, seer, sight—/ has ascended the three summits.' She speaks, too, of 'the mysterious devotee/ . . . freed from his shackles' who has become 'one with the vastness'. The crisp precision of her words seems to emerge from a wealth of subjective experience, suggesting that Lingamma knew whereof she spoke. Her language is marked by unadorned clarity and profundity and is described by scholar–translator H.S. Shivaprakash as 'cryptic but haunting'. She was married to Hadapada Appanna, also a committed spiritual traveller.

~

The mind grows dull
The body vanishes
The breath stops
The flame appears
The smoke spreads
The lake is all burnt down.
Unless you go in,
open the door
and immerse yourself in light,

there is no true freedom,
says Chennabasavanna, dear to Appanna.

*[translated by H.S. Shivaprakash]*

*

O all humans of the mortal world are dead,
drowned in darkness
Having learned to speak
uttering anxious words lost by a mouth full of holes
fond of the well of piss and the pond of shit
biting each other, driven mad—
the donkey–men wander.
Chennabasavanna, dear to Appanna
does not approve of them.

*

Sir, once a body burns in a blaze,
does it know distress?
When the self comes into its own,
does it rely on other human beings?
When the mind is fixed on the Immensity,
does any illusion remain?
For one who has transcended the body
is there any more to learn?
Does one who has seen the light
need darkness anymore?
O Chennabasavanna, dear to Appanna,
I bow down in joy to the devotee
who has overcome all this
and dissolved into the Great Divine.

*

Like a lamp on the threshold,
the self is the one who sees inward
and the one who sees outward.
It is the one who knows
and the one who forgets,
the one who has seen
and the one who cannot see.
The devotee who has overcome the three—
seeing, seer, sight—
has ascended the three summits.

The back door opens.

He watches; once he sees whence,
he revels in the Great Bliss.
His being needs no sowing,
growing, threshing
or winnowing.
As he grows beyond all this,
he sits on the ship mast and watches.
The ship is wrecked;
his wealth and possessions,
wife and children
drown.

Instantly, a cool breeze wafts in;
the mysterious devotee
is freed from his shackles
and becomes one with the vastness.

Look, he is none other than
Chennabasavanna, dear to Appanna.

*

Sir, why on earth don't they see
even when a ruby glows before their eyes?

Why talk of darkness
when the great devotee
stands before you?
It is akin to jumping into a stream
when you have an ocean of milk at your door!
Why search for other sacred forms?
That great devotee is none other
than Chennabasavanna, dear to Appanna.

*[translated by Ahalya Ballal]*

# Gangambike

## [Twelfth Century CE]

Basavanna, a visionary and leading light of the spiritual community in Kalyan, had two wives: Gangambike and Neelambike. Both women, as well as his sister, Nagalambike, were committed partners, actively engaged in implementing his vision of a spiritual revolution to establish a society based on equal opportunity.

As the daughter of a minister, Gangambike was born into a life of privilege and was accomplished in Kannada, Sanskrit, music, sword-fighting and archery. However, she seems to have taken willingly to a life of simplicity after her marriage. Basavanna was an obviously charismatic young man, but of modest means at the time. In time, he rose from clerk to prime minister at the court of King Bijjala. As his spiritual and social mission unfolded, he encouraged and drew on her intelligence, erudition and capability, inviting her to officiate over many proceedings at the Anubhava Mantapa, the lively academy for philosophical exchange. Gangambike appears to have believed deeply in the principles of equality and freedom on which this movement was founded. She fought valiantly to uphold this mission, eventually sacrificing her life for the cause. A memorial shrine stands on the banks of the Malaprabha river in Hubli, where she is believed to have breathed her last.

The selected poem speaks of a startling transformation—from predator to nurturer. It offers a glimpse of the powerful alchemical possibility that this spiritual movement proved to be for many.

~

Ah!
A tiger came
from a desolate land
to eat my young calf.
The tiger couldn't return
to the desolate land.
The tiger looked at the young calf
and turned into a mother.

What shall I say of this?
O Kudalasangamadeva, dear to Ganga!

*[translated by H.S. Shivaprakash]*

# Neelambike

## [Twelfth Century CE]

Neelambike (or Nilambike/Neelamma) was a poet and seeker, committed to the Sharana movement of her time. Married to Basavanna, she was a partner who stood by his side and actively supervised activities in his spiritual centre: hosting, feeding and attending to the many varied needs of the daily hordes of pilgrims while making time for her own meditative practices. An accomplished poet and singer, her melodious voice and devotional intensity are said to have inspired many. In one of her poems, she famously describes herself as his *'vichaarapatni'*, a discerning wife or contemplative companion. The couple had a son called Balasangayya, who died at an early age. She attained samadhi soon after her husband, on the banks of the river Krishna near Tangadige village in the Bijapur district in Karnataka.

~

Basava's wisdom has become free of all support
Basava's doing has become non-doing
Basava's bhakti merged into space and became non-space
Basava's, Basava, Basava—this word disappeared
and became wordlessness

*[translated by H.S. Shivaprakash]*

*

No one knows me,
I am neither godly nor emancipated.
No one knows me.

I am neither free nor bound.
No one knows me.

Since I am a woman,
formless in the Divine Companion,

no one knows me.

*

Sir, I do not entangle myself
in the female form.
I do not speak as a woman.

Sir, since I am not a woman,
I am neither of this world
nor of the other.

O Divine Companion,
since I have seen
the vastness that is Basava,
I experience
   and yet do not experience
   this duality.

*[translated by Ahalya Ballal]*

# Kalavve

## [Twelfth Century CE]

The voice of Kalavve, a Dalit poet in Kannada, is daring and satirical.
She was the wife of Urilingapeddi, a fellow poet and spiritual traveller.
Her unequivocal dismissal of caste points to her spiritedness as well as
the emancipatory ethos fostered by the Sharana movement. Here, we
hear her speak out against brahmin orthodoxy as well as the hypocrisy
of male custodians of faith. Her words hit like cudgel blows against
hierarchy in all its guises.

~

Those who eat mutton, poultry and fish
are said to be of noble birth.
Cobblers who eat the beast
that offers five ambrosias to Shiva
are said to be of low caste.
How are they of low caste?
And why do you demean castes?
What is eaten by Brahmins
adorns the grass.
The dog licks it and moves away.
What is eaten by cobblers
adorns both the grass

and the Brahmins.
This is how:
cow hide is turned into pouches.
Foolish Brahmins eat the ghee
and drink the water in these pouches,
assuming it to be sacred.
The worst hell lies in store for them.

The Lord of Urilingapeddi does not approve.

*

Those without dedicated work
are not devotees.
That which is bereft of truth and purity
is not dedicated work.
Desire is the seed of birth.
Absence of desire is abiding deliverance.
Know that with the Lord of Urilingapeddi,
this is no small matter.

*[translated by Ahalya Ballal]*

# Amuge Rayamma

## [Twelfth Century CE]

Amuge Rayamma, or 'Rayamma of the Spinning Wheel' (as her translator H.S. Shivaprakash describes her), was yet another Kannada poet of the Sharana movement, unsparing in her critique of religious sanctimony. A weaver by profession, she was the wife of Amuge Devayya.

Interestingly, her scathing critiques are directed at phonies and charlatans within her own circle. Once, when she saw a spiritually immature aspirant entering the Anubhava Mantapa to receive a linga, she remarked with some acerbity, 'Why make one who has no legs climb a ladder? . . . / Why a linga for one who knows no devotion, knowledge and dispassion?' And yet again, 'What if one holds a linga in his hand, can he become eternal?' In another poem, she wonders why a Sharana would bother with impostors 'going around with ochre robes on'. Her words are a reminder of the self-confidence engendered in seekers of her time by a vigorously inclusive spiritual movement. It also says something about the way her own inner journey bolstered a newfound sense of identity and self-worth.

~

Everyone can read the vachanas.
Everyone can speak of the divine.
Everyone can listen to the vachanas.

But everyone who speaks is not a guru,
and everyone who hears is not a disciple.

As long as one thinks
one has spoken or heard the divine,
it is a disgrace to the domain of dispassion,
O Amugeshwara!

*[translated by Ahalya Ballal]*

\*

Can you see the footsteps
of someone walking on water?
Or of the soul
riding a palanquin?
It is like searching for wisdom
when on elephant back,
seeking the light of the self
when in the midst of the wise.

If you can get rid of 'I' and 'you'
and stay your own self,
that self is Amugeshwara Linga, I say.

\*

If you can soar to the sky
why depend on a supporting stick?
If you can walk without touching the earth
why depend on the earth?
If you know the self
why have truck with those who gossip?
If you can move in ways unimagined,
why depend on women?

If you are a Sharana
aware of Amugeshwara Linga
why depend on wrong-doers
going around with ochre robes on?

*

Does the sun make a distinction
between this place and that?
It spreads its light everywhere
What if everybody denounces
the ascended wise one?
Is he inferior?
The one absolutely free,
whose every limb is Linga,
does not look after
only those that look at him,
only those that know him,
does not give up
those who give him up

He does not give up his determination—
The one who knows
Amugeshwara Linga

*[translated by H.S. Shivaprakash]*

# Nagalambike

## [Twelfth Century CE]

Nagalambike was the sister of Basavanna, the poet and spiritual pioneer. She received her spiritual initiation from him and was recognized as an advanced practitioner. She was married to Shivadeva and had a son named Chennavasavana, considered to be an important poet–saint in his own right.

Nagalambike was a woman of courage and capability, with considerable leadership skills. She played an active role in the spiritual debates and discussions at the Anubhava Mantapa, promoted the literary legacy of vachana poetry, fought the king's soldiers when a revolution broke out, and led fellow members of the Sharana community to safety when their lives were threatened. This spiritual warrior shed her body on the banks of Yennehole in Chikkamagalur district. According to legend, she camped at a temple near a stream, and when she found no oil for her lamp, she turned water from the stream into oil (*yenne* in Kannada), which is how the place is said to have received its name. Her fifteen poems use the signature address to Shiva, 'Chenna Sangayya, dear to Basavanna'.

In this poem, she offers a radical redefinition of the very notion of family. Her true community, she says, is a wandering tribe of poets committed to the same ideals.

~

With the guru as my parents,
the linga as my husband,
wandering mendicants as my in-laws,
devotees of Shiva as my relatives,
directed to the home of truth and principled action,
the term 'wife of a Sharana' rings true!
I shall live accordingly,
act without pondering the past or the future.

I shall follow the dictates of my conscience.
O Chenna Sangayya, dear to Basavanna,
I offer this at your feet.

*[translated by Ahalya Ballal]*

# Jira Dei

## [Twelfth to Thirteenth Century CE]

Little is known about Jira Dei. What is clear is that she was a yogini, a respected teacher in the esoteric Vajrayana tradition of Buddhism and a major representative of Odia Tantra. That seems evident in the crisp authority and assurance of her voice.

Her significant contribution is the authorship of the *Jhamaka Gita*, a commentary on the major philosophical work, the *Sisu Beda* (one of the core texts of the Odia Natha tradition, hailed as the fifth Veda). The tantric Buddhist tradition to which she owed her allegiance seems to have evolved around the tenth century in the Odisha region. It was a blend of Shaiva and Natha yoga elements.

Jiradei refers to herself as Dombi Mata, Mother of the Domba clan, a community scattered across southern Odisha and various parts of India, often viewed as the original inhabitants of the forest lands. Researcher, musician and archivist Prateek Pattanaik explains that references to a Dombi are found in the highly coded Buddhist songs, the Charyapada, authored by the eighty-four Mahasiddhas (Great Adepts of the Mahayana Buddhist tradition) between the fifth and tenth centuries. The Mahasiddhas hailed from every caste and class background and included kings, sweepers, cobblers, weavers and washermen in their midst. Four of them were women. Lakshminkara was one of them.

Pattanaik writes, 'The Mahasiddhas are still very popular in Odisha. Although Buddhism has declined through centuries. Their mystic, magical tales still survive. In the Jagannatha temple in Puri, Charyapada songs of the Mahasiddhas used to be sung atop the *ratha*, or chariot, long ago, but that was banned on grounds of obscenity. The metaphorical language of these Charyapadas is termed *sandhya-bhasha*. This is because they have an external and an internal meaning. Their interpretation, if taken literally, can be "dark as the night" and, if understood, the core tantric learning can be "bright as the day": this is the traditional Odia etymology. One can see Jira Dei coming out of this tradition of Odia Tantra, which respected knowledge irrespective of caste, class and gender. This is still the case in the Jagannatha temple, where a Brahmin can eat from the hands of an outcaste, and anyone who tries to discriminate is prosecuted, not the reverse.'

Jiradei's poems—a string of spare two-line and four-line verses—are mysterious, their images cryptic and resonant.

~

The mind grows watchful,
the wind falls still,
the soul aligns with the supreme,
and that's the inner heart of the mystery, says Mahadeva

*

It stumps the imagination,
blows the mind away,
Gorakhnath speaks the truth—
the spirit is a nomad, leaves the body behind.

*

A boat adrift in an ocean of time,
not a friend in sight
no shoreline even.
What use is the mind when your vessel's sinking?

*

As long as the body persists
attachment ensnares you,
but snap the threads—and there!
You're one with the stainless.

*[translated by Prabhanjan Mishra]*

# Muktabai

## [Thirteenth Century CE]

Mukta, or Muktabai, was one of the first women poets of Marathi literature and a sophisticated spiritual teacher in her own right. She was born into an exceptional family; her three elder brothers, Nivrutti, Jnaneshwar and Sopan were all advanced spiritual practitioners.

Born in the town of Alandi, Mukta was orphaned at a young age. Her parents were driven to suicide after the family had been excommunicated (for her father's decision to embrace the ascetic life while still married). The outcaste life led to much social derision and hardship for the children. However, her elder brother, Nivrutti, was initiated into the heterodox Nathpanthi sect (where caste considerations were irrelevant). He, in turn, proceeded to initiate his siblings into the spiritual journey. Mukta and her brothers now became the nucleus of what was to develop into the celebrated Varkari Bhakti tradition in Maharashtra—an egalitarian movement, centred on Vitthala or Vithoba (the presiding deity of Pandharpur), which held out the possibility of spiritual liberation for all castes and classes.

The lives of Mukta and her brothers were short, but their achievements were considerable. In a brief lifespan of nineteen years, Mukta was revered as a mystic and poet (forty-one of her cryptic poems are extant), an influential mentor, guide and role model for generations of women poets and spiritual aspirants.

She appears to have attained a formidable level of spiritual mastery at an early age. It was she whom Nivrutti approached, for instance, to initiate the once-hostile leader of the village into the spiritual path.

She was also responsible, we are told, for jolting the revered poet saint
Namdev from his spiritual complacency. Legend has it that she awakened
a corpse by simply repeating the name of Vitthala into its ears. She also
reformed an accomplished yogi and arcanist, Changdev, who eventually
bowed down and acknowledged her as his guru. (She was rumoured
to be only five years old at the time!) In one of her poems, we hear
her chiding her elder brother Dnyaneshwar (the author of the iconic
commentary on the Gita, the *Dnyaneshwari*) for his anger.

Mukta was only nineteen when she was last heard of. She appears
to have vanished during a storm—metaphorically, an appropriate end to
the life of a woman who seems to have been something of a spiritual
whirlwind. Yet, despite her brief life, her position as a foundational
figure in the Varkari tradition of Maharashtra and as a major mystic
poet was already assured.

~

**the zoom ant**

the zoom ant
swallowed the sun
the barren woman
begot a son

a scorpion went
to the lower depths
shesha bowed to him
with a thousand heads

a pregnant fly
delivered a kite
having seen it all
mukta smiled

*[translated by Arun Kolatkar]*

*

First came joy and on the morrow
Hard on her heels, a visit from sorrow.
Just as we had settled down to grieving,
She announced that she was leaving.
Joy and sorrow, what's the difference?
Both are sisters, born of ignorance.

Muktai tells Changya: Self-born, the soul,
Standing like a banyan, aloof and whole.

                        *

I sense Him here. My God.
                    From the temple
                    Here.
In my home.

The roof flies off.
I am open to the sky.

Until this happens, one is condemned
To play out those old roles of the ego;
To a heartbeat empty of love;
To be blind to the self-evident—
                        for fear of running mad.

Until you acknowledge the temple within
How can you experience compassion?

The rich and the poor struggle between
                        being and freeing.
Neither sees what is tangibly there.
This cloud of delusion, this house of doubt:
Welcome to Maya.

Muktai offers this milk of instruction:
One God; every possible emotional state.

*

## That Old Habit: Maya

In all that has form, the formless,
Which, of course, has no form of its own.
Our need for form? That old habit: maya.
Here's a warning from Him: the formless lurks
In the illusion, lives in everything, in everyone.
Yes, in you too.
Uproot the passive to become passive.
Muktai won't turn back now.
Not until she's free.
She's seen that it's all one.
All of it.

*[translated by Neela Bhagwat and Jerry Pinto]*

*

Listen,
from where has this anger come?
You are enlightened
You know well that people are the divine
we have pledged to serve,
and cannot get distracted from that path

When anger erupts, all yoga is wasted
So enlarge your vision,
                open the door,
                        Dnyaneshwara!

*[translated by Shruthi Veena Vishwanath]*

# Janabai

## [Thirteenth Century CE]

The poet Janabai worked as a maidservant in the home of the well-known male poet, Namdev. Hers is one of the most interesting and audacious voices in Marathi devotional literature.

Born in Gangakhed, Maharashtra, it is believed that she was taken as a five-year-old to the temple of the God Vithoba or Panduranga in Pandharpur—the pilgrimage centre in the Varkari Hindu tradition. Once placed on the threshold of the temple, the little girl found it impossible to leave and told her father she did not intend to accompany him home again. She was noticed by the poet Namdev, who asked about her antecedents. The five-year-old told him she was Jani and her parentage was, quite simply, 'Krishna'. Impressed, Namdev took her home and told his parents that she was now their responsibility. She worked in their household until the end of her days. Although she seems to have faced her share of domestic hardship, she considered Namdev to be her spiritual guide and mentor. She seems to have composed over 300 poems (although the authorship of some of these is debated).

The extraordinary intimacy of Janabai's relationship with her God imbues her poetry with a freshness of tone and texture. She often turns him into a female figure, addressing him as 'mother'—a reminder of the way in which goddess imagery subtly permeates so much devotional literature. There are times she asks him to help her with her daily tasks, and Vitthala obliges. He turns mother, even maidservant, grinding corn, doing the dishes, heating her bathwater, delousing her hair, and, at times, suffering blows on her behalf when she is beaten by Namdev's mother!

~

**i eat god**

i eat god
i drink god
i sleep
on god

i buy god
i count god
i deal
with god

god is here
god is there
void is not
devoid of god

      jani says:

god is within
god is without
and moreover
there's god to spare

*

**see the void**

see the void
above the void
on its top
another void

the first void
is red

it's called
the lower void

the higher void
is white
the middle void
is grey

but the great void
is blue
it contains
only itself

jani was struck
with wonder
when she heard
the silent bell

*

**god my darling**

god my darling
do me a favour and kill my mother-in-law

i will feel lonely when she is gone
but you will be a good god won't you
and kill my father-in-law

i will be glad when he is gone
but you will be a good god won't you
and kill my sister-in-law

i will be free when she is gone
i will pick up my begging bowl
and be on my way

let them drop dead says jani
then we will be left alone
just you and me

*[translated by Arun Kolatkar]*

*

Jana sweeps with a broom
The Lord loads up the garbage

Carries it in a basket on His head
Throws it away in a distant dump

So much under the spell of bhakti is He
He now performs the lowliest of tasks

Says Jani to Vithoba
How shall I return Your favours?

*

Among basil plants growing wild
Jani loosens her hair:

The Lord with butter in the palm of His hand
Gently massages her head:

'My poor little Jani has no one but me!'
He thinks as he pours down water:

Jani tells all the folks
'My boyfriend gives me a shower.'

*[translated by Dilip Chitre]*

*

## To Jana's Home, One Day

Vittho came to Jana's home one day,
Timidly, he asked for food.
What do I feed you, Lord?
I took His hand, I led Him in,
I served Him panchamrut and rice.
He belched His love all over me.
Jani says: Vittho found bliss that day.

*

## Dance Without Stopping

Only your name.
Fill my eyes.
I want to dance for you,
dance without stopping.
Only you,
in everything.
I wish the world were made that way.
So Jani prayed and night fell.
And with it, He came.

*

I have let my veil drop to my shoulders.
Bare-headed, I shall walk through the market.
In my hands the cymbals, on my shoulder the veena
Let who will try and stop me now.
Come wish me well, anoint my wrists with oil.
Jani says: I have become your whore, Keshava.
I have come now to wreck your home.

*[translated by Neela Bhagwat and Jerry Pinto]*

# Soyarabai

## [Fourteenth Century CE]

Soyarabai was a Marathi Dalit poet whose free-verse poems (sixty-two of which have survived) are sharply critical of the caste inequalities and hypocrisies of her day, even while they celebrate her devotion to her personal god, Vitthala of Pandharpur. She was the wife of Chokhamela, another Varkari poet.

Deeply moved by the life and verse of the saint, Namdev, Chokhamela decided to move with his family to Pandharpur and settle there. However, despite the breezes of freedom and equality blowing through the town, the orthodox upper castes seem to have objected to his entering the temple. This compelled him to build a hut on the other side of the river Chandrabhaga, where he lived with his family. Years later, Chokhamela and several other construction workers were crushed in a wall collapse. His tomb was built in front of his beloved temple, where it can be seen to this very day. Devotees believe that his interred bones continued to utter the name of Vitthala, the deity of the shrine that he was forbidden from entering all his life. Soyarabai's poetry is pervaded by an acute awareness of the injustices meted out to her and her husband.

'If menstrual blood makes me impure/ tell me who was not born of that blood,' she declares in one of her poems—a reminder of the ways in which the Bhakti traditions interrogated taboos around impurity and pollution. Scholar–translator A.K. Ramanujan points out that such critiques are found among several others too: Basavanna, the Kannada saint, offered leftover food to his god, just as Sabari, the tribal woman mentioned in the Ramayana, tasted every berry before offering it to her beloved Rama (a flagrant desecration of norms of purity), ensuring that he received the choicest and juiciest fruit. The bhakta's impulse 'to touch and merge' rather than 'to behold' (and rest content with darshan) was subversive. It resulted, even if 'often only in theory', says Ramanujan, 'in a breakdown of barriers and distinctions between caste and caste, between touchable and untouchable, between male and female . . .' The persistence of this poetry down the ages suggests that its innately disruptive potential cannot be erased.

Soyarabai's ringing voice still speaks today for those who are willing to listen. Her poems continue to raise questions around pecking orders. In the process, they also raise questions, perennially relevant to hierarchically ravaged human minds, around divisions between high and low, pure and impure.

~

You say some bodies are untouchable.
Tell me what you say of the soul.

You say defilement is born in the body.
If menstrual blood makes me impure,
Tell me who was not born of that blood.

This blood of mine fertilizes the world.
Tell me who has not sprung from this source.

Soyara says: this impurity is the cornerstone of your world.
That's why I praise only Panduranga,
Who lives in every body, pure, impure.

*

In this play of the five elements,
Remember, only the soul is pure.
Why one is spared, another taken,
Only He can know for sure.

Why carry these burdens on your head?
If the world still tempts you, all hope has fled.
Soyara says: I find it odd;
Those who know nothing, speak most of God.

*[translated by Neela Bhagwat and Jerry Pinto]*

# Nirmala

## [Fourteenth Century CE]

Nirmala was the younger sister of the outcaste Marathi saint poet, Chokhamela. She was married to a man named Banka. However, her brother was clearly her inspiration, and many of her poems invoke Chokhamela (and even demand divine union 'in Chokha's name'). Musician and translator Neela Bhagwat describes her as 'a spontaneous and outspoken woman', whose poems often speak of the burdens and ordeals of her life and her efforts to deepen her spiritual practice. The selected poem offers us the quintessential seeker's predicament: can the chattering mind ever be stilled?

~

Not one atom of happiness
in this life sentence.
I can't think. I can't pray.
My mind won't stop.
All day, all day: Tumult.

Nirmala says: Chokha, how do you do it?
            How do you hold on to Him?

*[translated by Neela Bhagwat and Jerry Pinto]*

# Lal Ded

## [Fourteenth Century CE]

The fact that Kashmir's most celebrated mystic poet is Lallesvari or Lalla Yogini to the Hindus and Lal-'arifa to the Muslims, points to the way in which her legacy has been embraced across boundaries of faith. She features in a hagiography of 1587 but was clearly a familiar part of the cultural consciousness well before that, as poet–translator Ranjit Hoskote points out.

Not much is known of Lal Ded's life, but vivid images endure: a spiritually inclined young girl; a woman abused by a husband and mother-in-law for her other-worldly preoccupations; a twenty-six-year-old renunciate who chose to throw off the constraints of the householder life; a spiritual initiate; a wandering mendicant (often presented as a naked figure); a self-realized being; an adept and finally, a teacher in her own right.

Her poetry suggests that she was profoundly acquainted with the mystical traditions of Kashmiri Shaivism, tantra, yoga, yogic Buddhism and Sufism. Despite her life of solitude and mendicancy, she became a hugely influential figure in Kashmir's religious life, inspiring the later mystic poet Rupa Bhavani and numerous other Sufi and Bhakti practitioners and poets.

The richness of her *vakhs* (utterances) suggests a versatile poet who could speak of yearning and fulfilment, devotion and mystical knowledge, quest and homecoming, even though her work could well have been authored, as her translator points out, by 'a contributory lineage' of diverse religious persuasions and gender identities. She embodies a tantric's quiet

authority when she speaks of knowing 'the password to the Supreme Place'
and how wisdom may be reached 'by breaking the rules'. There is also a
teacher's compassion when she speaks of disciplining the unruly mind:
unchecked thoughts, she says, are dangerous, but they are often no more
than 'children crying for milk'. Particularly interesting is the fact that many
of these are not poems of waiting but of *doing*. Lal Ded's work presents
the seeker as an active spiritual strategist and warrior. She feigns ignorance
to avoid unwanted attention. She pestles and roasts her heart in the fire of
love. She locks unbolted doors and looks her Beloved square in the eye. She
even strips off his skin 'with the whip of Om'.

Writes Hoskote: '[she] evolves from a wanderer, uncertain of
herself and looking for anchorage in a potentially hostile landscape,
into a questor who has found belonging beneath a sky that is
continuous with her mind.'

From seeker to finder to spiritual teacher, these luminous poems
chart an extraordinary journey.

~

They lash me with insults, serenade me with curses.
Their barking means nothing to me.
Even if they came with soul-flowers to offer,
I couldn't care less. Untouched, I move on.

\*

I trapped my breath in the bellows of my throat:
a lamp blazed up inside, showed me who I really was.
I crossed the darkness holding fast to that lamp,
scattering its light-seeds around me as I went.

\*

I, Lalla, wore myself down searching for Him
and found a strength after my strength had died.
I came to His threshold but found the door bolted.
I locked that door with my eyes and looked at Him.

\*

I locked the doors of my body,
trapped the thief of life and held my breath.
Chaining him in my heart's dark cellar,
I stripped off his skin with the whip of Om.

*

When the sun melts away, the moon remains.
When the moon melts away, the mind remains.
When the mind melts away, what's left?
Earth, ether, sky, all empty out.

*

When the scriptures melt away, the chants remain.
When the chants melt away, the mind remains.
When the mind melts away, what's left?
A void mingles with the Void.

*

Train your thoughts on the path of immortality.
Leave them unguarded and they'll grow
into monsters. But take heart, most of the time,
they're like children crying for milk.

*

My Master gave me just one rule:
Forget the outside, get to the inside of things.
I, Lalla, took that teaching to heart.
From that day, I've danced naked.

*

Shiva lives in many places.
He doesn't know Hindu from Muslim.
The Self that lives in you and others:
that's Shiva. Get the measure of Shiva.

*

Alone, I crossed the Field of Emptiness,
dropping my reason and my senses.
I stumbled on my own secret there
and flowered, a lotus rising from the marsh.

*

Wrapped up in Yourself, you hid from me.
All day I looked for You
And when I found You hiding inside me,
I ran wild, playing now me, now You.

*

As the moonlight faded, I called out to the madwoman,
eased her pain with the love of God.
'It's Lalla, it's Lalla,' I cried, waking up the Loved One.
I mixed with Him and drowned in a crystal lake.

*

I pestled my heart in love's mortar,
roasted it and ate it up.
I kept my cool but you can bet I wasn't sure
whether I'd live or die.

*

I hacked my way through six forests
until the moon woke up inside me.
The sky's breath sang through me,
dried up my body's substance.
I roasted my heart in passion's fire
and found Shankara!

*

Wisest to play the fool. Lynx-eyed, play blind.
Prick-eared, be deaf.
Polished, lie among the dull.
Survive.

*

Up, woman! Go make your offering.
Take wine, meat and a cake fit for the gods.
If you know the password to the Supreme Place,
you can reach wisdom by breaking the rules.

*[translated by Ranjit Hoskote]*

# Toral

## [Fourteenth Century CE]

Saurashtra, the peninsular region on the western coast of the Arabian Sea, has a fascinating cultural legacy of dacoits-turned-saints. The fact that they were from dispossessed backgrounds makes these interesting tales of social and spiritual rebellion.

The legend of Toral is a cocktail of romantic love and mystical adventure. Toral and her husband, Sansatia, led a life of prayer and devotion. One day, Jesal, a notorious bandit from Kutch who had heard much about her beauty, decided to abduct her. Her husband willingly agreed to part with his wife. This might have stemmed from helplessness, from an unbelievable spirit of altruism, or (as legend tells us) because he knew of an astrological prediction that his wife would transform the lives of more than one fallen man.

Toral then set off with Jesal to a new life in Kutch. A terrible storm broke out on the way. Jesal was terrified, but the brave and wise Toral retained her equanimity. Awed by her preternatural serenity, Jesal decided to mend his ways. The two lived together for several years as spiritual helpmates and partners. They are believed to have taken *samadhi* (consciously renounced their bodies) together, and their memorial shrines still exist in Anjar, Kutch. The legend of Toral, this remarkable saint and reformer of a hardened dacoit, lives on in the popular consciousness of the state of Gujarat, as does her poetry.

~

Jesal, think about it.
Death hovers over your head.
The world is but a dream.
Toral urges you,
'Come Jesal, let us meet in love.'

Diamonds are poured on an anvil
          to be crushed under a sledge.
If they break, they are fake;
          the real ones get known to the real.
'Come Jesal, let us meet in love.'

Bhakti is a dagger's edge;
          but the guru's grace is limitless.
What do the ones without a guru know?
          Their lives have been a waste.
'Come Jesal, let us meet in love.'

The guru's movement is subtle
          like the fragrance of the musk deer.
Trust the Lord's name;
          he will fulfill every wish.
'Come Jesal, let us meet in love.'

With a lifetime of experience,
          and the refuge of the true guru,
          we have set sail to the Lord's court.
The true guru will surely ferry us across.
'Come Jesal, let us meet in love.'

*[translated by Neelima Shukla–Bhatt]*

# Liral

## [Fourteenth to Fifteenth Century CE]

The folklore of Gujarat mentions several women saint poets named Liral. There are minor variations: one is referred to as Lidal and another as Lir. They belong to different historical periods, the most recent having lived in the nineteenth century (and who, like Toral, converted her husband to the spiritual path; her poem is included later in the book).

The earliest known Liral, however, was the daughter of a blacksmith, known as Devatankhi, and a mother named Meenalde. Her father was committed to the Mahapanth or Nijara Panth tradition. This was a spiritual path open to all classes, castes and genders, often allowing spouses to be jointly initiated. A certain measure of secrecy was evidently maintained around the practices, and in several cases, advanced women practitioners became initiators in their own right.

The guru, Ugamshi, and his disciple, Shelarshi, seem to have wandered through Saurashtra, imparting the principles and spirit of the Mahapanth tradition to a burgeoning tribe of disciples. Liral was initiated by Ugamsi, as this evocative poem of self-discovery indicates.

~

Who styled this brittle body?
Why was it fashioned so frail?

And yet,
>    within it are the moon, the sun, and a million stars;
>    within it, are the hammer and the billow that
>    shaped the self.

Within this jar are the tree, fruits, and the reaper.
>    Within it—the orchard, the tree-bed, water, and wind.
>    Within it—the lock, the key, and the locksmith.
>    Within it flow the Ganga and the Yamuna for one
>    to take a sacred bath.

At guru Ugamsi's feet, Liralbai proclaims,
'Here, I have found the precious True Word.'

*[translated by Neelima Shukla–Bhatt]*

# Loyan

## [Fourteenth to Fifteenth Century CE]

Loyan was yet another saint poet of western India who composed poems in Gujarati. According to tradition, she was a beautiful woman who belonged to the blacksmith caste. She was initiated into the spiritual life by her guru, Shelarshi, to whom she remained devoted.

She captured the attention of the local ruler, Lakho, who made attempts to lure and then abduct her. Loyan remained unmoved. On his second attempt to kidnap her, Lakho was struck with a skin disease. He realized the error of his ways and eventually became Loyan's disciple.

In her wise and cryptic poems, Loyan is a patient and spiritually refined preceptor. 'Leave aside your scheming,' she rebukes Lakha in one poem, and repeatedly urges faith in the figure of the guru: 'The key is in the guru's hands/ The lock will open only if the guru arrives.' As translator Neelima Shukla–Bhatt points out, Loyan was a guide to Lakho and, on occasion, to his wife, the queen, painstakingly mapping out the spiritual journey for both of them.

~

Lakha, a woman, Loyan, says to you,
    'The key is in the guru's hands.
    The lock will open only if the guru arrives.'

There is a lake brimming with milk, with embankments
of pearls.
>Those with a true guru
>>will drink there to their hearts' content.
Those without one will pass by thirsty.

There, a mango tree was planted.
Its trunk reached the sky
>and the branches extended to the heavens,
>>where only a skilled harvester might reach

Lakha, a woman, Loyan, says to you,
>'The key is in the guru's hands.
>The lock will open only if the guru arrives.'

*

Lakha, want to dissolve in the Ultimate?
Then seek an upsurge in love,
>leave aside your scheming.

Lakha, move inward to the carnival of light,
>leave aside all yearning.
Like a blade of grass is the world;
>see through its illusion.
It will be swept away with a single gust of time;
>and life will be lost to the wind.

Lakha, the guru's words will untangle within
>the knots of choices and resolutions.
Relish their flavour without fear.
So says Loyan, Shelarshi's pupil:
>absorb these words and drown in bliss!

*[translated by Neelima Shukla–Bhatt]*

# Kanhopatra

## [Fifteenth Century CE]

Little material exists about Kanhopatra's life, but like the chronicle of the Buddhist nun Amrapali, centuries before her, it is one that continues to fascinate hagiographers for its ostensible 'sex-worker-to-saint' storyline. The daughter of a wealthy courtesan named Shama, Kanhopatra was known for her spectacular beauty and talents in dance and music. A chance encounter with some pilgrims seems to have changed the course of her life. It led her from her hometown of Mangalvedha (home to Soyarabai as well) to the temple city of Pandharpur, which she eventually made her home. When the ruler of Bidar sought to make her his concubine, she is said to have turned to the god Vitthala of Pandharpur for deliverance. According to legend, she locked herself in the sanctum and died at the feet of the idol in the temple, like Andal before her—merging into oneness with the benevolent patron deity (as the canonical accounts tell us) or committing suicide (as an alternative version suggests, which could be seen as her act of rebellion against the status quo).

Colonial narratives and upper-caste folklore tend to present her either as a fallen woman yearning for acceptance in the eyes of the divine or as an unsullied maiden wedded to the lord. Above all, they present her as a passive victim of social circumstance and divine intervention, overlooking the complexity of Kanhopatra's life situation—much of which is left to our imagination. Her twenty-odd extant poems (sung even today) point to a rich subjective experience. They speak of her faith in Vitthala as well as the challenges and ordeals of her life. They also stoutly reject a world that seeks to objectify her. This is a voice of desperation *and* dignity, of devotion *and* independence. Like Janabai, she feminizes Krishna, turning him into a mother figure (as we see in the selected poems). No doubt this nurturing image was far more comforting than the predatory male figures with whom Kanhopatra was well acquainted.

The unique feature of her spiritual journey is the fact that there is no recorded evidence of any male guru in her life. Kanhopatra's spiritual relationship with her god seems to have been autonomous and unmediated. Writer Amruta Chowgule observes that it could be 'her matrilineal origin and her refusal to serve as an accessory to a male saintly figure' that have turned her into a relatively shadowy figure. Kanhopatra was buried in the southern part of the temple, and a tree still stands to mark the site of this unusual poet.

~

Mother Krishna in my innermost core,
From Your unseeing eyes, let mercy flow.

The world has forced me to be a whore,
From your unseeing eyes, let mercy flow.

The scriptures say: You raise the low,
From Your unseeing eyes, let mercy flow.

Time and again, Kanhopatra knocks at Your door,
From your unseeing eyes, let mercy flow.

*[translated by Neela Bhagwat and Jerry Pinto]*

*

No, my god, no!
No more of this ordeal
Life seems to flee my body.

The tiger has the fawn
between his fangs.
There is no place for me
in the three worlds
but at your feet.
Hurry, Vithabai.
    Mother,
        hurry.

I lose hope,
I grieve.

Shelter Kanhopatra within your heart.

My lord, I implore you,
don't deliver
my vulnerability
into the hands of my enemy.

The Vedas declare,
the six Shastras testify
that you are the saviour,
the protector of the helpless.

Now at your feet,
your supplicant,
    Kanhopatra,
repeats your definition to you.

                *


Nearest to my soul,
my mother Krishna,
my mother Kanha,
my dark one,
let your eyes show some mercy!

At the hint of scandal, people rush
to protect their reputation
my dark one,
let your eyes show some mercy!

The shastras declare you
the saviour of the defenceless
Prove them right,
my dark one,
let your eyes show some mercy!

Again and again
Kanhopatra surrenders before you,
my dark one,
        let your eyes show some mercy!

                    *


You claim the grand title
of saviour of the downtrodden
Then why this affliction for your devotee?
I am wedded to you, you to me,
so when another man claims me,
tell me, who is to blame?
When the jackal purloins the lion's prey,
it is the lion that is put to shame!

I surrender my body now.
All to uphold your title.

*[translated by Anjali Purohit]*

# Rami

## [Fifteenth Century CE]

The love story of Chandidas and Rami is legendary. The tale of the Brahmin musician–poet who broke all social taboos by falling in love with a low-caste widowed washerwoman has become an inspirational fable about human love and the way in which it can mirror the divine. The haunting poems of Chandidas celebrate a forbidden and immortal love. So do the lesser-known poems of Rami, his inspiration, who also happens to be the first acknowledged woman poet in Bengali literature. This literary legacy had a strong influence on later Bengali art, literature and Vaishnava spirituality.

Rami seems to have been a destitute wanderer who finally found work as a washerwoman in the Bashuli temple in the Bankura district. She composed devotional verses that were powerful and stirring. The poet Chandidas was the priest of the temple, and the two fell deeply in love. The social outcry was inevitable. Rami was fired and Chandidas was ostracized. In one poem, Rami bitterly reproaches her male neighbours for their slander, in a manner reminiscent of Radha whose forbidden love of Krishna also provoked much social censure.

Legends abound about what happened next. According to one, Chandidas fasted, died and was revived on the funeral pyre; another claims that he assumed the form of Vishnu. According to Rami's poems, Chandidas was invited by the nawab of Gaur to sing at his palace. He was then whipped to death while tied to the back of an elephant for having attracted the affections of the nawab's wife. Still another says that

Chandidas and Rami left their village and joyfully wandered through the dusty streets of Bengal, singing the praises of Krishna, echoes of their music drifting through the countryside to this day.

The story is unclear, and it seems impossible to tease history out of folklore. What remains is the poetry. Rami's bold and uninhibited voice lives on, expressing a revolutionary faith in love and freedom of choice and denouncing the hypocrisies of a convention-riddled society. Her articulation of her grief and rage makes her devotion seem that much more convincing.

~

[What can I say, friend?]

> What can I say, friend?
> I don't have enough words!
> Even as I weep when I tell you this story
> My accursed face breaks into laughter!
> Can you imagine the cheek of the sinister men?
> They have stopped worshipping the Devi
> And have started tarnishing my reputation.
>
> Let the thunderbolt crash on the heads of those
> Who from their housetops shout abuses at good people
> I won't stay any longer in this land of injustice.
> I'll go to a place where there are no hellhounds.

*[translated by Sumanta Banerjee]*

*

[Where have you gone?]

> Where have you gone,
> my Chandidas, my friend,

Birds thirst without water,
    despair without rain.
What have you done,
    O heartless lord of Gaur?
Not knowing what it means to love,
    you slay my cherished one.
Lord of my heart, my Chandidas,
    why did you break
the vows you made
    and sing in court?
Now evil men and beasts come swarming round;
    heavens turn to hell.
Betrayed by you, I stand in shame;
    you've crushed my honour in your hands
Once, heedless, untouched by Vasuli's threat,
    you told the court with pride
You'd leave a brahmin home, you said,
    to love a washergirl
Now, lashed to an elephant's back,
    you reach me with your eyes.
Why should the jealous king heed
    a washerwoman's cries?
Soul of my soul, how cruelly on your fainting limbs
    the heavy whip strikes and falls,
Cleave through my heart, and let me die
    with Chandidas, my love.

And then the queen fell on her knees,
    'Please stop, my lord,' she cried.
'His singing pierced me to the heart.
    No more of this, I plead.
Why must you thus destroy
    limbs made for love alone?

Free him, I beg of you, my lord,
    don't make love your toy.
O godless king, how could you know
    what love can mean?'
So spoke the queen, and then, her heart
    still fixed on Chandidas, she died.
Rami trembled, hearing her,
    and hastened to the place.
She threw herself at those queenly feet
    and wept the tears of death.

*[translated by Malini Bhattacharya]*

# Atukuri Molla

## [Fifteenth to Sixteenth Century CE]

According to a legend, Tenali Rama, the famed court poet of the Vijayanagar Empire, challenged a male poet from another village to prove his literary merit. It was an insult to the village. To restore the honour of her hamlet, Molla, the daughter of a local potter, took an oath that she would compose the Ramayana in Telugu in five days. The feisty young woman's rejoinder must have seemed laughable. How could a woman, particularly one of such lowly antecedents, with no background in intellectual learning or scholarship, accomplish such a task? But that is exactly what Molla did. In the process, she authored a Telugu version of the Ramayana in 138 verses, known even today for its simplicity, accessibility and unmannered diction.

What we know of Molla is that she was the daughter of Atukuri Kesanna, a potter and devotee of Shiva, who hailed from a Virashaiva background (one that was known for its heterodoxy and rejection of ritual and caste discrimination). She appears to have lost her mother early in life. In her work, she acknowledges her artisan father and the divine inspiration of Shiva (more specifically, Sri Kantha Mallesa, the deity of Srisailam). As scholars Susie Tharu and K. Lalita point out: 'Although it was the convention for poets in her time to claim divine inspiration, given Molla's own circumstances as a low-caste woman, it was perhaps mandatory that she do so, if her work was to be acknowledged or read.'

In an interesting departure from convention, she does not dedicate her work to any king or patron. Her stance reveals a self-confidence and an independence of spirit that are unusual, to say the least. Her poems speak of being 'untrained' with pride and suggest that she is making a case for a more robust, less precious literary idiom in Telugu. 'Obscure sounds and sense/ are no better than/ the dumb and the deaf,' she declares dismissively. Molla proved her credentials with the literary establishment of her time. She spent her last days in Srisailam, the site of the temple of her beloved Shiva, offering inspiration to the many seekers who sought her. She is believed to have consciously renounced her body at the ripe old age of ninety.

~

My father Kesava
was pious, friendly,
devoted to his guru,
and god in all his manifestations,
fixed and mobile.

Shiva's devotee
he was a guru in his own right.

I am god's gift to him;
they call me Molla.

*

I am no scholar
distinguishing the loanwords
from the native stock.

I know no rules of combination
no large vocabulary.

I am no expert
in composition and illocution,
semantics and style.

Nor do I know
phonetics, case relations,
roots of verbs and figures of speech,
meter and prosody, either.

Untrained though,
in composing poems and epics
in mastering lexicons and rules
I do write poems
by the grace of the famous Lord
Sri Kantha Mallesa.

                              *


As honey sweetens
the mouth readily
a poem should make sense
right away.

Obscure sounds and sense
are no better than
the dumb and deaf conversing.

                              *


The sun moved in the sky
from the East to the other end.

Fatigued and perspiring, he dived
into the western ocean
for a bath.

*[translated by B.V.L. Narayana Row]*

# Madhabi Dasi

## [Fifteenth to Sixteenth Century CE]

Regarded as the earliest female Bhakti poet in Odia literature, Madhabi Dasi remains an important presence in the Vaishnava tradition. Widowed as a child, she was initiated by her cousin into the devotional path associated with Lord Jagannath, the deity of Puri. She later went on to become a disciple of the celebrated mystic, Sri Chaitanya Mahaprabhu. However, since Sri Chaitanya was a monk, it was considered inappropriate for Madhabi Dasi to interact with him. In one poem, she speaks of watching him sing and dance in ecstasy, but from a respectable distance. Additionally, as a woman, her position was seen as decidedly subordinate to that of male disciples, and she was often considered an *ardha shishya* or 'half-disciple'. However, tradition suggests that her guru eventually acknowledged the sincerity of her devotion.

She was encouraged to study by her paternal uncle, but Madhabi Dasi's poetry is one of intense longing rather than philosophical reflection. Although her short poems were popular and sung during festivals, chanted at group rituals and performed by traditional dancers, not many are extant today. Her lyric poems in Odia, Bengali and Brajbhasa centre on the love of Radha and Krishna. Interestingly, as is evident in these poems, Krishna's longing for Radha is no less intense than hers for him. Perhaps this joyous image of requited love was the poet's veiled comment on a society that never quite offered her a relationship of mutuality with her guru?

~

Nanda's son, the prince of Braja,
       the venerated one, smeared with aromatic
sandal paste, reposes in Neeladri,
       the Lord of the universe, Jagannath.

The young Lord and lovely Radha,
       smitten with desire, lie in each other's arms
in soulful union in a secluded retreat,
       luminous in their sacred love.

The Gita Govinda, in its exquisite lines
       narrates the Lord's love for Radha,
his ecstasy in wrapping around his body
       a khandua sari emblazoned with her name.

Tying the same khandua sari as her very own headgear,
       the one with Radha's name, so dear to you, Krishna,
both your sacred names forever on her lips,
       Madhabi Dasi basks in your compassion.

She adorns her head with sacred basil leaves
                   surrendered at your feet.

*

Krishna savours the hour—
Radha in his lap, her soft body
pressed against him. He, the bee
thirsting for nectar; she, the lotus in bloom.

A growing rapture sets their hearts
aflutter; Radha, lying in Krishna's arms
in abandon, whispers,
Melt in me, Madhav, this propitious hour.

She hides her moonlike face
from his searching glances, his raging desire
to hear her sweet voice,
and behold her loveliness.

Radha's bewildered female companions
watch Krishna's besotted eagerness.
An awestruck Madhabi Dasi marvels,
What a blissful pair, truly made for each other!

                                        *

The handsome Gaur dances,
the gathered devotees following him.
They have all left home for Neelachala Puri,
they push and jostle to get closer to him.

Puri's houses are deserted, like rice-less husks;
Everyone seems to have fled behind Gaur.
The heralding chant 'Gaur-Hari' resounds in the air.
Madhabi Dasi is delighted to watch this dance.

Hands raised in the air, Gaur dances
in wild abandon, accompanied by his joyous companions.
The bemused folk of Puri watch, tempted
to join this whirling jamboree.

The clash of cymbals joins
the dholak's percussion to heighten the mood.
Madhabi Dasi witnesses the scene, enthralled,
and her soul resounds with Hari's name.

*[translated by Prabhanjan Mishra]*

# Meerabai

## [Sixteenth Century CE]

Chaste handmaiden to Krishna. Mad woman. Defiant rebel. Ecstatic poet. Meera (Mira/Mirabai) is all these and more. What's more, she is ubiquitous. She is the subject of novels, movies, calendar art and folklore, her poems translated into languages across the globe and her songs sung by classical, popular and traditional artists.

Yet, she remains elusive—now flesh and blood, now mythic ephemera. In his novel *Cuckold* (1997), author Kiran Nagarkar distils this enigmatic slipperiness in the portrait of 'Greeneyes' or the 'Little Saint', as seen through the eyes of her bewildered husband.

What we do know is that Meera was born in Merta, Rajasthan, and developed a childhood fascination with the figure of Krishna—a fascination that grew so all-consuming that she could not help but carry it into her marital home and her relationship with her husband, the crown prince of Mewar. Her in-laws were perplexed, then enraged, by her disregard of respectability and religious decorum. She let down her hair, wore ankle bells, sang herself hoarse and danced with the kind of recklessness that made many see her as crazy and a few as holy. Attempts were made by the clan to tame her and, when these failed, to eliminate her.

But the grace of Krishna seemed to protect his crazy devotee. Meera survived. And she was not cowed. She sang on. Later, she walked out of her home in the kingdom of Mewar and travelled to the lands of Vrindavan and Dwarka, places associated with her 'dark lord'. Here she presumably found a community of Krishna lovers as well as a guru.

Eventually, when her marital family tried to get her back (perhaps not entirely displeased with her burgeoning reputation of sainthood), she is said to have walked into the temple in Dwarka and merged into the idol of Krishna—like Andal and Kanhopatra before her.

She left behind a treasury of poems, suffused with the spirit of surrender and sensual abandon. The fact that millions of popular hymns in praise of Krishna are attributed to her, but very few authenticated, is testimony to the enduring trail of admirers and inspired imitators she left in her wake.

This selection includes fresh translations by Rahul Soni, as well as previously published translations by American poets Jane Hirshfied and Andrew Schelling, to offer a glimpse of the many ways in which Meera's work has piqued and catalysed the poetic imagination around the world.

~

rana
this shame is
so sweet

condemn or
commend me
I'll carry on

there's no
turning back
on this
one-way street

hermits
speak wisely
sinners
vilify

but girdhar's
my master

the sinners
can go die

\*

i dance
wearing
ankle-bells

people say
I'm mad
mother-in-law says
the ruin
of our clan

rana
sent me poison
I drank it
and laughed

offered
body and soul
for one look
at you

girdhar
my master
now let me come
to you

\*

fever-bird
stop crying
piya-piya

or
I'll tear off

your wings
cut off
your beak
rub salt
in your wounds

I'm aching
for my piya, my lover
I'm his
and he's mine
why should you
call to him

but
if your call
brings him to me
I'll gild
your beak
I'll crown you
king

crow
go tell my lover
his woman
can't eat
without him
she keeps
crying
piya-piya

come back soon
my master

you know all
don't you know

I can't live
without you

*

rana
i won't live
within
your walls

i've cast
my veil aside
the company of hermits
calls

left
my mother's home
shed
all attachments

my guru held
a mirror to my heart
now i dance
like a madwoman

rana
i don't want your
forts and palaces
ornaments and silks

i've seen
my true love
and he knows
my heart

my hair's
come loose

i dance
like a madwoman

*

i'm dyed
the colour of
my master

i went out to play
friend
wearing a blouse
of five colours

then i saw him
and the sight dyed
my body and soul
in his hue

those whose lovers
live far apart
they write and send
them letters

but i don't need
to come or go
my lover
lives in my heart

girdhar's
my master
night and day
i watch his path

*

i sit
awake

the world
sleeps

alone
in the palace
looking
for you

alone
in the palace
stringing
my tears

counting
the stars
waiting for
one moment of joy

girdhar
my master
to be parted after knowing you—
i cannot

                              *

struck
by beauty
i was struck
by your beauty

i went from body
to no body
the vessel i carried
fell

mother, father, brothers, kin
couldn't shake

your image
from my heart

my true love
was manifest
but the world thought
i strayed

besides you, my master
girdhar
who can know
my heart

*[translated by Rahul Soni]*

\*

The wild woman of the forests
Discovered the sweet plums by tasting,
And brought them to her Lord –
She was neither cultured nor lovely,
She who was filthy in disarrayed clothes,
She of the lowest castes.
But the Lord, seeing her heart,
Took the ruined plums from her hand.
She saw no difference between low and high,
Wanting only the milk of his presence.
Illiterate, she never studied the Teachings –
A single turn of the chariot's wheel
Brought her to Knowledge.
Now she is bound to the Storm Bodied One
By gold cords of Love, and wanders *his* woods.
Servant Mira says:
Whoever can love like this will be saved.
My Master lifts all that is fallen,

And from the beginning I have been the handmaiden
Herding cows by his side.

*[translated by Jane Hirshfield]*

*

Stumbling about,
  a clay pot on her head,
  the word for
  buttermilk gone from her tongue—
Who will take darkness, the Taker of Hearts?
Come take the taker, the taker!
The milking girl's lost in a
a dark body seizure,
      her mouth full of garble.

*

Take a yogin
  for lover, get nothing but grief.
  He beguiles you with intimate whispers—
      all worthless.
  Sister, he plucks your flower
  like a sprig of jasmine,
  then pulls on his robe and is gone.
  Mira says, Dark One,
  I saw you once,
      but tonight I'm an utter wreck.

*

You pressed Mira's seal of love
  then walked out.
  Unable to see you
  she's hopeless,
  tossing in bed—gasping her life out.

Dark One, it's your fault—
I'll join the yoginis,
I'll take the blade to my throat in Banaras,
Mira gave herself to you,
you touched her intimate seal
and then left.

*

Yogin, a single glimpse
    and I'd be exultant.
But life on this crazy planet is torment,
day and night torment.
Mad, raked by separation—
drifting from country to country—
look at Mira's black hair
        it's turned white.

*

Let them gossip.
    This mind never wavers.
Love fixes my mind on that enchanter of minds
like sorcery fixes on gold.
Birth after birth lost in sleep
until hearing the teacher's
word I awoke.
Mother, father, clan, tribe—
snapped like a thread!
Mira's lord can lift mountains,
he has aroused her.

*

Ten thousand thanks
    O astrologer
for announcing the Dark One's arrival!

Dizzy, ecstatic,
my soul goes into her bedroom.
Five companions converge,
five senses
to give him unparalleled pleasure.
One glimpse of his form
dispels anguish,
all my erotic longings bear fruit.
Shyam, the ocean of pleasure,
has come into me.

*[translated by Andrew Schelling]*

# Habba Khatun

## [Sixteenth Century CE]

The tomb of Habba Khatun on the Jammu–Srinagar National Highway stands dusty and deserted. The three Hindi films inspired by her life were never completed. She would not have been surprised. 'The divine blaze consumes only some/ Nothing will last, not a memory,' she famously said. Yet the voice of a woman considered to be the 'Nightingale of Kashmir' and its last great independent poet queen continues to pervade the valley, its music echoing through its chinar trees and saffron fields.

Like so many women poets of the land, Habba Khatun is more legend than fact. Born into a poor peasant family in the village of Chandhara, the beautiful Zooni (whose name means 'moon') seems to have been married to a man who had no patience with her poetic temperament and whose mother was even less sympathetic. She returned to her natal home, where one moonlit night, the last king of Kashmir, Yusuf Shah Chak, was spellbound as her voice wafted across to him over fields of purple saffron. The two fell in love.

Zooni entered his palace and took on the name of Habba Khatun. But in keeping with the tradition of love stories, tragedy struck. When the emperor Akbar arrested and exiled the emperor, a desolate Habba Khatun fled the palace with her daughter and settled down in a hut on the banks of the Jhelum. Here, she spent the rest of her life composing poems of loss and poignant separation that were to seep into the very rocks, trees and sapphire waters around her.

Another version claims that Habba Khatun was a poet–courtesan in the court of Yusuf Shah; yet another version claims she was a saint whose poetry was dedicated exclusively to the divine; and still another version insists that she never existed at all. What we do know is that her poems became a part of the oral tradition, making her an inerasable presence in Kashmiri poetry even four centuries after her death.

Translator Neerja Matto points out that Habba Khatun is 'one who is not content to just love and worship from a distance but demands fulfilment'. As she says in one of her verses, 'I read the Quran in one attempt/I didn't make a single mistake/ But I could not read the text of love.'

It is this presumption of intimacy that the female bardic voice brings so distinctively into sacred poetry. It empowers her to reproach, rebuke, dismiss and love all at once. Says Mattoo: 'Even when she is addressing the Almighty, her tone is more of a complaint against His ways than veneration.' Her distinct poetic form, the *lol* or the *loal*, embodies what poet Ranjit Hoskote describes as 'an intense and compelling state of longing . . . for the fleshly and the sublime all at once.'

This Kashmiri woman's verse of lament and longing speaks in many registers. Is this human love or sacred yearning? Do we view Habba Khatun as sybarite or spiritual seeker? The richness of her verse lies precisely in its ability to defy these categories. It is in this 'betweenness', this refusal to binarize flesh and spirit, that the genius of this poet, and so many other female bards, seems to lie. As for the line, 'Nothing will last, not a memory', it seems, at least in the case of Habba Khatun's verse, to have, to have been proved happily wrong.

~

Every pore of my body aches
He fills me with desire!

He looked at me from over the wall
I would have wrapped him in the finest shawl

Why was he so offended?
He fills me with desire!

He looked at me from the doorway—
Who showed him to my home?
For me, there's only anguish!
He fills me with desire!

He looked at me from the window
Long-necked beauty that I am
He left my heart so empty
He fills me with desire!
He looked at me from the skylight
Spoke to me like a songbird
Slowly, he vanished from sight.
He fills me with desire!

He looked at me from the attic
Like a trader, he entered my house
Bit by bit, he wasted me away
He fills me with desire!
He looked at me from the rooftop
He let me burn like a flaming torch
He left me nothing but regret
He fills me with desire!

He glanced at me as the moon was sinking
Why did he come like a man so mad
Why did he play that part
He fills me with desire!

He looked at me from the river bank
The rose's bud was lost forever
The fire of love consumed me
He fills me with desire!

*

In the heat of the summer I melt like ice
I'll only be whole in my mother's home.

I cook fine foods in the Shalimar
And light strings of lamps in Sona Laenk
If I don't see him, I'll cover myself in ashes
I'll only be whole in my mother's home.

Sick and wasted, I trail your steps
Winter winds blow away my leaves
Your deafness makes me a songless bird
I'll only be whole in my mother's home.

So much hostility! How much can I tell?
I bare my heart for you to see
My ears are deaf, I run to the woods
I'll only be whole in my mother's home.

How far you stray! I fall at your feet
Habba Khatun will waste away
What good's your regret, when I'm one with the earth?
I'll only be whole in my mother's home.

*

Forgive me my faults, God
What will you gain from my death?

I'm caught in a web, how do I pass the day
My basil's glow now pale as mint
The fire you lit smoulders in my heart
What will you gain from my death?

You may load yourself with untold treasures
But you'll be empty-handed in the grave
Why, my youth, were you so proud?
What will you gain from my death?

I read the Quran in one attempt
I didn't make a single mistake
But I could not read the text of love
What will you gain from my death?

Habba's body is in such pain
You didn't come to see her even once
Are you waiting till I'm in my grave?
What will you gain from my death?

*[translated by Neerja Mattoo]*

# Padmapriya

## [Sixteenth Century CE]

The first woman poet of the Assamese language, Padmapriya, was the daughter of the spiritual teacher, Gopaladeva, a direct disciple of the Vaishnava saint, Sankaradeva. A renowned polymath, mystic, poet, scholar, playwright and religious and social reformer, Sankaradeva spearheaded the Bhakti movement in Assam. His legacy of Vaishnavism, the new musical and theatrical forms he pioneered (such as Borgeet, Ankia Nat/Bhaona, Sattriya dance, and the literary language of Assamese Brajabauli), and the *sattras*, or monastic institutions that he established, continue to flourish as living traditions in Assam even today. While his spiritual movement was open to men of all caste and class backgrounds, women were evidently discouraged from such congregational participation. It is in this context that Padmapriya becomes such a significant figure.

While other girls did not receive an education, she was actively encouraged in her creative and spiritual pursuits by Gopaladeva, who had founded a sattra in Kaljhar, Bhavanipur. Her marriage alliance with Gopaladeva's prime disciple fell through when the young man politely declined. He viewed Padmapriya, he explained, as a mother figure rather than a partner. This made it easier for the young woman to devote her life to the spiritual life and the promotion of her father's legacy. After Gopaladeva's death, she founded her own sattra, becoming the first woman to do so. Her intensely devotional poems, composed in Assamese and Brajabauli, are not widely available, but the few that survive in the oral tradition establish her as Assam's first woman of letters.

~

O mind,
do not forget the Guru's words.
They will light my way
and holding fast to these words
I will navigate the river of life.

Son-husband-wealth are all mirages,
mere reflections on a drop of water—
here one moment and gone the next—
reduced to ash, devoured by time.

Life and youth are both illusions,
visions of a dream
that make you forgo the higher purpose
leaving only misery in their wake.

The thirsting mind and worldly attachments
are the ropes of Maya's great delusion,
says Padmapriya, as she bows
at the feet of Gopal, her refuge.

*[translated by Dibyajyoti Sarma]*

# Rupa Bhavani

## [Seventeenth to Eighteenth Century CE]

One of Kashmir's best-known saints, Rupa Bhavani, like Lal Ded before her, walked out of a marriage, charted her own course and refused to submit to socially assigned roles. Unlike Lal Ded's work, which was part of an oral tradition, Rupa Bhavani's poetry was written and 'remained the possession of the Kashmiri Pandit intellectual elite', says translator Neerja Matto. There is a certain gravitas, or what Mattoo terms 'a brooding intellectuality', about her work, making her not merely a mystic but an obviously scholarly and culturally refined woman of letters.

Rupa Bhavani was spiritually inclined from an early age. Born into a learned Kashmiri brahmin family, she seems to have grown up in an ethos that offered her exposure to Vedanta, Kashmiri Shaivism and Sufism. She was married at age seven, but gave up the householder life after an unhappy marriage, and returned to her father's home where she continued her spiritual exploration uninterrupted. Her father was not merely supportive, but was also the first to acknowledge her attainments. Like Lal Ded before her, she did not remain within her home for very long. She soon became an itinerant, wandering the countryside and entering into long spells of meditative absorption, her poems mapping the subtle aspects of her yogic journey.

She had her own loyal following that regarded her in her lifetime as an incarnation of the goddess Bhavani. 'The springs and secret grottoes associated with her mystic experiences are well-known to Kashmiris who venerate them as shrines,' says Mattoo. Conversant with Sanskrit, the language of Hindu scripture, and classic literature in Persian, the official language, Rupa Bhavani was recognized by some of the major Hindu and Sufi male mystics of her time, with whom she seems to have had conversations on an equal footing. These included Rishi Peer, Mohammad Sadiq Qalandar and Baba Asaruddin Quadiri. Her enigmatic poetry (composed in a mix of old Kashmiri, Sanskrit and Persian) was never deemed popular but has had a devoted readership of literary initiates over the centuries.

~

Give me the skill that solves the riddle
Give me the state where I find You in me
Give me all the attributes of Shankara
Or else it's only self-deception

*

Ferry the river with the wind as ferryman
No colour, no caste, no clan to consider
Weed your field and then do the rest
Who then the debtor and who creditor?

*

The body in bliss, a river of wine!
The cups of these eyes are open
O saqi, come and fill them to the brim, do!
Hu Hoo Ha! I cry in ecstasy, madness in my heart!

*

I thundered from my source and flowed like a river
I filled every vessel, every cup on my way
Who will drink from them? Only those who can.
These cups, I have filled them to the brim, drink!

*

I came like a thundering river of nectar,
Beautiful, dazzling and timeless,
Fulfilled and fulfilling, astride the three worlds,
Vast like the expanse of the ocean itself

\*

I have not bowed, I never will
The one who listens
Is resplendent, within me
That is worship, that's what I do

\*

The sword of meditation slung by my side
I mount the horse of twin breaths
The veena of the oriole's song fills the air
The conches resound all around
Cymbals ring, river of practice springs forth
That is how I worship Shiva

\*

Supported by the flow, I reached Him
The music of the *tamboor* held me in thrall
With streaming moonbeams I bathe Shiva
The parrot, grown sage, is now speechless

\*

The one who treads the path is motivated already
That divine form permeates her body
As though a sacrificial fire is lit by her
Nectar falls on her like a stream

\*

Inside this body-cave I fed on all the elements
Traversed this whole globe and the nether world
With the fire of breath control I melted the ghee
And from my own limbs made the Ganga spring forth

*

The ever-alert plays and dances as others do
Decks herself, good clothes she wears
Ever-conscious, herself is perfect
On Shiva's path, becomes Shiva Himself

*[translated by Neerja Mattoo]*

# Bahinabai

## [Seventeenth Century CE]

Bahinabai was a poet in the Varkari tradition of Maharashtra. Her autobiography is an account of a remarkable spiritual journey (and includes her memories of twelve previous lifetimes!) as well as her troubled marriage with an abusive husband. Unlike many women saints who remained single or walked out of married lives, Bahinabai chose to endure the ordeals of a difficult marriage until the end of her days. Her poetry in Marathi reflects the challenges of leading a life of conflicting priorities.

She speaks of an early spiritual encounter with a calf. When her husband separated her from this beloved animal, she was beside herself with grief. It was at this point that Vitthala, the patron deity of Pandharpur, and later the mystic poet Tukaram, appeared to her in visions and initiated her into the spiritual path of bhakti. Henceforth, Bahinbai considered Tukaram to be her guru.

Deemed alternately saintly and crazy by the world around her, Bahinabai stayed true to her spiritual calling until the end of her days. Alarmed and jealous at her attainments and growing fame, her hostile husband seems to have scoffed at her guru's low-caste background, physically abused, confined and even attempted to desert her on various occasions. But after years of inflicting such domestic violence, he was eventually convinced of her genuineness.

Bahinabai's poetry speaks of dispassion and adherence to social duty. While her attempts to idealize female adherence to marital vows at all costs could seem outdated today, they offer interesting insights into the challenges of brahmin orthodoxy as negotiated by a female spiritual traveller of her time. Her commitment to her own journey, despite the odds, also indicates a woman of steely determination.

~

Such happiness then, such happiness.
I could have sat there even to the end.
I bathed in the Indrayani and joy-soaked
I went to the temple. I looked upon
Panduranga. I felt his gaze upon me.

The words began to flow.

I bowed to Tukoba and went home.

Bahini says: The ocean is within me.
In the sky of my heart, God spoke in thunder.

*[translated by Neela Bhagwat and Jerry Pinto]*

\*

For her milk, you serve the cow.
For its fruit, you plant the mango.
Can't you see what you're doing?
Each act seeking its own reward?
Why pour milk on the roots of the vine?
Why seek out the rich with whom to dine?
Bahini says: These deeds
              are the route to ignorance.

\*

Who plants grass in a forest?
Who knows the heart's wild ways?
Who makes hillslopes home to the trees?

Who directs the birds? Who guides the bees?
Each does what its nature dictates.
Bahini says: The heart's desires multiply
      For that is its way.

\*

When I wind my ten senses around Hari's feet,
What will you make of that?
Go, mind, go, join those senses;
For this now I determine:
All will, all self, all thought and aim?
All offered up to the spirit.
Bahini says: No desire now.
      Just His feet.

\*

No darkness haunts
Even the dreams
Of the residents of the sun.
No illusion then;
for knowing Brahma
Is the cure for maya.
Does the touchstone know
Gold? Or iron?
No desires, no self, no temptations.
Bahini says: Can water thirst?
      In perfection feelings find purity.

\*

Words and meanings belong to the visible realm.
They disappear in the invisible.
Ask a Sadguru if you don't get that.
But even your friend-philosopher-guide

Will disappear in the invisible.
Your senses and what they sense
Belong to the universe of form.
They disappear in the formless divine.
Bahini says: That which yields not to words
                    Can only be explained by a maternal Sadguru.

*

Here's pride. There's ignorance of the heart's ways.
Here rules and mantras, but nothing to give one rest.
There five different postures of prayer.
Here sacred waters, there austerities and rites.
Here ceremonies and prescriptive rituals.
Bahini says: My mind cannot rest
                    On a battlefield of ignorance.

*[translated by Jerry Pinto]*

# Taj Bibi

## [Seventeenth Century CE]

Little is known about this woman, who has often been described as the 'Meera of the Mughals'. Some accounts say she was the wife of the Mughal emperor Akbar and the disciple of Gosain Shri Vitthalnath; others claim she was the wife of Akbar's heir, Jehangir. Some say she was a Rajput who married into the Mughal clan; others say she was the daughter of a Mughal nobleman. What is clear is that Taj Bibi knew that her love of Krishna was transgressive. This was not merely because it flouted the norms of a feudal social order. It also flouted the proprieties of faith.

It would be facile to view Taj Bibi as a symbol of the supremacy of one religion over another. Instead, what Taj Bibi represents today is the power of individual choice, the courage of a woman determined to follow the dictates of her heart rather than meekly abide by the rules of the collective. In a world where religions still have their overzealous gatekeepers, Taj Bibi points us to the surprises of the inner journey. For when the divine visits, it is not always in the shape or garb one expects. Taj Bibi was ambushed by the form of Krishna—a form that presented its challenges, given that she was Muslim, even as it produced a verse of intoxicated longing and love-maddened separation.

A charming story tells of Taj Bibi yearning for a glimpse of the deity in the local Govind Dev temple of Vrindavan. She believed she had no right to enter, for she was a *mleccha*, an 'impure' outsider. She hoped a priest would invite her in, but that, unsurprisingly, did not happen. Longing turned to despair. Despair turned to rage. She decided to give up food and drink and end her life. On the third night of her fast, her hut was filled with a blue radiance. She woke to find her beloved Govind Dev (or Krishna) standing before her with a plate of food and a jar of water. Food had never tasted so sublime, and water so nectarine. While the tale might well have been woven by a fertile local imagination, it remains poignant. For devotees might have their doubts and the doorkeepers of every faith might have their rules, but the domain of the sacred, we are reminded, is closed to none.

~

He's a dashing trickster,
Dyed in every possible hue,
Stubborn he is,
Utterly unique among the gods.

A garland bedecks him,
His nose pearl lustrous,
Earrings aglitter,
A crown of gold graces his head.

Saboteur of immoralists,
Protector of the wise,
Embodiment of consciousness,
Skilled connoisseur of love.

Beloved son of Nanda,
Slayer of Kansa,
Local youth of Vrindavan,
Krishna, lord of worlds,

   Is mine.

# Shenkottai Avudai Akkal

## [Eighteenth Century CE]

Shenkottai Avudai Akkal was a Tamil poet and saint whose poetry—alive with wonder, radiant with revelation, corrosively critical of orthodoxy—deserves to be far better known by Tamil speakers as well as seekers everywhere.

Born in the district of Tirunelveli, Avudai Akkal was married and widowed early. To describe the life of a child widow in the orthodox brahmin community of her time as hard would be an understatement. She would have had to undergo multiple rituals of austerity and mortification: tonsuring her head, giving up all ornamentation, wearing white unstitched cotton without a blouse, covering her head at all times, living in seclusion and leading a life of abstinence and celibacy. What is amazing is that Avudai Akkal's mentions none of this. Instead, she turns each one of these tropes inside out in her poetry, subverting every norm and ritual by imbuing it with her own fresh, radiantly original perspective. To read Avudai Akkal is to read not a woman reformed but a woman transformed by the life of the spirit.

The astonishing confidence of this poetry had much to do with a pivotal encounter: her meeting with her spiritual master. She sings of him with gratitude in poem after poem. Was he moved by this child widow's plight, or did he see in her an exceptional spiritual possibility? Perhaps both. What we do know is that on a visit to her village, he paused at the threshold of her home. That evening, he offered the young widow an initiation. A guru in the tradition of Advaita Vedanta, Sri Venkateswa Ayyawal did not offer mere scriptural instruction. Instead, he offered a key to transformation. The gratitude for what followed is summed up lyrically by Akkal: 'Like the full moon, brimming intoxicated/ I emptied into a radiant, infinite sky.'

The poems in this selection raise a series of superbly ironic questions about purity and pollution. Akkal makes effortless mincemeat of ideas of *ecchil* (the act of being polluted by another's saliva by consuming food or water from the same container) and *teettu* (ritual impurity). And in the final poem, a tour de force, she overturns the puberty ritual associated with menstruation by redefining it as a celebration of female bonding and community. There is an elaborate rite of sisterhood in which the sacred texts—personified as adolescent girls—dance around the menstruating girl and freely eat off each other's echhil! Finally, when every purity/impurity norm is punctured, Akkal gives us the image of the menstruating girl, secure in the knowledge of her desirability, preparing for her blissful union with the divine. The divine, it must be added, is deeply admiring of her, too!

Composed in colloquial Tamil, Avudai Akkal's poems were preserved by women in her district, who sang them and integrated them into their daily lives. Metaphysically sophisticated and yet anchored in daily domesticity, these poems have probably been companions over generations to many a desolate widow, chafing wife and thirsty seeker. Kanchana Natarajan's efforts have recently brought this extraordinary work into English translation.

~

O men! You lament: '*Ecchil! Ecchil*! . . .'
But there is no place without ecchil, Supreme One!
The forms of god are ecchil,
Honey is the ecchil of the bee,
And is not all nourishing mother's milk
Also ecchil, Supreme One?

The ecchil of the fish is in the holy waters,
The brahmins who bathe in holy rivers are ecchil.

Are not pecked fruits the ecchil of parrots, Supreme One?
The ecchil of the insect bores into and blights the coconut,
The little cats' excreta is everywhere, and I know
That space too is tainted with echhil, Supreme One!

The first sound is ecchil, the first form is ecchil,
The four Vedas of the brahmins are echhil.
Is not the tongue that chants the Vedas' ecchil, Supreme One?
The macrocosm and the microcosm, the various worlds,
Are all withdrawn into ecchil!
Do the dogmatic, frenzied religious men now even dare
Open their mouths to complain, Supreme One?

While mouth and body are ecchil,
Simply washing the feet every now and then
Will not purify anyone, Supreme One!

Only the Lord, the Truth, is not ecchil,
Because that Light has never become
The utterance or its meaning, Supreme One!

*

Yelling 'Teettu!' you take to your heels!
Now, who can understand the play of delusion
That overpowers you, Supreme One!
When the same teettu blossoms
And crosses your threshold
As a sculptured, nubile young maiden
Whom you so lustfully approach--
Does teettu then recede, Supreme One?

The young maiden, sweet as a ripe mango,
Absorbed in deluded self-admiration,
Became an ovum and then began

Adoring the sperm, Supreme One!
And fusing with it, firmly sprouted and spread
Into five branches in the world, Supreme One!
Sperm fertilized the egg,
They became the ninety-six cosmic principles,
And hence all lineages are superior, Supreme One!
Such is the cosmic tree that bears fruit--
Yet this incurable vertigo called lust
Continues to flourish, Supreme One!
Teettu appears, in superb order,
In so many varieties of forms,
But who can tell me why it so manifests, Supreme One?
Is not the son in your arms teettu from your loins?
With whom can I share this embarrassment, Supreme One?

The result of your earlier teettu
Is lying asleep in your cradle—and now
You unhesitatingly pick it up to kiss it!
How can it be that your remain so blind
To the Creator's illusion, Supreme One?
O man! When the teettu of your lust
Took the shape of the child in your arms,
You crawled off like a tortoise
To bathe in the holy rivers, Supreme One!

All scriptures, all castes, all divisions, all stations
And all holy men are teettu:
Do they know this, Supreme One?
Shiva and Shakti pervade everything,
But the ignorant fools believing in teettu
See only darkness, Supreme One!

The one reality without teettu
Is Consciousness Supreme!

If only the horned owl
Could see in broad daylight, Supreme One!
Recognizing Shiva, the Supreme Light of all lights,
That once consumed the lethal poison,
I transcended the three names, Supreme One!

Transfixed as though stung
By the fearsome black scorpion,
I no more see the ego or frantic motion
Of the deluded mind, Supreme One!

Will all the riches, the gold and precious stones
Accumulating in our treasure chests
Accompany us when we leave this world?
Tell me, Supreme One!
Stones, sugarcane, molasses, sugar—
Can the different sorts of minds
All be one, Supreme One?
Just as a stone flung at algae
Gashes the thick layer to reveal
The clear water ever-present beneath,
Only great sages see the hidden truth, Supreme One!

Like a babbling lunatic, like a corpse, like one drunk,
I forgot the body, Supreme One! . . .

                              *

He declared: 'Maya, I will not be caught by your snares!'
     dear friend.
He indeed is dangerous, dear friend;
This I have heard from many.

Like an upright respectable person, dear friend,
He manifested in this country.

Slowly and steadily, dear friend,
He approached the threshold of the house.

He softly and gently murmured, dear friend:
'You are indeed the Supreme.'
And then he asked me, 'Who are you?'
I stayed silent as though I knew nothing, dear friend.

He dampened and extinguished the fire of ego
        dear friend!
Entering me, he compelled the relinquishing of individuality
        dear friend!

He cast a propitious glance
At my illusion and ignorance, dear friend!
And the way he looked at me caused the waters
Of the ocean of birth and death
To evaporate, dear friend!

He placed his hands on my head, dear friend,
And reiterated, 'Brahman is the Truth, the only Truth.'
He asked, 'Do you know yourself?'
I stood mute, dear friend.

Impaling me on an iron hook of devotion,
He severed my mind, dear friend!
He beckoned me to the peepul tree, dear friend,
And proclaimed, 'I am indeed Brahman.'

He said, 'Know thyself,' dear friend,
And through gestures, explained how.
In blissful Oneness, dear friend,
I walked away, never turning back!

He transformed my delusions, dear friend,
Bestowing liberation upon me.

And then I renounced all attachments,
Including the bond between mother and child!

I meditated upon his lotus-like feet
As supreme, dear friend.
Like those snared in their own fear,
I too was terrified, dear friend.

Quoting many sacred texts, dear friend,
He said, 'Experience the Truth for yourself:
You were born because of your own will.'

He said, 'All creation is imagined by you,
You are the Light of all lights!'
He assured me with these words, dear friend,
As I stared at him with purified intent.

Like the solitary moon, dear friend,
I too merged into vast emptiness.
Like the full moon, brimming intoxicated
I emptied into a radiant, infinite sky.
. . . . . . . . .

*

In the menstruation room
Vidya spent the three nights
Called Waking, Dreaming and Deep Sleep
. . . . . .
At dawn of the fourth day, within the house,
Its floor swept and cleaned with cow-dung,
Scriptures, like adolescent girls, seated the young woman
on the ritual kolam.
Praising the Satguru, they anointed Vidya with fragrant oil
And then took her to lake Manasarovar,
Where even yogins dance in rapture.

Washing her hair with fragrant soap nut powder,
Anointing her with auspicious turmeric paste,
Cooling her body in the lake of Bliss,
They gave her an auspicious bath,
Then the maidens donned in various styles
A variety of gorgeous silk apparels
Called 'peace', that shone like moonlight.
They draped their breasts with the bodice called 'courage'
And combed out their long flowing hair,
Shaping it into elegant coils.
They put on the gold necklace
Called 'the transcendence of the worlds'.
They applied collyrium to their dark eyes
That saw the depths of all the worlds as Self;
As a sign of auspiciousness, they applied on their
foreheads
The special vermilion of 'equal regard for friend and foe'.
Adorning their fingers with a ring called Consciousness,
The girls sat by the lake called the Ocean of Bliss
And relished a variety of rice preparations.
Chattering about all manner of peculiar things,
The girls ate on another's echhil,
And after consuming generous amounts,
Enjoyed betel leaves as round as the full moon,
Containing the areca nuts called 'Vedanta',
Chewing these they rose and stood
Facing one another in straight lines.
In Light undimmed by illusion, they sang,
Clapping their palms to the refrain
'All manifest forms are our own forms,
All speech spoken is our own speech!'
Thus, they concluded the auspicious ritual.

. . . . . .

The Vanquisher of Illusion entered the chamber
And lay down. Immediately, Vidya was drawn
Into the infinitude of vast space.
Bashfully, with eyes lowered,
From the corners of her eyes
She beheld the Immaculate Light.
Taking cue, the All-Knowing Lord
Subsumed her in his arms.
'So young, yet abiding in Knowledge!'
Thinking thus, He praised her
And dissolved the 'I'-self;
Both became That.
Just as the wise ever abide in the Self
Like coolness in cool liquids, merged
Like as salt in water, like as camphor in flame,
Now ever free from bondage, Vidya
Became One with Brahman,
The Eternal Truth.

~

*[translated by Kanchana Natarajan]*

# Tarigonda Venkamamba

## [Eighteenth Century CE]

Venkamamba's passionate devotion to Lord Venkateshwara of Tirupati led many in her village to conclude she was insane. She remained undeterred. An inspired devotional poet from an early age, she had a spiritual education under an accomplished tutor, Subramanya Desika. Beautiful, talented and independent, her many gifts provoked admiration, fear and censure throughout her life.

Widowed as a child (she was married early, as was the custom of her time), she refused to act according to the conventions of widowhood. Her true lord, she declared, was Venkateswara, who was alive and well, and she refused to discard any of the signs of matrimony: vermilion, flowers in her hair, coloured apparel or her mangalsutra. Her rebellion did not end there. Her immersion in poetry, her independent spiritual orientation and her disregard for cultural norms scandalized her village.

According to one legend, the errant poet was summoned by the religious pontiff Sringeri Shankaracharya. She refused, however, to bow before him. When the outraged Brahmin elders insisted, she asked the Shankaracharya to rise. She then bowed before an empty seat that promptly burst into flames. Awed and chastened, the elders were compelled to accept defeat. It was clear that taming Venkamamba wouldn't be an easy task.

However, the poet decided life might be more congenial if she shifted residences. She moved to Tirumala where she was welcomed by the descendants of Annamacharya (the fifteenth-century poet who wrote in praise of Lord Venkateshwara). According to yet another legend, her beloved deity, Venkateswara, welcomed her into his sanctum every night, where she propitiated him with pearls and regaled him with her verse. When the priests discovered the pearls in the sanctum, they grew irate and exiled her to a cave fifteen miles away. However, god and devotee continued their nocturnal meetings through a secret passage.

Eventually, the priests relented and requested Venkamamba to return. She was now invited to participate in the worship of her cherished idol, and her composition (the *Mutyala Harathi*) has been incorporated into the last ritual performed at the temple to this very day. She created a substantial oeuvre of poetry in Telugu that encompasses religious verse, devotional hymns, lyrics for different cultural occasions (from lullabies to wedding songs), as well as several popular folksongs (most of which seem now to be lost) for Yakshagana, the traditional theatre of the region.

Musician and researcher, Dr Subhadra Desai, writes that Venkamamba's songs 'were sung locally in earlier times, . . . [but] she had many detractors among brahmin priests who could not accept her self-sufficiency.' Consequently, much of her work has not been preserved. Recently, scholars and musicians in Tirupati and Venkatagiri have done much to resuscitate the work of this legendary poet.

~

> Gently he lifts me up
> Wipes the stream of tears from my eyes
> Trails his fingers softly through my twisted hair
> Braids my tresses and decks them with flowers
> Gently requests I change my crumpled clothes
> Into a flowered raiment of his choice
> And adorns me with trinkets of gold and silver.
> On my forehead, he places the
> Vermilion mark of fidelity and artfully
> Darkens my reddened eyes with kajal
> And on my breasts, with his own hands,
> Playfully rubs a sandal salve to

Cool my burning flesh:
Slowly guides me to his chamber
And cajoles me with
Loving appeals to 'let me know'
The secret reason for my sulk
(As if he didn't know)
And I, like a fool, tell him
About the flower that he
Gave Rukmini, the other one,
Whereupon he laughs lightly.
'Oh that', he says sweetly,
'To poor Rukmini I have given
a single petal of the parijat.
To you, I'll present the whole
Tree if you wish.
And now come into my arms
I cannot tarry much longer.'
And so again, fool that I am,
I believe the charming rogue
And suffocate him with my kisses.
And as I lie in love-drugged sleep,
He leaves me, as is his wont,
For another bed.
Tell me, my dear, where Tarigonda's Lord is now.
Find him, my dear, the beloved libertine,
And bring him back into my arms.

*[translated by Srinivas Rayaprol]*

\*

## Light of the Self

My dear, see, the luminosity of this Light.
No clue how far how deep, but beyond space

infernal-celestial and time. In every life-form,
exulting, the supreme Self—Light.

No one can grasp it or say it is like this or that.
Joining Shiva's dance into a perfected moon-state,
it unites with the world to shine in many sages.
The Light of the Self.

Illusion of illusions, power inscrutable.
Bound by illusion yet beyond illusion.
Day or night make no difference
to this Light, the highest Self.

Takes many forms, remains itself.
In three sacred peaks
resting in the ocean of ever-bliss.
This knowing Light of the Self.

Golden-hued, it is visible now, now not.
Night or day its bluish-copper glows
along the kundalini path within
the body, this Light.

Omniscient witness known only by experience.
In the form of an atom, pervades the universe.
My Guru, my Moon, Tarigonda's Lord Narasimha
is This Light.

*

## What's Bad, What's Good?

So what if they call you bad, or good?
Why so much tossing and torment?

They mistook your body for you
and reproached you, yes?

But who has seen the inner Self
that they can berate it?

Why do you argue with the arrogant?
Your support, this Master who moves in everyone

O mind, is there anyone who has seen you?
Who has figured the mind's ways?

Who has pondered the real-unreal?
Why get all tangled in false words?

Why grieve when you hear insults?
Why puff up when you get praise? . . .

. . . The Lord of the Serpent-Mountain, Tarigonda's Master,
is witness to both wrong and right.

He listens to what people profess.
A mighty one, this boss, watches what's what.

(So be good, be truly good).

*

## A Poem Like a String of Pearls, An Offering of Light
[Mutyala Harathi]

To Him who lives on the Seshachalam peak.
To the Sun blazing the darkness of sins.
To that great God's consort constant
Alamelumanga who looks after us.
Joy Be, May It All Be Well,
May It All Be Always Good and Well.

To the deity called 'boon-giver' to refuge-seekers.
To Alamelumanga who reminds Him,

'don't forget your job'.
Joy Be, May It All Be Well,
May It All Be Always Good and Well.

To Him who resides in the inner temple of bliss.
To the deity who protects the wretched.
To Alamelumanga who honours Her Lord,
dispenses his gifts.
Joy Be, May It All Be Well,
May It All Be Always Good and Well.

To Him who says 'I liberate humanity'.
He reveals heaven in the palm of his hand.
(We know the gesture points to His feet).
To the Ocean's daughter who resides
on the chest of Her Lord, She confers
the material gifts.
Joy Be, May It All Be Well,
May It All Be Always Good and Well.

To the faultless Lord who intimidates.
Slyly He says 'bring, bring your bargains here'
and takes them on board.
To the Mother who gets nice treats made,
and feeds everyone tirelessly.
Joy Be, May It All Be Well,
May It All Be Always Good and Well.

And to rows of spectacular arbours of wonder
To temple corridors, to sacred springs
To sky-high towers and ramparts
To gold domes that remain forever
To the many places to stay for free
To gardens laden with fruit and flowers
To storerooms, treasuries

To mouth-watering kitchens
To personal mounts like Garutman
To parasols, to crocodile-flanked canopies (they are
heaven's gates)
To banners of many kinds, to musical instruments
To pavilions designed for divine weddings
Joy Be, May It All Be Well,
May It All Be Always Good and Well.

To weapons and tools like the conch and wheel
To gem-studded ornaments, sacred garment sets
To hands, to feet, with all the main parts
To the deity's gracious, sacred form
To good qualities like wisdom
To limitless power, infinite glory
To all the family gods in the surround
To staff who work so earnestly
To major religious and nonstop festivals
To delightful, daily celebrations
To the reason how the world runs
To wishes, prayers, that rise like towers
Joy Be, May It All Be Well,
May It All Be Always Good and Well

Know this is Tarigonda's Lord Narasimha.
To Lord Srinivasa who gives gifts
to all those who run after him.
And of course to Mt. Seshadri who bears
the earthly home of the omnipresent.
Joy Be, May It All Be Well,
May It All Be Always Good and Well.

*[translated by Mani Rao]*

# Sahajo

## [Eighteenth Century CE]

Sahajo was among the foremost disciples of Charandas, a spiritual master and poet who was strongly opposed to orthodoxies of ritual and caste. Sahajo and Daya were both poets in their own right and were regarded by Charandas (according to the twentieth-century spiritual master Osho) as his 'two eyes' and 'two wings of a bird'.

According to one account, Sahajo was beautifying herself after her wedding ceremony as she prepared to leave for her husband's home. A mendicant who happened to pass by made some pointed remarks in verse about the futility of self-adornment in a fickle and transient world. Deeply moved, Sahajo decided to forego her marital life and embrace a life of contemplation instead. The mendicant was Charandas, who then became her guru. (Another narrative holds that Charandas was, in fact, Sahajo's own brother.) She remained with him until the end of his days, after which she seems to have become a guide and mentor in her own right.

By the age of eighteen, she had composed her work, *Sahaj-Prakash*, a collection of eighty-five succinct poems that speak of the spiritual path, the importance of the guru and the significance of chanting. The selected poems emphasize an important distinction: the guide to inner freedom is far more significant than the divine as saviour or rescuer. It is a reminder of what the ultimate promise of *mukti* represents: freedom from concepts and crutches of every kind, including the very concept of the divine. If Sahajo chooses guru over god, it is because she chooses liberation over a life mired in duality.

~

Ram? I could perhaps abandon him,
but my guru? Never.

I am more indebted to my master
than I am to my Maker.

*

Into the mirage of doership
Hari seduced me.

To my innermost self
my guru introduced me

*

Hari ensnared me
in a dense web of kinship.

My guru butchered the ties
of every relationship.

*

And again Hari bound me
to the wheel of delusion

But my guru decimated
every illusion.

*

Hari did his damnedest
to stay concealed

but with my guru's lamp of clarity
he now stands revealed.

*[translated by Arundhathi Subramaniam]*

# Daya

## [Eighteenth Century CE]

Born in the village of Dehra in Mewat, Dayabai was a poet and disciple of Guru Charandas (and, after his time, of one of his three successors, Juktanand Swami). She seems to have been adopted as a child by the master and lived out most of her life as a renunciate. She is the author of two works: *Dayabodh* and *Vinayamalika*.

It is not surprising, says the mystic and spiritual teacher Osho, that we know very little about her: 'Daya belongs to those devotees who have left no information about themselves. They drowned so much in singing songs of the divine that no time was left for leaving information. Just the name is known . . .' What we do know is that she lived in Delhi.

Hers are not the poems of erotic spirituality, as we find in the works of Andal or Meera. Instead, they reveal a path of knowledge, meditation and devotion. At the same time, her poems about her tribe suggest a distinctly wild fellowship. She speaks often of those afflicted by the malaise of spiritual love: they reel around, restless and drunk 'with Hari's wine', laughing, singing, weeping, their speech slurred; 'they put their foot in one place and it lands somewhere else'. Nothing sedate about this lot!

The sadhu is a warrior in Daya's poems. This is not a path for the tame or the faint-hearted. The images are vigorous and martial; the implements invoked are club and mace; and the victor is the one who 'cuts off his head/ and lays it down as an offering/ to the earth.'

The metaphor here is of the practitioner as spiritual acrobat: 'I sank at first into the depths of the underworld,/ Till a great explosion hurled me up into the sky—/ My face took on the face of an acrobat-girl.'

Other poems speak of her meditative practices based around *ajapa japa*, or 'chanting without chanting' and taking the 'vow of the turtle' by withdrawing consciousness from the senses towards the breath. She is clearly an advanced spiritual traveller, evident from her assertion that all she now hears, throughout the day and night, is 'this infinite silence that is always so full of sound'.

From devotion to apprenticeship to self-realization, Daya's verse distils an eventful inner life.

~

How shrill and sudden, how full of joy—
This sound, this sign, this rising wave, this call to arms!
Time now for the weapons of wisdom;
The ancient battle with the enemy within.

*

Take care how you plant that first foot on the field!
To plant it firm is to never draw back:
All you who take arms against your own fake selves,
And turn willing to slay them in battle,
Shall surely assume the great form of Rama.

*

Death to your fear of death! There . . . now you're braced for the kill:
Demolish the ancient adversary who waits within!
Annihilate untruth to behold your true form!

*

Fearlessly the brave bear their scars in battle—
So also the pure-hearted one, the true renunciate,
Endures this world's baseless calumnies.

                              *

The weak are bound to quake
When they behold the sage in battle.
When he comes home at last,
To that serene place within him,
He cuts off his own head
And lays it down as an offering
To the earth.

                              *

I sank at first into the depths of the underworld,
Till a great explosion hurled me up into the sky.
My face took on the face of an acrobat-girl.
As she upon her ropes, so I, Daya,
Sought balance upon the thread of my own deep breath.

                              *

Behold her art:
Watch her leap and fall and leap once again,
Capering from moment to moment
Across the vaults of the sky.
Daya says: It was only when the Guru
Was truly pleased with me,
That I was set free from all fear.

                              *

By the grace of Guru Charandas my mind is now at peace.
Now, all day, all night, I hear it:
This infinite silence that is always so full of sound.

                              *

We think we have often heard them:
The clang of a bell, the beating of a drum
Or a lion in a forest roaring.
Yet few have truly *heard* these sounds:
It is only by the grace of the guru,
That the wise are granted pure hearing.

*

Ecstatic the note, ethereal the flute
That plays at the heart of the sky.
Though I heard it with my own ears,
My guru's mercy was what opened them to the sound;
It was by his mercy alone, that I, *Daya*—
Whose name means 'mercy'—
Arrived at the highest state.

*

Neither time nor fire survive here;
Neither cold nor heat hold sway—
Here, at this mysterious depth,
I find myself entirely at home.

*

Brighter than a million suns it was—
The shape I beheld, the form of my true lover.
The essence of all joy arose within me.
All suffering vanished in a glance.

**[translated by Anand Thakore]**

# Shija Laiobi

## [Eighteenth Century CE]

Born to the fifty-fourth king of Manipur, King Bhagyachandra, Shija Laiobi (literally the princess who turned Goddess) is often regarded as the 'Meerabai of Manipur'. Her devotion to Krishna might have been comparable to Meera's; however, her life circumstances certainly weren't. Unlike Meera, who was compelled to marry against her wishes, Shija Laiobi's unconventional spiritual temperament was actively nurtured by her parents. She lived her last days in Nabadwip (Nadiya), the birthplace of the Vaishnava saint, Chaitanya Mahaprabhu.

The story goes that her father introduced Shija Laiobi to the religious dance of the *raas leela* during the consecration of a Govinda temple. Since no idol of Radha was available, the temple priests suggested that the eight-year-old princess play the part. The king gave his permission, and thus began Shija Laiobi's commitment to a deity that was to last a lifetime.

As she grew, the princess' devotion deepened into an all-consuming passion. She was responsible for ushering radical innovations into the cultural and religious practices of her day. The *sankirtana*, or devotional music, in her time was performed only by men until then, but with her father's support, she initiated an independent women's group of congregational singers. She also introduced the women in the group to musical instruments that had earlier been the sole preserve of men. Shija Laiobi remains a fascinating figure in the cultural history of Manipur as the princess who turned poet–renunciate, defining her life role as consort

to the divine and living proudly single on her own terms until the end
of her days.

~

Gouranga is compassion incarnate.
O Sri Gourachandra, torrent of rasa,
for what fault am I denied?
You were Nanda's child indeed,
you played the flute, mellow tune on lips,
you appeared radiant at Nadiya,
to redeem sentient beings.

Only I was denied, why?

Your name, which redeems the wretched,
is hummed around your lotus feet
by nectar-craving, honey bee-like devotees.

I, a naive sinner, a parched, pining skylark
take refuge at your feet, O Gouranga.

*[translated by Robin Ngangom]*

# Gavari Bai

## [Eighteenth to Nineteenth Century CE]

Born in Dungarpur, Gavari Bai was married at the age of five or six but widowed within a few months of her marriage. She turned the tragedy to her advantage and immersed herself in the study of the Upanishads, following the *jnana* path of self-inquiry as her means of self-understanding. The king of Dungarpur built her a Krishna temple, where she spent over two decades devoted to the practice of yoga and often entered samadhi states for several days at a time. Her yogic attainments were widely acknowledged. When she went to Kashi on a pilgrimage, the ruler, Sunder Singh, recognized her as an advanced practitioner and asked her for an initiation on the yogic path. Musician Subhadra Desai states that she composed over 600 songs in Gujarati, Hindi and Rajasthani. As the poem included here indicates that she was a yogini of considerable accomplishment, with an experiential understanding of the mystical insight of *So-ham* or 'I am That'. The last line is a proud proclamation of her self-discovery: 'Gavari . . . is one with the Ultimate Truth.'

~

Repeat 'I am That! I am That! The Ultimate Truth!'
You are the true witness, hidden behind five sheaths.
You are the pure consciousness of the Ultimate.

You have neither old age, nor death.
You are beyond the order of time.
You are neither white, nor yellow or red.
You are beyond cold and heat.
You are neither bound, nor free.
You are beyond the rules of the body.
You are neither grand, nor subtle.

Gavari, controlled by the Self, is one with the Ultimate Truth.

*[translated by Neelima Shukla–Bhatt]*

# Muddupalani

## [Eighteenth Century CE]

A poet, scholar and courtesan in the court of the Nayaka ruler, Pratapasimha, in Thanjavur, Muddupalani was a woman of many accomplishments. Proud of her matrilineal legacy, she speaks in her poetry of her mother and grandmother, Tanjanayaki, a feted devadasi or courtesan of her time. She is not particularly modest when speaking of her own gifts, either. She talks of her peerless beauty, financial generosity, compassion, versatility, conversational skills and the number of literary works dedicated to her. This is clearly a woman with a high opinion of herself. No phoney humility here!

Muddupalani's great opus of 584 verses, *Radhika Santwanam*, focuses on the relationship between Krishna and Radha, Krishna's marriage to Ila, Radha's anguish and envy and her eventual appeasement by Krishna. The Radha–Krishna trope is not original in itself. But what makes this work original is the subjective female perspective. The articulation of a woman's sexuality is unapologetic. Radha here is not a coy heroine. She is an experienced woman who demands physical satisfaction and is capable of taking the sexual initiative. Her longings and ecstasies are carnal. Her admission of the contrary emotions of doubt, jealousy, rage, pain and love is searingly honest. There is no attempt to 'spiritualize' away their intensity. For Muddupalani, Radha and Krishna are not distant, dignified archetypes. They are densely human, fiercely corporeal.

Muddupalani was dismissed as a 'disgraceful' and vulgar 'prostitute' by the moral police of the nineteenth century. What a tragedy it would be, bemoaned one critic, Kandakuri Veerasalingam, if her 'crude' sexual imagery were ever to fall on the ears of respectable women. What was more tragic still was that it emanated 'from a woman's mouth'. The double standards, steeped in Victorian morality and upper-caste gentility, now seem obvious: erotic devotion was permissible from a man, not a woman. And yet, no one could dispute Muddupalani's scholarship. Or her literary and musical talents. It took another brave devadasi and gifted musician–scholar, Bangalore Nagaratnamma, to reinstate Muddupalani and to publish a de-sanitized version of her text in 1910. 'As it is not only written by a woman but by a woman who was born into the same community as mine, I intend to edit and publish it in a proper form,' she declared.

However, the outrage persisted; legal charges of obscenity were filed; and the publishers hounded and raided. It was only after Indian Independence that the ban on the book was revoked and Muddupalani found her rightful place in the Telugu literary canon.

Even today, Muddupalani is not for the faint-hearted. There is nothing spiritually anaemic about her poetry. She can be sexually graphic, and Radha's mix of pain, jealousy, vicarious curiosity and erotic fantasy can be unsettling in its candour. But Muddupalani is not interested in being politically correct. She is concerned with the truth of subjective experience. Her gods are real and so are their passions and vulnerabilities. Her work reminds us that to ignore sexual desire and wounded emotion would be sidestepping life itself. There can be no sublimity, she seems to tell us, that has not made peace with the wild fever of the hormones. Or the dark turbulence of the human heart.

~

## The Definition of Bad Poets

They know how to take a book apart.
They know where to find its minor faults.
It clashes with the canon, say the
evil folks. Whatever you do, don't
imitate them.

*

## A Manifesto for New Poetry

Can your poems stand in the field, girl,
alongside all the great poems of all the great
poets? Absolutely.
Doesn't the bee gorged on honey
from the great lotus still savour
the humble flower's nectar?

*

Worldly stuff and worldly ties may be given up,
and even the body's inseparable breath.
But to give up her man to another woman—
what woman can bear it?

*[translated by Subhashini Kaligotla]* [2]

*

## Radha Instructs Ila, Krishna's New Bride in the Arts of Love
[Radha has dressed up the young bride, while Krishna waits in the bedroom.]

'How will the lips of this young girl
suffer his bites? He is the killer of the demon Kaitabha.
How will her breasts bear his clawing? He's a lion of
a cowherd.
Can her tender thighs take his vigour? He wrestled
Chanura to the death.
Will her smooth body survive? He's an elephant killer.'

---

[2] [All poems translated by Subhashini Kaligotla are in consultation with Kaligotla Asoka Kumari and Velcheru Narayana Rao]

All the women were joking like this, and Ila bowed
her head
in shyness, her face all red. Radhika drew close to her
and offered comfort:

'When your husband holds you,
push him gently with your breasts.
If he kisses your cheek, touch his lips with yours.
When he gets on top of you, move against him from below.
If he gets tired while making love, quickly take over
and get on top. He's the best lover, a real connoisseur,
extremely delicate. Love him skillfully,
and make him love you. That's my advice.
But you know best.

Loving has its own laws.' And she taught her.
Then she said, 'Go quickly. The good hour
is passing. Meet your lover. Don't delay.'
And she led her gently to Krishna and said to him:

'Her breasts are tender as young buds. Unlike mine,
they won't hold up if you claw at them.
Her lips are like leaves. Mine are full-blown coral.
Don't bite too hard.
My thighs are used to wrestling with you,
but hers are soft as bananas.
Her whole body is a fragile vine. Mine is tough
as gold. In a word, she's not me.
Not equal to you in love.
Innocent. New to the art.
You have to know how to handle her.
Do you need me to tell you?
You're good with women . . .'

Then she handed Ila over to Krishna.

But really, she wanted to come too,
and held on to Ila's sari. Ila loosened her fingers:
'I'll be back soon,' she said.
And Radha went, her mind a jumble
of misery and joy.

Lying on her bed, alone, she thought to herself:

'You can give money.
You can give away your own family.
You can give your very life, that isn't easy to give up.
But to give your own husband
to another woman—what woman can do that?
By now I'm sure she's sucking at his delicious lips.
Or already pounding his naked chest with her breasts.
Probably moaning like doves.
He's on top of her and she's pressing against him.
She's quite skilled to begin with. Maybe a bit shy,
but by now he's won her over, freed her
from any reticence. He's brought her close,
touched her everywhere. Taught her everything.'

She kept thinking. Tortured by love,
she couldn't close her eyes.
Inside her, she was burning.
As for Krishna, he was busy
with the girl.

*[translated by Velcheru Narayana Rao and David Shulman]*

# Mah Laqa Bai Chanda

## [Eighteenth Century CE]

Chanda Bibi (or Mah Laqa Bai, her court title) was an accomplished courtesan of Hyderabad, famed for her beauty and her skills in dance and verse. She was the author of a collection of poems entitled *Gulzar-e-Mah Laqa* (Mah Laqa's Flower Garden). The reason she remains little known is perhaps obvious: she was perceived as 'a mere tawaif–poet'. As scholar Scott Kugle points out, her work offers interesting insights into how a woman whose life was limited by patriarchal norms learned to manipulate them to achieve her own ends as an unmarried woman, performing artist and seeker.

Political astuteness was a must to survive the changing fortunes of court life. As a single woman, Mah Laqa Bai had to be particularly adroit in the way she navigated her journey. Many of her poems are, not surprisingly, *qasidas*, or paeans, to her court patrons. When she gifted her poetry collection to John Malcolm, a British East India Company official, it was no doubt a canny act of social networking as well.

Mah Laqa Bai's ghazals were often written in the male voice, singing the praises of a female beloved (in which she was frequently the implied subject). This was in accordance with the literary norm of her time and was a means of ensuring a position of dignity for herself in a precarious power dynamic. Yet, much of her work is also permeated by themes of mystical longing. Was this born of a genuine spiritual urge or was this presentation of self a means to ward off unwanted male attention? Perhaps both. In one of the poems included here, she sings her own praises as a dancer. She sees her art not merely as a key to her social success at glittering parties but also as a key to the hereafter. In another poem, she implores Imam Ali (regarded by Shia Muslims as the first 'Imam', the true religious and political successor to the Prophet Muhammad) to bless her well-wishers and destroy her adversaries. 'Those who show her ill will guide their heads to the sword,' she declares unapologetically.

Mah Laqa Bai's poetry was certainly about working the status quo to her advantage. At the same time, her work wove the tropes of Shia spirituality into a Sunni court and memorably distilled the romantic and the mystical into lyric verse. Her words echo down the centuries as she proudly stakes her claim to both the sensual and the sublime: 'Why shouldn't Chanda be proud, O 'Ali, in both worlds?/ At home with you, she eternally astounds with dance.'

~

Cups of crimson wine are circling in rounds of dance
If the beloved is glimpsed, this party abounds in dance
God has made this beloved peerless in my view
Everything before my eyes resounds with dance
You captivate beasts and birds along with people low and high
Each in its way obeys your command in bounds of dance
Leave the party of my rivals and come over to mine
I'll show you a star whose very name sounds like dance
Why shouldn't Chanda be proud, O 'Ali, in both worlds?
At home with you she eternally astounds with dance

*

Why make a drama of reaching for your sword?
My head is a bubble on the rippling current of your sword
Don't summon her healing glance to salve my heart's wound
Her saber tongue makes incisions as sharp as any sword
I stood strong, leading the corps of your lovers

Till my head fell at your feet as if before a double sword
To those half-gone in throes of love a breath of life remains
Have mercy, glance their way as a coup de grâce's sword
O 'Ali, grant prestige to those who wish Chanda well
Those who show her ill will, guide their heads to the sword

*[translated by Scott Kugle]*

# Gangasati

## [Nineteenth Century CE]

Born into a royal family in Saurashtra, Gangasati appears to have been spiritually inclined ever since her birth and was married to a man who was either similarly oriented or persuaded by her to walk alongside her on her journey. According to one account, a maid and friend called Panbai accompanied her from her parental home to her marital one. Other accounts hold that Panbai was her daughter-in-law.

Gangasati and some of the women saints of the region, such as Toral, Loyan and Liral, belonged to the Mahapanth movement. Eclectic and subaltern in spirit, this popular form of bhakti placed greater emphasis on the path of liberation through the guru, the figure of Shakti and aspects of nature than through the conventional worship of Vishnu or Shiva. Researcher Neha Joshi points out that this vibrant popular tradition was shaped by 'multifarious faith groups that were greatly influenced by tantric sects', and developed parallel to mainstream bhakti movements.

Gangasati's household became the nucleus of much devotional activity, abuzz with congregational music, discourses and conversations with visiting sadhus. After a while, the family decided to retire to a forest, where they met their guru. He was to have a profound impact on their lives. Gangasati's husband decided to voluntarily give up his body and enter into samadhi. His wife was keen to join him, but her husband suggested that she wait until their daughter-in-law, Panbai, was spiritually mature and capable of serving as a conduit of wisdom for the family. Gangasati agreed. For the next fifty-two days, she offered poems of counsel to Panbai. On the fifty-third day, when her work was complete, Gangasati also renounced her body.

Gangasati's songs are part of the oral tradition of poetry in Gujarati, and are sung by devotional singers in Saurashtra to this very day. Unlike women mystics such as Andal, Lal Ded, Akka Mahadevi and Meera, Gangasati and several other Gujarati women saint poets seem to have combined their spiritual pursuits with householder lives (although these were not without their challenges). What is remarkable is the self-assurance and clarity of these poems, leaving one in little doubt that Gangasati was an advanced practitioner and gifted teacher. The spiritual life is not a path for the fearful or the cowardly, Gangasati reminds us. For devotion takes courage. 'Forget about bhakti/ if you are scared', she says in one poem, for this is a domain where the 'head is slain but the body fights on./ Such is the mettle of a warrior.'

~

## Let Mighty Meru Rumble and Shake

Let mighty Meru rumble and shake,
let the cosmos itself crumble to dust,
those who remain resolute in adversity
are the only ones god calls his own.

Neither joy nor woe raised a hiccup
in the brave who moved in Satguru's wake,
they laid down their lives without a care
and earned the self-respect they craved.

The ever-present company of the true
ensures bliss all hours of the day. Neither
resolve nor recourse makes the heart dither
for one who has broken the web of illusion.

Such is the path for the devout—
always remain in Satguru's thrall.

Gangasati says: listen to me, Panbai,
believe in the Word, above all.

*

## Keep it hidden

Be discreet, if you get my drift,
hide it well, hide it deep. Do not
be enamoured by a sweet tongue
that conceals a heart full of a deceit.

Incorrigible and indiscreet, turn away
from such a guru, have a care,
his unchaste speech is lugubrious with lust,
you can have no meeting of minds there.

Every vice, brimful in his envious mind—
ego, affection, aspiration, ambition.
If you are taken in by his fake naiveté,
you only open yourself to derision.

Have no faith in the words of the one
whose heart simmers with rage,
Heed Gangasati's counsel, or else
find yourself in a fine mess.

*

## Neither Joy nor Woe Raises a Hiccup

Thread your pearls in flashes of lightning
or else, all may suddenly go dark.
While you waste days in fruitless quests
twenty thousand days would have passed.

Some willfully choose ignorance,
no drilling sense into the half-witted,

this hidden truth is a complex game
only an unravelled ego can comprehend.

Cleanse yourself before you enter the field.
Understand the ways of the living.
Let me show you the union of opposites,
Let me recast you into a different being.

The Guru stands apart from the universe,
let me take you to this sacred place.
Gangasati says: there is no cloak
of illusion in the Guru's grace.

*[translated by Smita and Mustansir Dalvi]*

*

### Get Ready to Live like a Pauper

Get ready to live like a pauper,
If you're serious about bhakti.
Melt away your ego,
Feet of the guru is where lies mukti.

The world of the divine has no place
For caste, gender or race
Shed this phantom chain,
Be cool and take it easy, man.

The mantle of His woman is for those to claim,
Who are blind to flaws of others.
What do they care for hope and hanker,
Simply revel in abiding faith, sweet sister.

Be such a devotee, if you so desire,
And confide in the power of vachan.

Says Sati Ganga, listen O Panbai
Don't settle for anything less, be His woman.

*[translated by Hemang Ashwinkumar]*

*

Abandon wandering, once the self awakes
and sever ties with the discordant ones.
Embrace solitude at all times
girded by the shield of the guru's grace

No need for pilgrimage and rites now,
no need to become guru to anyone else
Abandon all these trappings
when the splendor within is unveiled

When you see the world as pervaded by Him
drop the wheeling and dealing
Cast all illusion aside
and behold His glory to your heart's content

Carnivals and canopies are pointless,
they are only for the half-baked
Says Gangasati to Panbai,
See only Ram, the perfectly Perfect!

*[translated by Neelima Shukla–Bhatt]*

# Liral

## [Nineteenth Century CE]

A significant poet in the Mahapanth tradition, Liral was born into a devout family in a village near Porbandar, Gujarat, and was initiated by her family guru, Sant Jivandas. Her husband was perplexed by his wife's spiritual temperament, and the result was a volatile relationship in which Liral suffered much abuse.

Despite the torment, Liral raised children. Her spiritual commitment remained steadfast. Her poetry reveals the conflicts she faced as well as her resolve to never disclose the wisdom of the heart to the spiritually immature. Eventually, her husband realized he was married to a woman who was decidedly his spiritual superior. Like Toral and Loyan, who converted male lovers into their disciples, Liral emerged triumphant. Her husband eventually joined her on the spiritual journey. In addition to her spiritual pursuits, Liral was a champion of caste and class equality and ran an open dining hall for the underprivileged along with her husband. When she attained mahasamadhi in 1876, she seems to have already been regarded as a saint of considerable importance in the region.

In this poem, the woman mystic asks her teacher an interesting question: once one has witnessed the sacred within, how does one conduct one's spiritual life externally? The teacher—channelled in the poem by Liral herself—suggests that she keep it simple: remember the divine, feed the hungry, and continue to meditate. This was clearly an advanced practitioner on the spiritual path.

~

Tell me, my guru, how do I worship?
I have caught a glimpse of the inner dweller.
Tell me now, how do I worship?

'Repeat His name
and feed the hungry, if you can.
The diamond of devotion
lies right before you.
Pick it up if you can.
String yourself to the prayer beads
and release yourself from worldly frivolity.'

The subtlest of the subtle
is my gemlike Guru.
Only rare ones reach Him,
passing through labyrinthine inner streets.
Meditate deeply on the void
and hear the fine music of the inner strings.

Liral says: After much effort, I have met my beloved saint.
The earth and the sky roll, as he parts the veils of the Self.

*[translated by Neelima Shukla–Bhatt]*

# Peero

## [Nineteenth Century CE]

The tale of Peero is dramatic. Like Amrapali, Sule Sankavva and Kanhopatra before her, she was a courtesan who embraced the spiritual life. However, what makes her distinctive is the spirit of confidence and autonomy in her poems. The story is drawn from her autobiographical verses (authored in the mid-nineteenth century), in which she speaks of her life as a Muslim prostitute who escaped the red-light district of Lahore to follow the dictates of her heart. Her quest led her to the sanctuary of Guru Gulabdas, the charismatic Sikh founder of an unorthodox spiritual community.

Ensuring that the gates of his community were open to all, irrespective of caste or creed, her guru promoted an eclectic spirituality, drawing upon principles from Sikh, Hindu and Sufi traditions. Here, Peero found not merely spiritual anchorage but love as well. She and Guru Gulabdas entered into an intimate relationship that they made no effort to conceal or deny. Unsurprisingly, outrage ensued. She was shunned by the conservatives of both religious establishments.

Condemned for apostasy and sexual licence, Peero retaliated with her poetry—a defiant rejoinder to fundamentalists of all hues, an anthem to love and freedom and an assertion of the importance of the spirit over the letter. Her poems speak of abduction and rescue, of the viciousness of puritanical clerics and of the eventual triumph of love. It is a dazzling story of a woman's bid for self-determination that, understandably, has inspired modern-day dramaturges in both India and Pakistan.

Scholar Anshu Malhotra draws attention to the way in which Peero echoes Punjabi mystic Bulleh Shah before her. While Bulleh Shah speaks of the love of the spiritual master in terms of the high-voltage, forbidden love of Heer and Ranjha ('calling out to Ranjha, I became him'), Peero asserts, 'Peero herself is the lover, not separate from him'. Time and again, she declares her impatience with the bogus promises of exoteric faith: if moustache and circumcision make a Muslim and sacred thread and hair-tuft an upper-caste Hindu, 'women cannot be made thus'. Like Akka Mahadevi and Meera and all the women mystics before her, whose verse celebrated an authentic, even if illicit, romance over a loveless marriage, she says, 'I will not accept the companionship of a lie/ Those that are separated will never meet, just like a broken thread/ Not family, not your in-laws, not your age-mates, nor even your friends/They disperse as people do when they disembark from a boat.'

Like Heer and Ranjha, the archetypal lovers, Peero and Gulabdas were buried together in a single grave in Chathian Wala, modern-day Pakistan. Her voice reaches us clear and strong across the years in Neeti Singh's fresh new translation: 'These Muslims I quit,/ nor will I settle for these Hindus./ Bursting the Sharia threshold,/Peero dived/into the limitless pool . . .'

~

Flung in the company of foolish zealots
who piteously whine in piety;
the qazi, the Brahmin pandit
goad me to read the Kalma, the Purana.
They seek in the written script,
my ferryman Lord
who stands outside
and beyond all this.
I say, says Peero,
how will they lead who themselves are lost?

*

They bring me no profit, these men
who bound me to the Sharia.

In eternal debt I stand before the wise
who fashioned my release.
These Muslims I quit,
nor will I settle for these Hindus.
Bursting the Sharia threshold,
Peero dived
into the limitless pool . . .

*

My lover is casteless,
beyond the binaries of Hindu–Turk,
beyond gender, beyond birth-wheels,
unbound, boundless is He.
In resplendence unmatched,
His play limitless.
Peero says, the Guru will bring you to Him
whom your eyes could not see.

*

The lover's presence, Peero can sense:
here, there: an omniscience.
Without him I am not, for him it is the same.
We are neither separate nor feel the need to merge.
In an all-embracing dream we breathe,
Guru-disciple fused as One.

*

Let us go where the mendicants live, come Peero!
their words drop like nectar in the heart's chalice;
contemplating on the spoken word
will ease this birth.
Wherever the lost ones meet,
a carnival begins!

*[translated by Neeti Singh]*

# Andavan Picchai

## [Twentieth Century CE]

Andavan Picchai was a south Indian poet, music composer and devotee of Muruga. Born in Chennai, Maragathavalli (her name at birth) was an exceptionally quiet girl who married at the age of nine. Shortly before her tenth birthday, she underwent a transformative experience. The story goes that lord Muruga—yogi extraordinaire, the eternally youthful god who travels the world on a peacock, son of Shiva—appeared before her and said, 'You may appear crazy to the world, but devote yourself to me even while you are busy with your daily work.' In an initiation, reminiscent of the one given centuries ago to a Tamil saint poet named Arunagiri, the god asked her to open her mouth and wrote 'Aum' on her tongue with his spear. The silent little girl was transformed into a poet, and eloquent verse after verse poured forth from her.

In a foreword to her biography, Andavan Picchai wrote, 'Once the Lord had entered the secret chamber of my heart, there was no room there for anything else . . . This experience of mine found expression in a song: I dived deep into the ocean of the Lord's love and took out the pearl called Muruga.'

Even as she composed her poems, Andavan Picchai led a householder's life, becoming a mother to several children. However, on one occasion, when she entered an inspired trance and proceeded to compose 600 verses in praise of Muruga, she was oblivious to the cries of her newborn infant. Her mother-in-law decreed that enough was enough. Andavan Picchai took an oath—to which she adhered even after her mother-in-law's death—never to compose songs on Muruga or mention him again. It was a terrifying oath. But it did not dishearten her, she says, since he remained alive in her heart.

Andavan Picchai fell seriously ill in 1948, and in an interesting twist to the tale (relished by those with a taste for arcana), it is said that a south Indian yogi named Ramakrishna now began tenanting her body (to fulfil his spurned wife's curse that he be reborn as a woman to know the pain of rejection). Even though two entities now apparently occupied her body, her life as a poet did not come to an end. Muruga reappeared and commanded that she begin composing again. When she protested that she had taken an oath, he insisted: 'You are but a pen-holder who is dipped in different-coloured inks. I am the eternal poet . . .' And so the inspiration continued to flow, and Andavan Pichai resumed her compositions.

Her spiritual attainments seem to have been recognized by twentieth-century figures, such as Ramana Maharishi, Swami Sivananda (who initiated her into sanyas), and the Shankaracharya of Kancheepuram. As for her literary and musical attainments, these continue to be widely acknowledged. Andavan Pichhai became a well-known figure in Chennai in the 1950s, with prominent musicians and congregational music groups performing her songs. She lived in Rishikesh for several years and died in Chennai in her family home in 1990 at the age of ninety, leaving behind a vibrant legacy of poems in Tamil, Telugu and Sanskrit.

~

Dear Mind,
if you want to dance,
try coming to me as a peacock.
You think I'd ever let you escape
into the forest after that?
You think we'd ever be parted?

      Surrender, dear Mind,
      Surrender.

Like mother and child reunited,
it's time to make our peace, you and I,

to drown our differences
in the vastness of sky,
in the mother tongue of silence,
in the awakening of wisdom.
Let all suffering cease.
When I order you to stop, obey!

      Surrender, dear Mind,
         Surrender.

We were born conjoined,
hence our undying bond.
We're as inseparable
as inner world and outer.
It's time make our peace, you and I,
to drown our differences
in the sky of unstruck sound,
in the embodiment of the ultimate name,
in the wisdom of illumination,
Only when *you* are can *I* be!
Let's hit the stage then,
dance our duet.

      Surrender, dear Mind,
         Go on. Surrender.

      \*

Call him a madman.
Call him a ghost.

Still
he draws me, Mother.

The thunder of his footsteps,
his wild dance of infinity,

his electrifying tandava—

    that bigshot of Chidambaram.

Call him a madman.
Call him a ghost.

Still
he draws me.

The cosmos trembles,
his serpent garland shudders,
pearls and gems scatter
    as he whirls into formlessness,

blue-throated,
consort of young Sivakami,
the one who charred a love god to ash
with his inflammable gaze—

    that lord of lords.

Call him a madman.
Call him a ghost.

Still
he draws me.

*[translated by Arundhathi Subramaniam]*

# Sharika Devi

## [Twentieth Century CE]

Part of an illustrious lineage of yoginis in the Kashmiri tradition, Sharika Devi was the prime disciple of spiritual master Swami Lakshman Joo. She led a life of quiet commitment to her path and her teacher, who recognized her as a *jivanmukta* (one who is liberated when alive) and a *brahmavaadini* (female sage). It is said that when she was about to set out on a journey, her guru held a mirror before her and asked her to behold Devi, the supreme goddess, and seek her own blessings before she departed.

While her life was simple and her demeanour unassuming, her translator points out that 'many were witness to her spiritual powers while she was alive'. Her poems, collected and compiled by her sister, speak of the breathtaking inner world that opened up for her through meditation and the grace of her teacher. 'Like a honeysuckle vine, I bloomed,' she says in one poem. She herself never drew attention, however, to her spiritual accomplishments. As she says: 'The musk was within me, but its scent burst out, never contained/ With a bow and arrow they chased me, but never could they grasp my essence.'

~

Oh, what a mistake I made, what a blunder it was!
I was dressed in heavenly robes,
The moths of desire and anger made them their nest.
Holes were bored in them by the rats of duality.

. . . What a mistake I made, what a blunder it was.
Be aware, all the time, and you will hear
The inner music of the soul.
But in the midst of its resonance, I fell asleep.

What a mistake I made, what a blunder it was!
But once I assumed a universal form through
meditation,
No longer aware of my individual self,
The Cosmic Power was before me, all of a sudden!

What a mistake I made, what a blunder it was!
When I renounced the world and
Entered a state of seclusion,
Full knowledge of things stood before me.

What a mistake I made, what a blunder it was!
One day I knew who I was.
Once bathed in the light of sat-chit-ananda,[3]
In disgust I turned away from desires,

When I felt the benediction of shaktipat[4],
The whole world seemed a reflection of my own self.
Like a honeysuckle vine I bloomed,
Everything wore an imprint of where I had come from.

Everything I saw as an extension of myself.
Then it was that Time itself was vanquished.
Everything I saw an extension of myself.
Everywhere I saw nothing but all-pervading bliss.

*

---

[3] Sat-chid-ananda: consciousness-existence-bliss

[4] Shaktipat: the transmission of spiritual energy from guru to disciple; shaktipat
can be transmitted with a word, a syllable, a look, a thought or a touch.

Ah! A tree bereft am I, never stepped out of the threshold,
My head I kept bowed always, never raised it at all.
With eyes closed, saw everything, never opened them at all.
Like a deer, the forest was my abode,
but never bounded or frolicked in it.
The musk was within me,
but its scent burst out, never contained.
With a bow and arrow they chased me,
But never could they grasp my essence

[These last words by Sharika Devi are often viewed as a pithy summation of her own life.]

*[translated by Neerja Mattoo]*

# Indira Devi

## [Twentieth Century CE]

Born in 1920, Indira Devi belonged to an affluent family but chose to renounce wealth and family ties in pursuit of the spiritual life. She became the disciple of singer and musicologist Dilip Kumar Roy, who was, in turn, a direct disciple of Sri Aurobindo and the Mother (of modern-day Puducherry). With the sanction of his gurus, Dilip Kumar Roy initiated Indira Devi into the yogic path.

In 1949, Indira Devi began to experience mystical states, in which she remained for hours. In these altered states of consciousness, she is believed to have met and interacted with the sixteenth-century saint, Meera or Mirabai, who shared her songs with her—an interesting symbiotic relationship between two women lovers of Krishna, both born on the festival of Holi. Over 1000 *bhajans*, or devotional songs, from Mirabai, received by Indira Devi, were transcribed by Dilip Kumar Roy. 'It is evident,' wrote Sri Aurobindo in a letter to Dilip Kumar Roy authenticating this phenomenon, 'that Indira is receiving inspiration for her Hindi songs from the Mira of her Vision and that her consciousness and the consciousness of Mira are collaborating on some plane . . . Such things do happen on the occult planes, they are not new and unprecedented.'

This tale of spiritual teamwork presents a fascinating example of an esoteric sisterhood. According to one legend, the thirteenth-century saint poet, Namdev, appeared in a dream to the seventeenth-century poet, Tukaram. Namdev revealed that his vow to compose a vast number of poems in praise of Krishna had remained unfulfilled. He urged Tukaram to complete his mission, and Tukaram did his bidding. The partnership between Mirabai and Indira Devi bears a certain resemblance to this creative relay, with one woman poet passing on the baton to another across the centuries.

In an account recorded in 1951, Indira Devi speaks of a particular exchange Meerabai had with her lord, Krishna, the wit and repartee of which suggest a playful relationship between the two:

13 July 1951: Mira gave another example of how Krishna loved provoking people . . .

'But then Mira,' he argued, 'I am supposed to be as fickle as any. So beware, lest I push you away after a while.'

'But you can't, my Lord', I answered, 'for I am like a swing: the stronger your thrust, the greater the speed with which I will come back to you; beware.'

'Mira', he pursued, 'you keep saying that you want to be with me and yet retain your identity. But I am like a lake, so if you want to be with me, you will be drowned, I warn you.'

'But no, my Lord', I returned, pointing at a lotus in a lake. 'Like that, I will float in the deep water of your love, draw my sap from your waters, and yet not lose my identity as your *dasi* (servitor).'

Together, Indira Devi and Dilip Kumar Roy founded the Hari Krishna Mandir in Pune, a sacred space open to 'devotees of all castes and creeds'.

Two volumes of Dilip Kumar Roy's translations of Indira Devi's work, named *Indiranjali*, have been published. This selection includes new renditions of her work (based on these translations as well as the originals).

∼

There's a desire in the heart, a longing for you,
but I've no clue how that longing works.

It is your feet I yearn for, your lotus feet,
and yet, I have no idea how they are attained.

> I love you, but can't quite figure how it works,
> I'm clueless about this grammar of union,
> I play the veena, but know no music,
> Defeat and victory—I understand neither.

I'd renounce the entire world for you,
but tell me, how do I reach you?

> I know neither beauty nor sentiment,
> I'm qualified in neither yoga nor ritual.
> Mine is simply the penance of passion.
> This is the love I offer at your feet.

I long to share my heart with you,
but I have no clue how to share it

> Nothing is concealed from your gaze.
> My heartbeat is merely your flute song.
> Fuse your flame with me, dispel this dark,
> I'm done with these lifetimes of fooling around!

One with you, I'd sing you,
but tell me how,
    how do we become one?

*

To what land do you belong, traveller?
Where are you bound?
Travel-blinded, have you forgotten
the point of your journey?

This world's a mere wayside inn;
your destination's still remote,

Lighten your karmic burden,
so you never need gather it again

The oysters by the shore are seductive,
but why get sidetracked, then weep?
If it's the pearl you're seeking,
Come now, plunge into the deep
The seed born in filth unfurls
into a radiant flower
Yes, your home's distant, the path an ordeal,
but don't settle now, traveller!

*

Tell me, friend, who enters my courtyard?
Who's the strange thief who brings radiance into the gloom?

His eyes pure nectar, decked in garland and crown,
anklets around his flower feet, a flute at his lips,

his ways curious, his theft more curious still,
a wily, heartless crook, his face pure innocence.

It isn't grand palaces he's after; neither gold nor youth,
The colony in the heart—that's all he's out to loot,

Hari, Govind, Keshav, Shyam, Murari—his names
are abundant,
He's monarch of three worlds, and yet, every lover's
supplicant

He's Mohan to every Radha, Kanhaiya to every Meera,
Mariner of life's wild ocean, he's burglar *and* sustainer!

Tell me, friend, who enters my courtyard—
who's this strange thief who brings radiance into the gloom?

*

She's stormed out of her childhood home,
Meera's headed to her lover's abode
No one can stop her now,
Meera's headed to her lover's abode

> Dad, mum, playmate, companion, friend,
> They've all been cast away, guardians and confidantes,
> She's walked out to meet her Hari alone
>> Renouncing her life of lavish abundance

The slur of the world is her forehead's vermilion
The scratches of thorns are henna on her feet
Her devotion to Hari oozes out of every pore
> She's armoured by a love so incredibly sweet

She's off to dissolve at the feet of her lover
To infuse her devotion in all she meets
To discover the vast ocean at the core of creation
> To sing, to proclaim it, in every street

She's the royal queen who's now turned mendicant
No one can figure the workings of her heart
Friends and strangers call her 'lunatic'
> They abuse her, their every word a dart!

Sowing his love seeds, striding the world,
She's the undying flame on devotion's stage,
A rare gem in the treasury of lovers,
> The flower that blooms in every age.

*[Translated by Arundhathi Subramaniam]*

# PART TWO

*'I've No Relatives Here and Everyone Here Is My Relative.'*
—Nammalvar

# Women as Protagonists

# Introduction

This book could end with the voices of these fifty-six women poets.

But it doesn't.

Two more sections—shorter, eclectic, but significant—seemed necessary to complete it.

The journey of a book, not unlike the journey of the heart, has its own logic—precise but not always schematic. So, when another tribe of wild women came a-knocking, it felt right to open up the doors.

My fascination with Indian classical dance started early. So did my impatience. There was much that enthralled me: the pulsating lines, the iconography, the electrifying precision, the iconic grandeur.

But there was discomfort too. For while I loved the stylization and the heightened intensity of emotion, I gradually found myself uneasy with the servility of female love that pervaded so much dance poetry. Why did the heroines insist on waiting interminably for absconding male lovers? Why were they so content to sigh, to wilt and to look mournfully out of windows? Why on earth didn't they get a *life*? There was something farcical and reductive of human complexity here, something that seemed to trivialize desire into a coquettish pantomime of moues and grimaces.

What made it worse was that it was explained in the language of facile allegory. This was not mere erotic love, most dancers declared. This was nothing less than the individual soul pining for the universal soul. To my gaze, it seemed like both sexual and spiritual union were about turning into a puddle of treacle and servitude. I wanted none of it.

It was only later, as my own existential questions deepened and my reading intensified, that I made other discoveries.

For one, I found that there was always a difference between a good
dancer and a mediocre one. In the hands of a good dancer, love was never
just about simpering femininity. It always seemed to suggest something
more. There was the hint of a human condition too unnamable to be
told except through the language of archetype.

Besides, as some of my habitual indignation subsided and my
glibber judgements abated, I realized that the quest for the sacred could
indeed be sensuous. And the other way around. I realized, too, that
waiting wasn't meek compliance. There was perhaps a reason why inner
work entailed a particular kind of female wisdom. For the deepest acts
of creation and renewal happen in invisible realms that require a subtle
mix of intensity and non-doing, alertness and grace. Fallow fields are far
from lifeless, for much churning happens deep within the soil. Here was
an insight about the alchemy of waiting and the power of living stillness.
Conscious 'being', I began to understand, could be far more significant
than 'becoming'.

That drew me to many of the sacred–erotic poems I had grown up
with, never quite guessing their capacity for surprise or sedition. They
began to reveal to me places where life is not just divided into puritanical
or epicurean binaries. Where spirituality isn't just an angst-ridden quest
but entails a welter of inner states in which the passionate is inseparable
from the profound. And so, it was with a more complex understanding
of love and art that I began to approach this work.

In the second section of this book, therefore, the spotlight is
on women, not as poets but as protagonists. The authors are almost
entirely male poets who invoke female characters or channel the
female voice or declare their longing to experience the condition
of femininity. Women here are actors, speakers, doers. They wander
through the different seasons of love—yearning, immersion,
possession, grief, anger, exultation, freedom.

It is possible at first glance to dismiss these poems as perpetuating
old clichés and hierarchies. One could argue that they turn women into
puppets of circumstance, their moods governed by the mere presence
or absence of male lovers. The trope of the subservient female devotee
can get predictable. The figure of the elusive male god can get more
predictable still. The misgivings are valid. Yet, on deeper reading, one

sees that some of the best poems are rich in psychological nuance. They offer portraits of extraordinary protagonists—emotionally rich, expressive, intelligent, sensual.

The women in these poems stand tall, take centre stage and exhibit remarkable agency. In the poems of Kabir and Shah Abdul Latif, the seeker is aware, active and bristling with choice. Ready to flout social decorum, she sets out on a journey on which success means no return. This is love as voluntary self-sabotage. Yet she cannot disregard the summons—the call of the wild, the voice from the other shore, the tug, the dim, unrelenting memory of her truer home.

This is not dumb waiting. This is a forbiddingly courageous decision to hold out. A refusal to settle for the seductive bargain. A refusal to broker the easy deal. A refusal to barter freedom for respectability. This is devotion as terrifying courage.

Consider the seeker in Kabir's poem: 'I ate the neighbour lady for breakfast/along with the wise old mother./ Poor thing! Then spreading the easy bed,/I stretched my legs and slept/ Now I don't come, don't go,/ don't die or live . . .' Or in Shah Abdul Latif: 'When oneness is the bride/ the groom is cut to pieces/The gallows are the bedroom/ of true lovers.'

In the poems of *saguna* bhakti (where god has a name and form), the theatre of duality is even more vivid. As Jayadeva's Krishna pines for Radha, or as Narsinh Mehta's milkmaid ties Krishna's arms to the bedpost, the women who wait are far from powerless. In these poems, the women do not merely bill and coo. They bare their teeth. They snarl. They remind their gods of the need for reciprocity. If the male lover doesn't keep up his end of things, the courtship will come to an end. He is never allowed to forget that he is equally implicated. God here is not boss; he's birthright.

The woman in these poems seeks, but the seeking is no longer one-sided. A new protagonist—a woman of adventure and sexual inventiveness—replaces the tormented male seeker. She is secure enough to argue and even reject her divine lover's overtures. Jayadeva gives us a Radha who, as scholar–translator Barbara Stoler Miller points out, is 'neither a wife nor a worshipping rustic playmate', but 'a jealous, solitary proud female' and one who is 'difficult to please'. The divine must work hard at wooing her. In Jayadeva's poetry, Krishna knows the seasons of remembrance, desire and desolation, as well as his beloved Radha.

Later, Kshetrayya's sexually mature courtesan speakers are amused by the bashfulness of the divine: 'I found him wandering the alleyways,/too shy to ask anyone . . . / *And he rules the worlds.*' This god is both eternal and endearingly human. And while the social context inhabited by Kshetrayya was widely different from Jayadeva, the poems make one thing clear: if devotion demands the unconditional surrender of the devotee, it expects nothing less of the divine.

Significantly, the woman's yearning is not passive. It is both energetic and alchemical. As the seasons around her change, the woman becomes a site of transformation herself.

As her experience of incompleteness deepens, she is imperceptibly born into a new wholeness. What's more, the male lover now turns from a distant object of desire to an ardent paramour. The incredulous woman in Narsinh Mehta's poem realizes that the tables have turned; as a woman, she has the upper hand: 'What merit have I earned to be born a woman? Hari pleads with me with such meekness.'

At the close of Jayadeva's poem, Radha sits triumphantly astride Krishna. God turns supplicant. Devotee turns goddess. The union is complete. 'Displaying her passion/ In loveplay as the battle began/ She launched a bold offensive/ Above him/ And triumphed over her lover . . .'

But this is not a simple tale of one-upwomanship either.

For the journey in sacred poetry is always a symbolic movement away from power towards radical vulnerability. Both Krishna and Radha are vital pieces of the existential puzzle. They may stray. They may sulk. They may misunderstand. But when they surrender to each other, they return to a condition that is more than the sum of its parts. Stoler Miller describes this 'dual divinity' not as 'an incarnation . . . of Vishnu, but as the source . . . of all the incarnate forms he himself assumes in order to save the world'.

Widening the male poets' view of spirituality and sexuality, the female voice ushers in a new timbre into poetry. No longer is spirituality about mere 'efforting'. It now spells possession, intoxication, erotic vulnerability. Self-flagellation gives way to the dance of courtship. When he adopts the female voice, the male poet has the chance to forge a far more equal relationship with the divine. Gradually, the hierarchical role-play—entreating seeker and elusive god—falls away. The woman does not merely seek, but is sought. Nammalvar's devotee may know she will dissolve in the explosive experience of ultimate union, but there's no guarantee that her god will make it out unscathed either. If we are left with Radha's victory at the close of Jayadeva's poem, it is because Radha embodies love. And, as scholar John Stratton Hawley points out, love will endure—in divine absence *and* in divine presence, in longing *and* in union.

Wisdom in these poems lies in cross-dressing on many levels—sartorial and spiritual. In the case of Kshetrayya, we may well be listening to a woman poet (or several women poets) who chose to adopt a male pseudonym. This brings yet another flavour into the mix. In one of these poems, the female speaker engages in some sexual experimentation with another woman, only to find this is one of Muvva Gopala's pranks! 'And he touches me expertly/and makes love to me./ *Those women, they told me he was a woman!*' Learn to listen to what *feels* right within, the poems remind us, for nothing is aberrant for the true lover.

When boundaries begin to blur, the game of otherness is coming to an end—this is the logic of sacred poetry. In the heart's dark forest, where the river flows noiseless and moonlit, where lovers wait with eyes like night lilies, divisions grow smudgy. Definitions crumble. Identities melt. Things are not as they seem. In the heat of the anticipated sexual and sacred union, the familiar world collapses.

This is a liminal space. A space of possibility. A space where the mystic Bulleh Shah might don the attire of a female dancer; where Krishna might wear a yellow sari and braid his hair; where the devotee might turn divine and the divine devotee. As duality becomes a festival rather than a battle, as the seeker trusts the logic of the body and the heart, every frontier softens into irrelevance. Biological, cultural and existential barriers—between male and female, head and heart, night and day, heaven and earth—fall away. The entire world seems plunged in a dark and rapturous dishevelment.

'Who can tell/ who is the man/ and who the woman/in this ecstasy?' asks Uddhabadas.

Taking our cue from the poetry, we might reply: spring is here, and who really cares?

# Nammalvar

## [Ninth to Tenth Century CE]

Foremost of the twelve alvar saints of Tamil Nadu, Nammalvar remains one of the most original poets of mystic delirium in the world. His work, which precedes the *Gita Govinda* of Jayadeva, laid the foundations of a great inheritance of sacred–erotic literature in the Vaishnava tradition. His origins were humble, and legend tells us he was mute until a conversation under a tamarind tree with the poet–scholar, Madhurakavi (who followed a light in the southern sky until he reached the boy prodigy). After this pivotal meeting, poetry poured out of him. The composer of four major literary works (including the celebrated *Tiruvaimozhi*), his poetry pervades the Vishnu temples of the south to this day.

Capable of combining philosophical refinement with a poetic love of the concrete, Nammalvar's poetry breathes dramatic aliveness into the stories of Vishnu. This is not the poet as pundit or as expounder of scripture, but as seer and visionary. Vishnu in Nammalvar's poetry is a living figure and the host of female characters around him—lovers, mothers, girlfriends and gossiping elders—are vividly here and now.

Here is a poet whose work reminds us that the longing to touch, to eat and to make love can be a perfectly legitimate path to the divine. What's more, it can be the most natural, sensually rewarding and effortless path there is. Sexuality in Nammalvar is not an allegory for spirituality. His verse offers us the thunderbolt immediacy of metaphor—where a naked-wire encounter with the divine becomes hormonal and holy all at once. There is the possibility of reaching a state where the divine and devotee view each other as joyously equal: '[He] thought of me what I thought of him/ and became my own thoughts.' Transformed and empowered by this explosive love, the female protagonist is capable of proclaiming that she has reached the supreme state of non-dual self-realization: 'I've no relatives here/ and everyone is my relative./ I'm the one who makes relatives relate.'

The divine lover can be tantalizingly separate, but he is accessible. He is elusive, but also a mere heartbeat away. Exploring this paradox, Nammalvar offers a poetry of romantic ardour as well as a map of deepening states of spiritual immersion—from longing to obsession to radical possession.

~

## He And I

He who took the seven bulls
    by the horns
    he who devoured the seven worlds

made me his own cool place
    in heaven

and thought of me
    what I thought of him

and became my own thoughts.

\*

*What Her Foster Mother Said*

She's young:
    breasts not even full-grown;
    hair thick, soft, but much too short;
    her dress doesn't cover her waist
    and her tongue stammers;

but her eyes,
    so priceless
    earth and sea cannot buy them,
    they flash everywhere.

She's learning to say,
    'Is Venkatam
    the hill of our Lord?'

Will she ever get there?

                         *


For the sake of that girl,
    her mouth red as a berry,
    you broke the seven bulls;

you bent the long bow
    and finished off the king
        of the island of towers;

and you broke the tusk
    of that pedigreed elephant.

I haven't worshipped you
    with flowers and holy water
    at proper times;

but then
    my heart is the only sandalwood
        to rub and perfume your body with,

    your body
    dark as *kaya* blossom.

                         *

*What Her Mother Said*

O women,
    you too have daughters
    and have brought them up.

    How can I tell you
    about my poor girl?

    She talks of the conch shell,
    she talks of the wheel,
    and she talks, night and day,
    of the basil in his hair,

what shall I do?

*

*What Her Mother Said*

When she sees kings,
she says, I see my lord.

When she sees shapes and colours,
she leaps up, saying,
I see him who measured the world.

All temples with gods in their wombs
Are, she says, places of the lord dark as the sea.

In terror, in love, in every mood,
she wants
the Dark One's anklets.

*

**Love Poems: A Case of Possession**

1.

'I made the world
    surrounded by the sea,' says she.

'I became the world
    surrounded by the sea,' says she.

'I once redeemed from the demon
    the world surrounded by the sea,' says she.

'I pitchforked with my tusks
    the world once drowned in the sea,' says she.

'I devoured once
    the world surrounded by the sea,' says she.

Such talk!

Can it be because our lord
    of the world surrounded by the sea
has come and taken her over?

How can I explain
    my girl who lives within this world
        surrounded by the sea

to you people of this world
    surrounded by the sea?

2.

My girl, who's just learning to speak
says,
                'I'm beyond all learning.
                I'm all the learning you learn.'

'I'm the cause of all learning,
        I end all learning,
I'm the essence of all learning,'
                        says she.

Does my girl talk this way
        because our lord of all learning
                has come and taken her over?

How can I tell you,
                O learned men?

6.

. . . My little girl says,
        'I've no relatives here
                and everyone here is my relative.'

        'I'm the one who makes relatives relate,'
                                she says.

        'I also end relations,
           and to those related to me
           I become all relations,'
                        she says.

Can it be the lord of illusions
                beyond all relations
has come and taken her over?

How can I tell you,
my kinsmen,
what she means?

*[translated by A.K. Ramanujan]*

# Basavanna

## [Twelfth Century CE]

Basavanna, or Basaveshwara, was a mystic, teacher, poet, social reformer and statesman of the twelfth century. He was a proponent of equality across the barriers of gender, caste, class and religion, and a leading figure of the Virashaiva Sharana movement.

Born in Bagewadi, North Karnataka, he grew disenchanted with the inflexibility of his social and religious context early in life. He found a spiritual guide in Kudalasangama and forged a deep connection with the deity Shiva at the local temple. Later, he entered public life, becoming finance minister to the Chalukyan king in Kalyana. A charismatic spiritual leader, Basavanna revitalized a tradition for fellow Sharanas based on egalitarian ideals, which became the nucleus of a remarkable galaxy of saints and mendicant devotees. He left behind a legacy of vachana poetry, celebrated for its spiritual insight and virtuoso command of metaphor and rhythm.

This poem pays homage to a self that shape-shifts seamlessly between gender identities, reiterating in its own way, like the other oft-quoted poem by the Kannada poet, Devara Dasimayya, that 'the self that hovers in between/ is neither man nor woman'.

~

Look here, dear fellow:
I wear these men's clothes
only for you.

Sometimes I am man,
sometimes I am woman.

O lord of the meeting rivers
I'll make war for you
but I'll be your devotees' bride.

*[translated by A.K. Ramanujan]*

# Jayadeva

## [Twelfth Century CE]

Jayadeva was not merely the author of a major erotic-devotional poem in Sanskrit, the *Gita Govinda*; he also offered the world the earliest extant paean of the Krishna–Radha love story—twelve cantos that explore the illicit secret romance between divine lovers, between god and his sacred partner.

As moonlight descends upon the River Yamuna, an ancient rite of spring is enacted that never loses the fever of sexual passion or the many contrary shades of psychological complexity. At the same time, it offers a sophisticated ideal of divinity in which male is inextricable from female, god from goddess. God here is a participant in the human drama of love and loss. He is vulnerable. He is fearful. He longs. He suffers. He is unfinished without the love of his human consort.

Born in Kenduli, near the temple city of Puri, in modern-day Odisha, Jayadeva seems to have received an education in Sanskrit, poetry and the performing arts. According to legend, the wandering poet fell in love with Padmavati, a dancer at the Jagannatha temple, who appears to have shared his devotion and aesthetic. Jayadeva's work proceeded to inspire centuries of Vaishnava mystics and Bhakti poets thereafter. While some of the poet's compositions live on in the Sikh sacred text, the *Guru Granth Sahib*, the strains of the *Gita Govinda* infuse the Odissi classical dance form to this very day.

Legend has it that when Jayadeva reached the climactic moment of the *Gita Govinda*, in which Krishna tells Radha to place her foot on his head, the poet baulked at his own gumption. Could the divine really submit to the human? Could the divine Krishna be tamed by a mere milkmaid? But when Jayadeva went to bathe, Krishna appeared in the poet's guise and wrote the couplet himself. He then ate a meal prepared by Padmavati and left. When Jayadeva returned from his bath, he realized what had happened. Inspiration had melded with divine decree. Beauty had converged with verity, poetic imagination with truth. The *Gita Govinda* could end in no other way.

~

After struggling through the night,
She seemed wasted by the arrows of love.
She denounced her lover bitterly
As he bowed before her, pleading forgiveness.

*The Seventeenth Song, sung with Raga Bhairavi*

Bloodshot from a sleepless night of passion, listless now,
Your eyes express the mood of awakened love.
    Damn you, Madhava! Go! Kesava, leave me!
    Don't plead your lies with me!
    Go after her, Krishna!
    She will ease your despair.

Dark from kissing her kohl-blackened eyes,
At dawn, your lips match your body's colour, Krishna.
    Damn you, Madhava! Go! Kesava, leave me!
    Don't plead your lies with me!
    Go after her, Krishna!
    She will ease your despair.

Etched with scratches of sharp nails in the battle of love,
Your body tells the triumph of passion in gold writing
on sapphire.
    Damn you, Madhava! Go! Kesava, leave me!
    Don't plead your lies with me!

Go after her, Krishna!
She will ease your despair.

Drops of red lac from her lotus feet wet your sublime breast.
They force buds from the tree of love to bloom on
your skin.
     Damn you, Madhava! Go! Kesava, leave me!
     Don't plead your lies with me!
     Go after her, Krishna!
     She will ease your despair.

The teethmark she left on your lip creates anguish
in my heart.
Why does it evoke the union of your body with mine now?
     Damn you, Madhava! Go! Kesava, leave me!
     Don't plead your lies with me!
     Go after her, Krishna!
     She will ease your despair.

Dark Krishna, your heart must be baser black than your skin.
How can you deceive a faithful creature tortured by
fevers of Love?
     Damn you, Madhava! Go! Kesava, leave me!
     Don't plead your lies with me!
     Go after her, Krishna!
     She will ease your despair.

Why am I shocked that you roam in the woods to
consume weak girls?
The fate of Putana shows your cruel childhood bent for
killing women.
     Damn you, Madhava! Go! Kesava, leave me!
     Don't plead your lies with me!
     Go after her, Krishna!
     She will ease your despair.

Jayadeva sings the lament of a jealous girl deceived
by passion.
Listen, sages! Heaven rarely yields such sweet elixir.
 Damn you, Madhava! Go! Kesava, leave me!
 Don't plead your lies with me!
 Go after her, Krishna!
 She will ease your despair.

*

Displaying her passion
In loveplay as the battle began,
She launched a bold offensive
Above him
And triumphed over her lover.
Her hips were still,
Her vine-like arm was slack,
Her chest was heaving,
Her eyes were closed.
Why does a mood of manly force
Succeed for women in love?

Then, as he idled after passionate love,
Radha, wanting him to ornament her,
Freely told her lover,
Secure in her power over him.

*

*The Twenty-fourth Song, sung with Raga Ramakari*

Yadava hero, your hand is cooler than sandal balm on
my breast;         /
Paint a leaf design with deer musk here on Love's
ritual vessel!

She told the joyful Yadu hero, playing to delight
her heart.

Lover, draw kohl glossier than a swarm of black bees
on my eyes!
Your lips kissed away the lampblack bow that shoots
arrows of Love.
She told the joyful Yadu hero, playing to delight
her heart.

My ears reflect the restless gleam of doe eyes,
graceful Lord.
Hang earrings on their magic circles to form
snares for love.
She told the joyful Yadu hero, playing to delight
her heart.

Pin back the teasing lock of hair on my smooth
lotus face!
It fell before me to mime a gleaming line of black bees.
She told the joyful Yadu hero, playing to delight
her heart.

Make a mark with liquid deer musk on my moonlit brow!
Make a moon shadow, Krishna! The sweat drops are dried.
She told the joyful Yadu hero, playing to delight
her heart.

Fix flowers in shining hair loosened by loveplay, Krishna!
Make a flywhisk outshining peacock plumage to be the
banner of Love.
She told the joyful Yadu hero, playing to delight
her heart.

My beautiful loins are a deep cavern to take the
thrusts of love—
Cover them with jewelled girdles, cloths and
ornaments, Krishna!
> She told the joyful Yadu hero, playing to delight
> her heart.

Make your heart sympathetic to Jayadeva's splendid speech!
Recalling Hari's feet is elixir against fevers of this
dark time.
> She told the joyful Yadu hero, playing to delight
> her heart.

*[translated by Barbara Stoler Miller]*

# Amir Khusrau

## [Thirteenth to Fourteenth Century CE]

Poet, scholar, musician and mystic, Amir Khusrau remains an iconic presence in the Indian cultural landscape. Born to a Turkish father and Indian mother, his legacy is unique in more ways than one. It lay in the brilliance with which he wrote in Persian, the court language of the Delhi Sultanate, and the vernacular language of Hindavi. It lay in his contribution to Indian classical music (he is said to have played a pioneering role in evolving styles such as the *khayal* and the *tarana*, and even an instrument like the sitar). It lay in his contribution to sacred music (he evolved the devotional singing style of the *qawwali*). It lay in his contribution to poetic form (he is considered the father of the Indian ghazal) and metre (he is considered a master prosodist). It lay, too, in the way he became emblematic of a composite culture in which both Islamic and Hindu elements were creatively synthesized.

A disciple of the Sufi mystic of the Chishti order, Nizamuddin Auliya, Khusrau's spiritual journey started young. The worlds of the courtier and the mystic could not have been easy to reconcile. Khusrau's career as a court poet began at the age of twenty. It continued until his death in 1325. (He was in the service of princes and nobles, and later at the court of the Delhi sultan.) However, he never abandoned his spiritual pursuits, and was eventually buried next to the tomb of his master. While he probably wrote some of his ghazals for the court and others for his master's sacred assembly, many work in both contexts as poems of human love and mystical longing.

~

Khusro, this night of union
I spent awake with my beloved
    This body mine, the mind his
    The two became one colour

    Khusro, this game of love
    I played with my beloved
      If I win, he'll be mine
      If I lose, I'll belong to him

    Khusro says, the river of love
      Flows in strange ways
      One who escapes, drowns
      One who drowns is saved

*[translated by Vipul Rikhi]*

*

Stealthily, he came through my door last night,
hair like a thief's lasso slung over his shoulders.
I stumbled to my feet, lost my footing,
and fell faint when he sat down.
Gazing on his beauty, I was stunned
and laid waste, swooning and drunk.
His bewitching, half-intoxicated eyes:
gazelle fawn in a rabbit sleep.

Whoever sees you for just one day
forgets the kingdom of this world and the next.
Without you, nectar turns to nettles,
and nettles turn to nectar in your hand.

Put a ring in Khusrau's ear.
He is your slave and heeds your call.

*

## When Our Eyes Met

I dressed myself up to go see my lover,
but when I saw him, I forgot myself.
You robbed me of everything
When our eyes met.

You made me drink love's elixir
and I got drunk
when our eyes met.

I was left staring—
you made me an ascetic
when our eyes met.

Fair arms and green bangles—
you caught my wrist
when our eyes met.

You became the charming lover—
you left me breathless
when our eyes met.

Khusrau dies for Nizam—
you made me a married woman
when our eyes met.

*[translated by Paul E. Losensky and Sunil Sharma]*

# Vidyapati

## [Fourteenth to Fifteenth Century CE]

Priest, playwright, linguist, philosopher and court poet, Vidyapati was a polymath whose influence on the later poets of eastern India (from Chaitanya to Chandidas and centuries later, on Tagore) was considerable. It led to his being christened 'the new Jayadeva' by the king of Mithila, Sivasimha (1402–1406).

A devotee of Shiva who also wrote ardent love songs about Krishna and Radha, Vidyapati's poems broke with tradition in various ways. For one, they were composed in Maithili rather than the court language of Sanskrit. For another, they chose to focus extensively on Radha's point of view. We see her here in various moods of love—desire, confusion, embarrassment, anguish.

The voice in these selected poems is that of a woman in deep longing, but also a woman aware of her charms. She is passionate and self-aware, and her bashfulness is clearly more posture than reality. The lush eroticism is offset by the poet's voice, which occasionally brings in a counterpoint of sardonic disbelief. This tonal oscillation between soaring desire and pragmatic scepticism offers a textural richness to the work. Falling in love with a god is a risky business, the female lover warns us, for it offers an odd brand of sanctuary that leaves one 'utterly dispossessed'.

~

O friend, I cannot tell you
Whether he was near or far, real or a dream.

Like a vine of lightning,
As I chained the dark one,
I felt a river flooding in my heart.
Like a shining moon,
I devoured that liquid face.
I felt stars shooting around me.
The sky fell with my dress,
Leaving my ravished breasts.
I was rocking like the earth.
In my storming breath
I could hear my ankle bells,
Sounding like bees.
Drowned in the last waters of dissolution,
I knew that this was not the end.

Says Vidyapati:
How can I possibly believe such nonsense?

*

In that night of rains
as I walked to your doors,
snakes hissed at my feet
and the darkness grew deep.

Listening to the sound of desire
as I stood stabbed
by love's five arrows,
my heart shrank at my daring.
Am I rejected then,
my man of miracles?

I shall close down the tryst
for all women.
That sport of love,

this wonder of passion,
is only a faraway cry.
Even beholding you
fills me with doubts.

The night is crawling to the fourth watch,
I must now go home . . .

*

O friend,
My love has left for that terrible land
where kokilas do not sing,
bees do not hum
and flowers do not blossom in the wood.
Where the seasons do not change,
and love has no power.
Where the people do not speak
or hear of love.
And my love has marched to that fearful land.

My heart is filled with shame—
have I only been a fool?
Has Krishna then no taste
for the art of loving?

*

I was unaware
of the power of love
and I thought my lover
was forever mine.
Bewitched,
I had taken shelter in his love
but to be utterly dispossessed.

While I prayed
and offered my life,
my love abruptly departed
without a single word.
I hold his loveliness now
in the core of my heart
but as a constant pain.
And I live only for the moment,
like a lamp without oil.

*[translated by Deben Bhattacharya]*

# Chandidas

## [Fifteenth Century CE]

The figure of Chandidas, the priest–poet who addressed his love poems to a low-caste washerwoman, Rami, has become so iconic that it is difficult to separate the original from a barrage of legend. It is also difficult to separate Chandidas' work from the multitude of inspired imitators spawned in his wake. What we know is that this forbidden love was, for him, a profound bond, analogous to the archetypal love of Krishna and Radha.

The poems suggest that Chandidas was a village priest in the Bankura or Birbhum district of Bengal who refused to abandon either his priestly office or his subversive love. Indeed, he refused to see any distinction between the two. According to one version, when the social disapproval grew intense, he resolved to fast unto death but came miraculously to life on the funeral pyre. Another version says he assumed the form of Vishnu. A third says he was whipped to death while tied to the back of an elephant for having ignited the interest of the wife of the nawab of Gaur.

What remains are around a thousand poems of such intense musicality that they were inspirational to Vaishnava spirituality in Bengal. These also foregrounded a love that was earth-bound and sensual. It proudly wore its human credentials, suggesting that there could be no sacredness that bypassed the human experience. 'The supreme is man, nothing more important than this,' is a celebrated line from his verse.

The tantric tradition of Vaishnava–Sahajiya (*sahaja*: 'natural') spirituality in Bengal viewed an unlicenced or forbidden love as more sacred than conjugal love, for it prioritized intensity and authenticity over social convention. Radha was seen, therefore, as the ideal *parakiya* woman (one who belongs legally to another), and her relationship with Krishna was celebrated as true, unfettered by moral and normative constraints.

Radha in these poems is unafraid and unapologetic about her transgressions. 'The elders chatter/ and the wicked gossip' about her immodesty and wantonness. But while their gossip is limited to a town as small as their minds, Radha's love leaps effortlessly from the local to the universal. Possessed by an all-consuming madness and an energizing passion, she is empowered to 'reach for the moon'.

~

How can I describe his relentless flute,
which pulls virtuous women from their homes
and drags them by their hair to Shyam
as thirst and hunger pull the doe to the snare?
Chaste ladies forget their wisdom,
and clinging vines shakes loose from their trees,
hearing that music.
Then how shall a simple dairymaid withstands its call?
Chandidas says, Kala, the puppet master, leads the dance.

*[translated by Edward C. Dimock and Denise Levertov]*

\*

The ignorant shout at me
saying, 'Out, out with you,
you scandalous slut!'
And I cannot divine
whom I have robbed.
None ever speak to me
and I live in ceaseless fear.
But this is a disgraceful lie
since he and I are not on speaking terms.

\*

I met a connoisseur
of the flavours of love,
and desire mounted in me.
O my life's dear love,
as I counted the nights for you,
flames of fire rose in my heart,
spreading and growing,
till I was bodily scorched by love.

*

She lingers out of doors.
She rushes in
And she rushes out,
Her heart is restless.
Breathing fast,
She gazes at the kadamba wood.
What has happened
That she is not afraid?
The elders chatter
And the wicked gossip.

Is she possessed
By some enchanting god?
Forever restless
Careless of clothes,
Startled, she jumps in her dreams . . .

Her desire inflamed
By passion and longing,
She reaches for the moon.

Chandidas says that she is caught
In the snare of Kaliya, the dark.

*[translated by Deben Bhattacharya]*

# Kabir

## [Fifteenth to Sixteenth Century CE]

He has probably been translated more than any other Indian mystic. His voice—abrasive and disruptive—has been sung and recited by millions in north India for seven centuries and still echoes in streets and seminar rooms around the world. What's more, it is difficult to know where he begins and ends; he has generated an entire literary tradition and countless poems bear his imprimatur in the oral tradition. His voice still cuts through orthodoxy, pretention and punditry of every hue.

There is an urgency in Kabir. His is a relentless project to wake people up to an immediate, intimate experience with truth. This truth is formless, nameless, creedless and casteless, as he tirelessly reiterates. And yet, on occasion, the poetry employs the female archetype to make its point more emphatically. Sometimes, the powerful woman is Maya, the cleverest conwoman in the cosmos. And yet, she is not merely a beguiling seductress. To the awakened one, she is everything: 'she alone is root, flower, garden,/ she herself plucks and eats.' At other times, the woman is the seeker yearning for a truer home. She travels the world in search of truth: 'Looking my best,/ I go in search of Hari.' But she must return empty-handed only to realize that 'we live under the same roof,/ sleep in the same bed'.

Then there are those times when she is an agile spiritual adept. She cannot be contained by domestic borders or pigeonholed by her marital identity. She is the unbridled natural one who devours her husbands, ties up her mother-in-law and sleeps when she pleases, stretching her legs out unapologetically!

Here, a taste of Kabir.

~

*Ram's bride has looted the market.*

She looted the cities of gods and snakes,
looted the three worlds, making a racket,
looted Brahma, Shiva, the great sage Narad,
put Shringi in his place, ripped Parashar's belly,
looted Kashi with a whisper long ago.
After thinking about it, she looted
the lord of yogis.
I escaped by the lord's grace, got across
on the cord of the word.
Kabir says listen friends, seekers,
when that swindler comes,
stay awake

\*

*My mind has gone mad, o lord.*

Fair one, stop prancing. Your lover
is in your own body.
The one he loves
is the true blessed bride.
Who cares
about dark or fair?
Stone by stone, people build
a palace and say, 'My house'.
Not my house! Not your house!
We're birds, just here for the night.
The traveller ties his bundle and camps
at an inn. Traveller, if there's someone to meet,
meet now! This is it!
A woman flings her hair and weeps:

my mate—our bond—broken.
Kabir says, listen seekers, friends,
the one who joined you
broke you.

*

*I don't feel right in my parents' place.*

My lord has a city of perfect beauty
where no one comes or goes,
there's no moon or sun,
no water or wind.
Who will carry this message?
Who will tell the lord of my pain?
I can't see the path ahead,
and going back would be a shame.
Oh beloved, how can I reach
my in-laws' house?
Separation burns fiercely.
The juice of sensuality
keeps me dancing.
Without a true guru
no one is ours,
no one can show the way.
Kabir says, listen friends, seekers,
even in a dream my love won't come
to put out these flames.

*

*Oh friend, that house*
*is utterly other*
*where he lives, my man,*
*my complete one.*

There's no grief or joy,
no truth or lie,
no field of good and evil.
There's no moon or sun,
no day or night,
but brilliance
without light.

No wisdom, no meditation,
no recitation, no renunciation,
no Veda, Quran,
or sacred
song,
action, possession, social
convention, all
gone.

There's no ground, no space,
no in, no out, nothing like
body or cosmos,
no five elements, no three qualities,
no lyrics, no couplets.

No root, flower, seed, creeper.
Fruit shines
without a tree.
No inhale, exhale, upward, downward,
no way to count
breaths.

Where that one lives,
there's nothing.
Kabir says, I've got it!
If you catch my hint, you find

the same place—
no place.

\*

Saints, a huge surprise:
If I tell, who will believe it?
Just one man, just one woman—
imagine that!
In just one egg all eight-four,
and a universe
lost in delusion.
Just one woman spread her net,
The world filled with confusion.
Searching, they couldn't find the end,
nor Brahma, Vishnu or Shiva.
The snake-noose tightens in the body,
the world's plundered, they struggle
without the sword of knowledge,
no one can lay a hand on her.
She alone is root, flower, garden,
she herself, plucks and eats.
Kabir says, only those are free
whom the guru has shaken.

*[translated by Linda Hess]*

\*

## What A Match She Found

What a match she found, that crazy girl
How hard she courted and wooed
My awareness is a brand-new bride
She's taken God as groom

Endless wandering in endless lives
Today your chance has come
If you blow this moment again
You'll never find your ground

Anointed with the lotion of love
The fragrant oil of the Name
Five friends sing to the bride
Under a canopy adorned with gems

Truth decorates the wedding arbor
The gathering brims with love
Their hands join in an unbreakable bond
A union blessed by the One

In a colourful palace, my nuptial bed
My awareness fully awake
My heart is now hitched to my love
I'm in the company of saints

Lost, astray and wandering for ages
At last, I brought home my groom
Say Kabir, my swan rejoices
And bursts into joyous song!

*[translated by Shabnam Virmani]*

\*

Lying beside you,
I'm waiting to be kissed.
But your face is turned
And you're fast asleep.

Though a buzz saw on my neck
Would sound sweeter than your snoring,

I'll put my arms around you
And whisper in your ear:

I have one husband: you.
You have one wife: me.
Who's there to come between us?
Beware, says Kabir,

Of the man you love.
He can be a tricky customer.

*

Hari, the thug,
Has thugged us all,
But, Mother,
I can't do without him.

Who's it you call husband?
Or call wife?
Who's it you call son?
Or call father?
Who is it who dies?
Who is the mourner?

I've taken a shine
To this thug, says Kabir.
I've caught him out,
And stopped his thuggery.

*[translated by Arvind Krishna Mehrotra]*

*

Mother, I've poured glory on both families!
I ate twelve husbands at my father's house

and sixteen at the in-laws.
I tied sister-in-law and mother-in-law
to the bed, and insulted
brother-in-law.
I burned the part in the hair of that hag
who nagged me.
In my womb I got five
plus two plus four.
I ate the neighbour lady for breakfast
along with the wise old mother.
Poor thing! Then spreading the easy bed,
I stretched my legs and slept.
Now I don't come, don't go,
don't die or live.
The master has erased all shame.
Seizing the name, I dropped the world.
I caught the name—
so near!
I saw the name!
shouts Kabir.

*[translated by Linda Hess]*

# Narsinh Mehta

## [Fifteenth Century CE]

Regarded as the foremost poet of the Gujarati language, Narsinh Mehta is widely known as the author of '*Vaishnav jana to*', a poem much loved by Mahatma Gandhi and inspirational to many during the Indian freedom struggle. Following the norm of so many narratives around saint-poets, we are told he was mute until the age of five. Being asked to intone the words '*Radhe Shyam*' miraculously infused speech into the little boy. According to legend, he escaped one day into the forest to escape the taunts of his sister-in-law and spent several days in meditation beside a Shiva linga. Pleased by his devotion, Shiva transported him to the lush moon-drenched groves of Vrindavan where he was offered a ringside view of Krishna's dance with his gopis, the magical *raas leela*.

Narsinh was never the same again. He spent the rest of his life singing the glory of that scene. What's more, he did not forget to thank his sister-in-law for catalysing his spiritual journey! Henceforth, caste, class and gender considerations were thrown to the winds; Narsinh Mehta belonged to a sangha of the divinely-transformed—those he defined as compassionate, empathetic, free of egotism, bigotry and prejudice.

Narsinh Mehta's oeuvre is substantial, including poems that are autobiographical, narrative, devotional, didactic and erotic. The poems in this selection are love poems in which the female devotee is presented as a bold and innovative lover. Krishna, on the other hand, is playfully quiescent: he allows his sweetheart to tie his arms to the bedpost, and is even willing to cross-dress to add an exciting element to their amorous play. The poetry flirts with such effrontery with barriers between woman

242

and man, devotee and divinity, self and other, that the female speaker
asks in ecstatic disbelief, 'What merit have I earned to be born a woman?
Hari pleads with me with such meekness.'

~

## To the Foot of the Bed

To the foot of the bed I'll fasten your arms
with flower-ropes shamelessly.
Who will free you from the temple of my body?
Rivals? What can they do but flame in anger?

To the foot of the bed I'll fasten your arms.

You are the gardener, I the flowering vine;
Why plant me if you will not water me?
    You are the honey bee seduced by my love,
You, dying in the fragrance of my lotus heart.
To the foot of the bed I'll fasten your arms.

Love's essence and lover should be one—
    Yours is the divine surrender of body and mind.
Says Narsaiyo: Gopi, won't you teach me
how to burrow into his heart and win?

To the foot of the bed I'll fasten your arms.

*

## Strange Ecstasy and Joy Unique

Strange ecstasy and joy unique:
the son of Nand conjures a leela
to pleasure his beloved proud,
dons garments and adornments strange
            Here's ecstasy and joy unique

He oscillates upon the swing,
studded with pearls and gems, the swing.
The gopis through their half-drawn veils,
unseen themselves, gaze at his face.
          What ecstasy and joy unique

Body and limb in saffron paste
anointed; unmatched his attire—
an elephant-pearl drops down his nose,
to wet, impassioned lips;
          What ecstasy and joy unique.

Garbed in yellow silk, with love
He wears a sari splashed with dark,
his ringing anklets dance away,
to humour her he wears a bodice.
          Strange is the ecstasy of joy

Red lacquered are her tender feet,
studded with gems the anklet-bands,
bracelet and bangle are of gold,
a black braid swaying down the back;
          Strange ecstasy and joy unique

Floral garlands round the head,
the eyes lined with antimony
Narasaiya's Swami, great to meet you
Who can pen your pure resplendence?
          Strange is this joy and ecstasy.

*[translated by Keki Daruwalla and Meena Desai]*

                *

What merit have I earned to be born a woman?
Shri Hari pleads with me with such meekness!

The one they call eternal, unfathomable,
the beloved of the lotus-eyed goddess,
embraces me.

The one you can't see even in dreams, through
opulent sacrifices,
deep meditation,
or painful rites,
him, you may grasp with a single loving glance.

He who reclines on the luxuriant bed of the serpent king
and inhabits the imperishable celestial realm of Vaikuntha,
enters my nuptial bed in yellow silks.
Even greater than Vaikuntha is my home!

His title is 'Lover of Devotees.'
So proclaim the sacred texts.
Blessed is meeting Narasaĩyā's Lord.
Seeing me so vulnerable, he deluges me

                              in his grace.

*[translated by Neelima Shukla–Bhatt]*

# Guru Arjan Dev

## [Sixteenth Century CE]

The fifth guru in the Sikh tradition, Guru Arjan Dev's contribution to the spiritual culture of his day was considerable. He completed the construction of the Golden Temple in Amritsar, vitalized the cultural climate of the city, composed a beloved prayer entitled 'The Prayer of Peace' and collated the hymns of various mystics into the first edition of the Sikh sacred text, the *Adi Granth*. This laid the foundations of the later scriptural compilation, the *Guru Granth Sahib*. His aim was to systematize the oeuvre, weed out distortions, and create a text that would offer enduring revelatory guidance to future generations. Above all, he aimed to craft a work that abided by the casteless, inclusive vision so central to the Sikh faith. A gifted poet with exceptional command over rhythm, metre and form, Guru Arjan Dev contributed 2218 of his own poems to this work. His widespread influence among people of diverse faiths alarmed the orthodoxy and, eventually, the Mughal regime. He died tragically in 1606, becoming the first of the two gurus to be martyred in the Sikh tradition.

This *shabad*, or sacred song, set to the raga Bilaval, assumes the voice of the female beloved or bride—not an uncommon occurrence in the Bhakti tradition. Both Guru Nanak and Guru Arjan Dev have employed it as a trope. The 'muscular physicality' of the verse, however, says translator Avtar Singh, is the poet's own. Guru Arjan Dev's verse mentions the name of the Sikh founder and first guru, Nanak, and makes no mention of the author's. This was not an uncommon practice, either: the name in the signature line, for many devotees, was intended to represent 'authority', not 'authorship'. Avtar Singh points out that all the gurus in the Guru Granth Sahib used the name 'Nanak', 'believing it was his flame that illuminated their poetry'.

The 'thudding rhythm of the last couplet', says the translator, cannot be rendered in translation. And yet, this utterance retains its unvarnished freshness. There is no ornamentation, no erotic surplus. But it is clearly time for celebration. For when the beloved blooms within the bride's body, her very bed rejoices.

~

My Lord's name is without limit and beyond price
My Beloved is as life; I depend on Him. I crave Him as
the betel chewer does the leaf.

With the Guru's guidance I have become one with Him.
My body bears His colours.
Good fortune showed His face to me. We are wedded;
my devotion won't waver.
I need neither beauty, nor incense, perfume, or light. He
blooms within me.
Nanak: the Lord has joined his bride to Himself. My bed
is the better for it.

*[translated by Avtar Singh]*

# Bulleh Shah

## [Seventeenth to Eighteenth Century CE]

The verse of Punjab's foremost Sufi poet and mystic, Bulleh Shah, embodies a flamboyant disregard for orthodoxy and is characterized by a human empathy that extends across barriers of class and gender. It explains why his poems are sung centuries later by itinerant street musicians, rock bands and renowned concert artists, from Nusrat Fateh Ali Khan and Abida Parveen to the Wadali Brothers.

Reared and educated in Kasur (in the Punjab province of modern-day Pakistan), Bulleh Shah appears to have studied at a reputed local madrasa. He chose, however, to depart from tradition and compose poetry in the Punjabi vernacular. Later, he went to Lahore, where he met the Sufi master, Shah Inayat Qadri, and became his disciple. The relationship between disciple and *murshid*, or master, was intimate and explosive, as Bulleh Shah's poems indicate. It is reminiscent of other celebrated bonds such as those between Rumi and Shams, Amir Khusrau and Nizamuddin Aulia, Gorakhnath and Matsyendranath, and more recently, Sri Ramakrishna and Swami Vivekananda. Bulleh Shah died in Kasur in 1757. He was declared a heretic by some orthodox clerics, but others knew better. His funeral services were conducted with due ceremony, and a tomb with his Punjabi verses inscribed in calligraphy still stands in Kasur.

According to tradition, Bulleh Shah's family objected to the lowly class antecedents of Shah Inayat. Swayed by this reasoning, Bulleh Shah left his master. But the wandering poet soon realized the folly of his ways. Contrite, he tried to return to his murshid, who spurned him. Bulleh Shah then decided to atone by throwing respectability to the winds and joining a community of dancers. After twelve years, he donned female attire, wore ankle bells, braided his hair and danced before his master. It was an act that would have horrified his family and the religious establishment of his day. Shah forgave his errant disciple, however, and the relationship was resumed.

The poems are infused with a jubilant knowingness that life is not about the costumes we wear—whether of faith, class or gender—as much as about the quest for the true self, naked and stainless. 'O naïve Bulleya, what did love steal . . .?' asks the poet with rhetorical aplomb, and adds a classic line of mystic paradox, 'Love looted even god of his godliness.'

~

## Your Love Has Made Me Dance

Your love has made me dance like mad
Come quickly, O healer, or I'll be dead

Your love has built a home in my heart
This cup of poison, I drank of my own accord
O my complete guru, now you must save me
*Your love has made me dance . . .*

The sun has set, only redness remains
I'd give my life for just one glimpse of him
I forgot you, O teacher, I let you down
*Your love has made me dance . . .*

In the forest of this love, a peacock calls out
My love is more beautiful than any holy place
He wounded me, then forgot all about me
*Your love has made me dance . . .*

Bulleshah is called to Shah Inayat's door
He who coloured me in red and green

He who was always lying in wait for me
*Your love has made me dance . . .*

*

## Love Stripped Me

Once I went to the office of love
Love stripped me of my swagger

I'd gone to garner love's praises
Love robbed me of my vanity

Love swindles saints and prophets
It strips mighty kings of their kingdoms

O naïve Bulleya, what did love steal of yours?
Love looted even god of his godliness!

*

## My Beloved Has Come Home

My beloved has come home, friends
Get rid of the watchman
That dratted timekeeper!

My love has come home
Allah brought us together
An incredible benediction

Time and again he clangs the bell
And disrupts my night of union
If he understood my heart's desire
He'd toss that clock away!

The limitless melody sounds so sweet
A wonderful singer, rhythm and beat

All ablutions and prayers forgotten
O bartender, hand me the cup of wine!

A glimpse of him is a marvellous thing
It softens all life's stings
May this night never end, do something!
Erect a wall against the morning

Bulleshah's bed is ready and made
I'm in love with the one who saves
This time has come after eons of trying
Now we'll never be parted again!

*[translated by Vipul Rikhi]*

* 

## Rituals

Fasting, pilgrimage, and the call
to prayer, love has drowned them all.
    Can any artifice survive
    when messages of love arrive?
    On the ears only its sounds fall.
        Fasting, pilgrimage, and the call
        to prayer, love has drowned them all.

The moment Love came toward me,
rituals went by the board.
Love, only love, was then to be seen,
over and over, around, between.
The loveless noticed nothing at all.
        Fasting, pilgrimage, and the call
        to prayer, love has drowned them all

*[translated by Taufiq Rafat]*

# Shah Abdul Latif

## [Seventeenth to Eighteenth Century CE]

Widely considered the greatest Sufi poet of Sindh, Shah Abdul Latif left home at the age of twenty and met many a saint and yogi during his nomadic years across Gujarat, Rajasthan and Sindh. The result is a mysticism that has inspired both Muslims and Vedantic Hindus to view his work as an invitation to a deeper faith.

Widowed early, Shah Latif did not remarry. Instead, he chose to lead a life of verse, music and contemplation and was viewed in his lifetime as a saint–poet, beloved of his people. His work was compiled into a single work known as *Shah Jo Risalo*, celebrated in folk songs to this day and compared by scholars to the work of Rumi. He died in 1752, and a mausoleum was built over his grave. This grave in the village of Bhit Shah was to become a popular site of pilgrimage.

His translators, Vipul Rikhi and Shabnam Virmani, relate an interesting anecdote about how he confounded sectarian labellers. When asked if he was Shia or Sunni, he replied that he was 'in between'. 'But there is nothing in between,' pondered his disciple. 'Precisely,' was Shah Latif's reply. 'I am nothing.'

When Shah Latif adopts the female voice in his poetry, it is to invoke the great folk legends of Heer–Ranjha, Sohini–Mahiwal or Sasui–Punhu. These are no longer typical stories of star-crossed love. Instead, the eventual death of the heroine is presented as ecstatic oblivion rather than tragic annihilation. The ultimate bedroom is the gallows. The ultimate surrender is waiting for the Beloved to 'drop the blade'. This is the path of the brave, for 'to choose safe waters/ is the route of impostors'. Sohini, who drowns when swimming to meet her lover, is the courageous heroine who knows that true lovers will not settle for the shallows but must 'take on the mighty rivers'. What seems like a tale of doom becomes one of triumph. Slaughter here is sacred death, butchery a blessing. The divine 'unites his favourites to him' in what is seen as the ultimate snuffing-out, *fanaa*, the end of duality, freedom. 'When oneness is the bride', says Latif, 'The groom is cut to pieces.'

~

people swim in summer
she delights in wintry waters
slipping into the crippling cold

how unfair the river
is to the lover

*

she jumps in

to choose safe waters
is the route of impostors

those who love
take on the mighty river

*

the river heralds continuously
she answers the clarion call

in the darkness she plummets
into the icy water

*[translated by Anju Makhija and Hari Dilgir]*

*

I look for the head but can't find the torso
I look for the torso but can't find the head
Hands, wrists and fingers chopped
And dropped who knows where
When oneness is the bride
The groom is cut to pieces

The gallows are the bedroom
Of true lovers
To turn back or hesitate is a shame
Their love belongs to open fields
The vow to embrace death
Is a sign of true lovers

I am wedded to him who
Wields an axe in his hands
In the field of love
No place to hesitate
Let me put my head on the block
Let the beloved drop the blade

*[translated by Vipul Rikhi]*

*

They didn't take my consent
These eyes
Before falling in love

They've strayed into
A dangerous market
Where no one haggles
And the price is steep

You offer your life
To close the deal

*[translated by Shabnam Virmani]*

*

## No Time for Loitering

He's not found by sitting on your ass
He's not found on a soft, warm bed
   He's found by those
Who walk on the path and weep for him

   If you wish to die tomorrow
  The beloved will come tomorrow
    Or never at all
    It has never been
   That one living in comfort
    Found him

Don't wail without a true cry
Don't walk without a true gait
Don't burn without true fire
Don't weep without true tears

Burn as long as you live, Sasui!
There is no rest without burning
In heat and cold, keep walking
 This is no time for loitering

*

Don't leave the house, Sohini
Or don't return!
Smash duality
Take hold of oneness

\*

He is This and he is That
He is death and he is life

He is the beloved's body
And its breath

He is enemy and well-wisher
Both here and there
Also hiding in the heart

He is the one looking at himself
In his own light

*[translated by Vipul Rikhi]*

# Kshetrayya

## [Seventeenth Century CE]

The work of this poet suffuses the dance and musical traditions of south India. Believed to be an itinerant poet–singer who wandered from one town to another, his Telugu poems centre on his deity, Muvva Gopala. (Muvva is ostensibly a reference to the village in which Kshetrayya was born.) Approximately 300 of his poems have survived.

These brief lyrical poems of love and longing for Gopala or Krishna (often seen here more as patron than deity) are dramatized through the erotic dalliance of a courtesan and a man, where a woman of independent spirit speaks of her sexual adventures with a whimsical male. These poems were performed in the devadasi tradition until they found their way, in more gentrified versions, into the hands of upper-caste performers.

Interestingly, however, recent scholarship by Harshita Mruthinti Kamath argues that Kshetrayya was not a historical figure, much less a male. He was, instead, a literary construct authored by multiple women, many of whom were courtesans in the devadasi tradition. A combination of Victorian morality, nationalist fervour, upper caste unease, the zeal of the anti-nautch movement and changing literary weather unleashed this process of cultural bowdlerization. The result was the persona of the male saint–poet. This was clearly a more respectable figure than the 'dissolute' devadasi as an author. Dancer Swarnamalya Ganesh offers a series of names of courtesans who might actually be the authors of these poems.

Is Kshetrayya then just a pseudonym? A female creation? If so, these playful poems—with their sometimes-reticent male god/ customer and female devotee/ courtesan, brimming with sexual initiative and skill—make for even more compelling reading.

~

### A Woman to her Lover

How soon it's morning already!
There's something new in my heart,
    Muvva Gopala.

Have we talked even a little while
to undo the pain of our separation till now?
You call me in your passion, 'Woman, come to me,'
and while your mouth is still on mine,

    *it's morning already!*

Caught in the grip of the Love God,
angry with him, we find release drinking
at each other's lips.

You say, 'My girl, your body is tender as a leaf,'
and before you can loosen your tight embrace,

    *it's morning already!*

Listening to my moans as you touch certain spots,
the pet parrot mimics me, and O how we laugh in bed!

You say, 'Come close, my girl,'
and make love to me like a wild man, Muvva Gopala,

and as I get ready to move on top,

*it's morning already!*

\*

## The Madam to a Courtesan

Woman! He's none other
than Cennudu of Palagriri
    Haven't you heard?
    He rules the worlds.

When he wanted you, you took his gold—
but couldn't you tell him your name, your address?
    Some lover you are!
    He's hooked on you.

    *And he rules the worlds.*

I found him wandering the alleyways,
    too shy to ask anyone.
I had to bring him home with me.
Would it have been such a crime
    If you or your girls
had waited for him by the door?
You really think it's enough
To get the money in your hand?
Can't you tell who's big, who's small?
    Who do you think he is?

    *And he rules the worlds.*

The handsome Cennudu of Palagiri,
    this Muvva Gopala,
has fallen to your lot.

When he said he'd come tomorrow,
        couldn't you consent
        just a little?
Did you really have to say no?
What can I say about you?

                *And he rules the worlds.*

                                    *

## A Senior Courtesan to a Younger One

Are you done with your anger?
Have you finally talked, my dear,
to one another,
you and your Muvva Gopala,
and stopped being angry
at last?

Have your hearts cooled off
and found a little peace?
Tell me the truth:
is all that grieving
over for today?
Could you finally have
one good day?
He over there,
you here,
with these endless sighs in between?

                *Are you done with your anger?*

Have you looked
at each other's faces,
taken sweet kisses
from your lips,
pressed body against body?

Why treat one another
like a hunter and his prey?

*Are you done with your anger?*

Today, at least,
have you shared a single bed
and praised, I hope,
each other's skills in love?
You've finally come together,
haven't you,
you and your Muvva Gopala,
confessing over and over
that you listened to slander
like fools.

*Are you done with your anger?*

\*

## A Young Woman to a Friend

Those women, they deceived me.
They told me he was a woman,
And now my heart is troubled
by what he did.

First, I thought
she was my aunt and uncle's daughter,
so I bow to her, and she blesses me:
'You'll get married soon,
don't be bashful. I will bring you
the man of your heart.'

'Those firm little breasts of yours
will soon
get round and full,' she says.

And she fondles them
and scratches them
with the edge of her nail.

'Come eat with me,' she says,
as she holds me close
and feeds me as at a wedding.

*Those women, they told me he was a woman!*

Then she announces:
'My husband is not in town.
Come home with me.'
So I go and sleep in her bed.

After a while she says,
'I'm bored. Let's play
a kissing game, shall we?
Too bad we're both women.'

Then, as she sees me falling asleep,
off my guard,
she tries some
strange things on me.

*Those women, they told me he was a woman!*

She says, 'I can't sleep.
Let's do what men do.'
Thinking 'she' was a woman,
I got on top of him.

Then he doesn't let go
he holds me so tight
he loses himself in me.
Wicked as ever, he declares:

'I am your Muvva Gopala!'
And he touches me expertly
and makes love to me.

*Those women, they told me he was a woman!*

\*

## A Woman to Her Reluctant Lover

Because I'm a good woman, I forgave you this time.
Would any other woman have let you off?

You follow me around like a servant,
you say humble things,
yet when I ask you to come home, you don't.
Why do you hurt me like this?

Now I've got you all alone.
If I hold you prisoner in this house,
who is there to release you?

*Because I'm a good woman*

You hold my hands; you say nice things.
But when I ask you to get into bed,
you say, 'I've taken a vow,' and do nothing.

Now I've caught you.
If I tie you down to my bed,
who is there to release you?

*Because I'm a good woman*

Only for a bet in a game you enter my bedroom.
When I call you, 'My handsome,

my Muvva Gopala!' why this indifference, dear parrot
in the hand of the Love God?

If I choose to make love to you now,
Who is there to stop me?

*Because I'm a good woman*


**[translated by A.K. Ramanujan, Velcheru Narayana Rao and
David Shulman]**

# Uddhabadas

## [Eighteenth Century CE]

Born in the second half of the eighteenth century in the village of Tenya–Baidyapur, Bengal, Uddhabadas was the disciple of the poet Radhamohandas. He wrote in both Bengali and Brajbuli. Vaishnavism in Bengal, which received a great impetus from Sri Chaitanya Mahaprabhu's bhakti in the sixteenth century, explored the many dimensions of the Radha-Krishna theme: Radha's intense experience of separation, the magical music of Krishna's flute and their adventures on the banks of the river Yamuna. Although much of the poetry was authored by men, the focus is on the subjective experience of the woman in love. Krishna in these poems is the cowherd of Braj, the lover of Radha as well as the ruler of the universe—now tactile, now transcendent, now playfully immediate, now bewilderingly unattainable. The themes of love, laughter, food, colour, song and dance permeate this world where life is a festival of abundance. The sacred is discovered in and through the festivity.

While Krishna beguiles the world, Radha beguiles even him; who then is superior? And where does one end and the other begin? Here again, we see the divine–human divide, personified in the Radha–Krishna trope, dissolve into a state of rapturous non-duality.

~

Hear my words on the game of enchantment:
Toying together in the festival of Spring,

265

the lovers have transfigured into each other.
Blind with the red dust of the seasons' rites,
wiping their eyes, they kiss
and the syringe ejects torrents of crimson dawn.

Who can tell
who is the man
and who the woman
in this ecstasy?

*[translated by Deben Bhattacharya]*

# PART THREE

*'Will I Eat You? or You Eat Me?'*
—Ramprasad Sen

# Goddesses

# Introduction

Since she represents the wisdom of the number three, perhaps it is appropriate that this unique woman is the focus of the third section of this book.

Enter the Goddess.

Who is she—this figure who looms across all cultures of the world, so inexplicably familiar and yet just beyond our reach?

There are many ways to view her. For the devotee, she is deity, mother and protector. For the seeker in quest of transformation, she is guide and key to experiential wisdom. For those seeking a more just, ecologically sustainable, gender-sensitive world, she is inspiration. For a humanity seeking to recover from a brutalizing history of skewed power equations, she is equalizer and balancer. For those seeking to repair psychic wounds and ancestral pain, she is healer and harmonizer. For dreamers, seekers, artists, she is a reminder of the ultimate mystery. For the lost, she is home. But whether inner or outer, subjective or objective, real or imagined, one thing is clear: the Goddess cannot be erased. She is one wild woman who never quite goes away.

She looks, one imagines, somewhat quizzically, at the lurching tempests of a dualistic world. One wonders what she makes of the battles of supremacy among nations and faiths dominated by territorial male gods. She knows she merely needs to blink for the whole kabuki to fizzle to a stop. For she is the energy that animates the drama. The embrace within which this universe is contained. The matrix within which the theatre unfolds. She represents the compassion of the umbilical cord, the nourishment of the breast, the sanctuary of the womb.

To historically date the Goddess might be seen by her lovers as a tad impertinent. It is a bit like asking one's mother for her birth certificate as proof of her existence!

Archaeological evidence suggests that she was part of Palaeolithic settlements in central India and pervaded tribal culture and rural folklore a long time before she emerged in mainstream poetry. She is cited in Vedic literature and the Mahabharata but explodes into full-fledged iconic existence in the *Devi Mahatmyam* between the fourth and sixth centuries. We see her here in a fearsome martial form in which she slays demonic energies, routs adversaries and drinks blood, consumed by a frenzy of bloodlust. And yet, she is not what she seems, for while she disrupts civilizational order, she restores cosmic order.

Over the centuries, she has taken on diverse names and forms. There are regional, theological and esoteric variations. There are also innumerable distinctions: between Kalikula, the clan of the Black Goddess, and Srikula, the family of the Auspicious Goddess; between left-hand and right-hand practices; between Hindu, Buddhist and Jain conceptions; as well as between Shaiva, Shakta and Vaishnava-based practices. The Goddess speaks to multiple orientations—yogic, tantric, devotional and, in recent times, global New Age and feminist.

A planet awakening to the urgency of ecological awareness seems to need her more than ever. The imperative need for an earth-nourished spirituality may have much to do with her return. She was never lost, but she seems poised to surge—not just into domestic altar and roadside shrine but into collective consciousness.

She returns perhaps to remind us that the pursuit of power is an adolescent phase that we urgently need to outgrow; that the spirit of conquest is self-destruction; that compassion is not cowardice.

Author Linda Johnsen writes that those who seek the tradition of 'the living Goddess' would do well to begin their search in India, 'where not for one moment in all of human history have the children of the living Goddess forgotten their Divine Mother'. It is a proud legacy. But regrettably, it has not always made for gender justice. Divides have been created between what one might term the 'Divine Feminine' and the 'Dispensable Feminine'. And that is perhaps not surprising, for as long as the human gaze is divided, hierarchies are inevitable. Unfortunately, goddesses have been treated very differently from women of flesh and blood.

Yet, the uninterrupted goddess traditions have had a discernible impact on the land. If the experiential wisdom traditions of the subcontinent are still alive, we probably have our goddess traditions, in some measure, to thank for them. If holistic healing systems and traditional arts are still exuberant, if cultural, linguistic and religious diversity lives not just in museums but in homes, on streets and in hearts, we probably have our goddess traditions, in some measure, to thank for them. And if fundamentalist excesses are still checked by spiritual anarchy that returns us time and again to confusion, wonder and uncertainty, we surely have our goddess traditions to thank for it. For the Goddess grounds. She refuses to be refrigerated in text and temple. She stands for an anchorage in everyday sacredness, in the organic mess of life. She is the creator who dares to become her own creation, refusing to remain an unmoved mover or dispassionate conjuror.

The Goddess invites us to become conduits, not custodians, of the divine.

The contradictions abound. And still, there are reminders, especially within tantric traditions, of the need to honour all women, irrespective of social or religious background. A Vajrayana Buddhist text (excerpted in this book) offers an unequivocal rationale for this. 'Women who are served will, for their part, instantly grant/ accomplishment to all those seeking/ to benefit living beings.'

In the Shakta traditions of the subcontinent, the Goddess as Shakti is both creation and creator, the manifest and the unmanifest world. Her pre-eminence does not imply the subordination of the masculine; instead, it represents the supreme truth beyond all duality. In the eighth-century hymn, the *Saundaryalahari*, attributed to the mystic philosopher Adi Shankara, we are reminded that the physical universe is born of the union of Shakti and Shiva. However, in the absence of Shakti, Shiva is inert, transcendent, a latent possibility. For Shakti is the creative power that infuses dynamism into all of creation: 'Only when with her can he stir/ Shakti, she's Shiva's power/ Even Shiva who's a god/ Only prevails when paired with her.'

And this is why she is so difficult to obliterate.

The Goddess does not stand aloof. She gets involved. She does not live outside our reality, but in it. She turns creation into a sacred event. Her involvement tells us that this is not an alien or hostile planet into which we have fallen, or to which we have been exiled. We tread on her body; we inhale her breath; we are her messengers 'between moon and mud'. Our bodies are the 'anthem of muck' she sings into existence. It explains why caste and patriarchal prejudice, as well as ritual ideas of pollution, are often so conspicuously absent in Goddess-based spiritual practices. She is the continuum between spirit and embodiment, between abstraction and incarnation, journey and destination.

You reach her *through* her.

But human minds must separate, and so we do. We separate her into the goddess of pure wisdom and the goddess of maniacal laughter. We separate her into the goddess of birth and the goddess of cruel termination. Of winsome youth and haggard cronehood. We separate her into chaste consort and unruly independent power.

She indulges us. But she is a trickster, a consummate actress. Her guises are many. She looks out at us through a bird at the window, the gaze of a pet dog, a glowering teenager, a blooming cabbage patch, an old woman on the train muttering to herself, and always through the mirror.

One way to celebrate her is to sing her many names. This section can be read as a garland of goddess appellations: Devi, Durga, Mahakali, Mahalakshmi, Mahasaraswati, Tripurasundari, Amba, Ambika, Yogamaya, Vajradhatvishvari, Mei Hukum, Yellamma, Kali, Abhirami, Parashakti, Mahashakti, Neeli Mariamman, Linga Bhairavi. And they represent just a fraction of the names—articulated and unnamable—by which we know her. This selection represents a small mosaic of poems in her praise. They range from the outpouring of lovers to the voices of advanced practitioners; from tones of worship to those of complaint; from invocations to her as mother to addresses to her as daughter; from poems by men to poems by women; from the voice of the devotee to the crisply authoritative voice of the Goddess herself; from classical Sanskrit odes to folk songs and tribal poems in praise of the living Earth; from praise of her purity to her joyous involvement in the lives of the contaminated and the forsaken.

Some of these are not mere devotional poems. They are esoteric texts that understand the mechanics of the inner journey. When the bhakta meets the shakta, we have the birth of a new science of intimacy.

These poems mark the explosive site where devotion meets awareness. This is where erotica meets exactitude. This is where love meets the technology of ego-combustion. For many Goddess poets are not mere devotees; they are initiates. And the Goddess is not just divinity; she is a device. She is not just a transcendent truth; she is a catalyst and a solvent, a tool to dismantle the limited identities we mistake for ourselves. 'Isn't it funny/ that though she's Mother of the Universe/ we warble/ about her lotus-bud breasts? . . . / Hilarious really,/ all the hype/ when she's beyond it all—/ description, explanation,/ perception,' says Abhirami Bhattar.

Interestingly, while devotion can demolish the seeker, it is, on occasion, capable of demolishing the deity as well. Both acts are rooted in love.

The Goddess who first manifests in her warrior form in the *Devi Mahatmyam* gradually turns into a nurturing mother figure. She loses none of her voltage. However, her ferocity is that of the mother who destroys only to renew and liberate. This relationship allows poets to speak to her as a confidante. They have the implicit right to sulk, argue and revolt, if they choose. In the Gujarati garba, sung by women, the deities of various temples are playfully reprimanded. 'O goddess of Pavagadh, give me your darshan!' they sing, 'Or give me my quarter back.' If the local goddess doesn't keep up her end of the bargain, the devotee humorously threatens to shift allegiance to another shrine, another goddess.

In the poems of the fifteenth-century poet, Annamacharya, we see the Goddess as lover. Even here, she is no pushover. She is argumentative and contrary, and she will not be won over by blandishment or power. 'Unless I want it myself,' she says dismissively, 'it doesn't count as love.' These poems speak of a mutuality that is both romantic and spiritual. 'He's the master,' says Alamelumanga in one poem of her beloved god, and adds with equal ease, 'He's my slave.' She reminds her god on more than one occasion that he cannot take her for granted. She enjoys their flirtation, but she will not succumb to force or coercion.

This bond of intense familiarity is vividly enacted in the poetry of eighteenth- and nineteenth-century Bengal. Ramprasad Sen famously declares: 'Will I eat you? Or you eat me?/ Today is the day of reckoning.' There is Kamalakanta Bhattacharya's unabashed irreverence towards the naked Kali: 'Who is this/ dressed like a crazy woman,/ robed with sky? . . . / Mother,/ are you going to rescue Kamalakanta/ in *this* outfit?'

This is the *ninda–stuti*, a tantrum in verse that allows devotees not merely the freedom to love but also to reprimand the divine. This prosody of rage, in fact, becomes part of the subcontinent's remarkable inheritance of sacred poetry.

The result is a goddess you can laugh with, quarrel with, reproach, and swear at in the sheer ferocity of your passion. The divine never takes offence because she knows the volatile nature of love. She knows its rituals and games of make-believe. Kazi Nazrul Islam writes: 'Don't you have a place to play/ that's not a crematorium? . . . / Oh bone-burning, bothersome girl!/ Where did You get Your necklace of bones? . . . / Yet even when I hold You to my chest,/ still I die of pain;/ that's why I abuse you, Ma.'

The Goddess persists.

Even in a world deforested of dreams, illuminated by reason, she finds a way to leak through the crevices. And how could it be otherwise? For she is unafraid of physicality, unwilling to stand apart from the terror and beauty of her creation. She invites us to a path where engagement is not at war with freedom. She does not ask us to transcend the world without experiencing it. She leads by example. She plunges into the materiality of Earth, its many vegetal and animal surprises. She births, caretakes and participates in the joys and losses of the journey. And she laughs and weeps with her creations through it all. The American poet May Sarton writes: 'Every creation is born out of the dark,/ Every birth is bloody. Something gets torn./ Kali is there to do her sovereign work/ Or else the living child will be stillborn.'

Her mysteries are many.

She is many and she is one; she is form and she is emptiness; she is stillness and she is energy. And perhaps most inexplicably, she is concealment and revelation. She is *maya Shakti*, the power of make-believe, and she is *chit Shakti*, the power of consciousness that peeps out through the darkest fog of abandonment. She demands that we acknowledge a truth beyond duality. Paradox is her domain. She reminds us of the power of the third way, beyond the human impulse to cleave and binarize. She turns division into delirium. And her language is (and how could it be otherwise?) poetry.

Her intimacy makes her unique. She isn't squeamish about the slime and muck of existence. She drinks blood, chops heads and is altogether terrifying until humans realize they are hers, pretending to be separate. While we splinter our realities, believing we are separate, she takes apart only to make whole. Our bodies, although we believe otherwise, are her own. That is the last illusion that she must divest us of.

That divestment can be scary. And hence her dark face.

Which brings us to yet another mystery: she is both auspiciousness and horror. The poets sing of both: her benevolence and fury; her youth and antiquity; her beauty and fearsomeness. And so, we have Kali, the goddess of darkness and death, and Sitaladevi, the goddess of disease, and many in between. The goddess Yellamma is eulogized in a Kannada folk poem: 'Her body ravaged by leprosy/ Yellamma roamed the wild forests/ But when she went to the saints Yakkai and Jogya/ Her life was transformed . . .' Yellamma is born to goddesshood through agony, and is believed to summon only those whom she believes are ready for such transformation.

Indeed, no culture seems to escape the Goddess' dark face. Hecate, the Greek goddess of crossroads; Baba Yaga, the Slavic crone goddess of death; Ereshikgal, the Sumerian goddess of the underworld; The Morrigan, the Celtic goddess of war; Tiamat, the Babylonian goddess of chaos; Sekhmet, the Egyptian goddess of war; Lilith, the mother of demons; the Black Madonna, the primal mother—all represent a radical shift in consciousness. They point us to a primal, less disinfected, more inclusive experience of life itself.

Bede Griffiths, the contemplative Benedictine monk (who settled in south India) spoke of an experience in the year 1990, towards the end of his life. It was a stroke in medical terms, but nothing short of a mystical event, in his experience. It was the experience of the Dark Goddess whom he referred to variously as Shakti, the Earth-Mother, the Black Madonna, 'the Void', 'the Dark Mother who is Love itself'.

'[She] symbolizes for me the Black Power in Nature and Life, the hidden power in the womb . . . I feel it was this Power which struck me. She is cruel and destructive, but also deeply loving and nourishing.' Later he wrote, 'I was overwhelmed and deluged with love. The feminine in me opened up and a whole new vision opened . . . It led me to the conviction that there is no absolute good or evil in this world.'

As long as we are seduced by polarities, existence is happy to oblige us with our own smorgasbord of horrors. This is the reminder that the Goddess' dark face represents. But implicit in those horrors is an invitation. An invitation to venture into those closets in our psyche, ruled by guilt and fear and ancestral conditioning, and allow the sunlight to enter. She summons us to the alchemical process that she is— capable of transforming matter into moksha through the sheer furnace of her gaze.

This is her ultimate promise.

And if she is sometimes breathtakingly casual in the way she treats her creations, it is because she has fashioned them from her own cauldron of wholeness. Time and space are ingredients she plays with in her cosmic kitchen—chopping, slicing and sautéeing—in a fever of creativity. She does not stand for some dismal creed of transience. She stands for the ecstasy of shape-shifting. Nothing is terminated in her fantastic workshop. It is merely transmuted.

Her repulsive face is the last myth of separateness. When that last terror falls away, we are hers once more—restored to her body as one of her many limbs, reinstated to her tree of life as one of its many singing branches.

It is also why the human imagination can never erase her, even if it sometimes forgets her. For wherever we end up, battered and shipwrecked, the Goddess' mudra of fearlessness assures us that there is no zip code that is ever outside the dark hospitality of her womb.

And her language is (and how could it be otherwise?) poetry.

# Devi Mahatmyam

## [Fourth to Sixth Century CE]

The *Devi Mahatmyam*—literally, the Greatness or Glory of the Goddess—is one of the earliest extant texts in the subcontinent that speaks of the worship of the sacred feminine. The female principle is venerated here both as a personified goddess (a creator with name and form) and as a transcendent truth.

While this verse eulogy emerged between the fourth and sixth centuries, there is no doubt that it was preceded by a centuries-old tradition of honouring the female principle. Comprising 700 verses and thirteen chapters, the work is part of the *Markandeya Purana* and is seen as one of the core devotional texts of the Goddess tradition of India.

The Goddess is described here as Tridevi, or the triple Goddess; she manifests as Mahakali, Mahalakshmi and Mahasaraswati, each symbolic of her destructive, sustaining and creative powers. She is also viewed as the unmanifest basis of creation, in an eternal state of latency. This same latency is viewed as the potential within every human being, waiting to be realized.

The work invokes a metaphoric battleground in which Devi manifests as the fearsome Durga to vanquish the trickster demon, Mahishasura. After delusion has been routed, the world is restored to peace and clarity. But only for a time. When two more antagonists, Shumbha and Nishumbha, begin to wreak havoc, the world is plunged into delusion again. Defeated and divested of power, the helpless male gods of the universe turn to Devi as their saviour once more. They bow down before her and begin their homage. The result is a poem that is still chanted in goddess temples across the country, venerating Devi as both supreme deity and inner reality, the sacred crucible in which all contradictions coexist.

~

## To That Goddess That Abides in All

Salutations to the Divine Mother who is ever auspicious.
Salutations to Her who is the primordial cause and the sustaining power
With deference, we make obeisance to Her.

Salutations to Her who is terrible, to Her who is eternal.
Salutation to Gauri, the supporter of the universe.
Salutation always to Her who is of the form of the moon,
    moonlight and happiness itself.

We bow to Her who is welfare
Salutations to Her who is prosperity and success.
Salutation to the consort of Shiva who is Herself the good fortune
As well as misfortune of kings.

Salutation always to Durga who takes one across in difficulties,
Who is essence, who is the author of everything;
Who is knowledge of discrimination;
And who is blue–black and also smoke-like in complexion.

We prostrate before Her Who is at once most gentle and most terrible;
Salutation to Her who is the supporter of the world.
Salutation to the Devi who is of the form of volition.

Salutation again and again to the Devi
Who abides in all beings and is called Vishnumaya.

Salutation again and again to the Devi
Who abides in all beings as awareness.

Salutation again and again to the Devi
Who abides in all beings in the form of intellect.

Salutation again and again to the Devi
Who abides in all beings in the form of sleep.

Salutation again and again to the Devi
Who abides in all beings in the form of hunger.

Salutation again and again to the Devi
Who abides in all beings in the form of shadow.

Salutation again and again to the Devi
Who abides in all beings in the form of vigour.

Salutation again and again to the Devi
Who abides in all beings in the form of craving.

Salutation again and again to the Devi
Who abides in all beings in the form of forbearance.

Salutation again and again to the Devi
Who abides in all beings in the form of class.

Salutation again and again to the Devi
Who abides in all beings in the form of shyness.

Salutation again and again to the Devi
Who abides in all beings in the form of peace.

Salutation again and again to the Devi
Who abides in all beings in the form of faith.

Salutation again and again to the Devi
Who abides in all beings in the form of brilliance.

Salutation again and again to the Devi
Who abides in all beings in the form of affluence.

Salutation again and again to the Devi
Who abides in all beings in the form of thought-movement.

Salutation again and again to the Devi
Who abides in all beings in the form of memory.

Salutation again and again to the Devi
Who abides in all beings in the form of compassion.

Salutation again and again to the Devi
Who abides in all beings in the form of contentment.

Salutation again and again to the Devi
Who abides in all beings in the form of mother.

Salutation again and again to the Devi
Who abides in all beings in the form of delusion.

Salutation again and again to the all-pervading Devi
Who constantly presides over the senses of all beings
    and governs all the elements.

Salutations again and again to Her
Who pervading the entire world abides in the form of
consciousness.

*[translated by the Arunachala Archive]*

# Saundarya Lahari: Wave of Beauty

## [Eighth Century CE]

Attributed to the mystic–philosopher Adi Shankara, this Sanskrit hymn is a work of adoration and auspiciousness. This wave of beauty (*saundarya* signifies beauty, and *lahari* wave) washes over the reader as a song of oceanic wonder. Dedicated to Shakti, the radiant feminine divine, the consort without whom Shiva is self-confessedly powerless, the text combines madness with method, panegyric with procedure, inspiration with instruction.

The Goddess here is not merely a deity (in this case, the beauteous Tripurasundari). She is existence itself, clad in verbal and visual attire. The praise is the outermost veil of the text. When readers commit to becoming seekers, they are invited to penetrate beyond the epidermis with an advanced adept as their guide. It is only then that they begin to unpack the delicately coded software of mantra and yantra, sacred sound and mystic diagram, that underpins the whole enterprise. This is poetry as an audacious power project. For, on this tantric level, Shakti is not an external icon who needs to be appeased. Instead, Shakti and Shiva are seen as the inseparable basis of every human being. When fully realized, every individual participates in the triadic reunion, the glorious family homecoming, the ultimate reintegration, by which the human becomes the embodied divine.

It is said that when Adi Shankara visited Mount Kailash, Lord Shiva entrusted him with a manuscript of 100 verses in praise of the Goddess. On his return, however, the precious manuscript was ripped apart by

Shiva's bull, Nandi, who took one half of it away with him. Shattered, Shankara raced back to Shiva to relate his miserable tale. The Lord consoled him and instructed him to write the rest of it himself. The first half of the *Saundarya Lahari* is, therefore, believed to have been written by Shiva, while the remaining verses are said to have been composed by Shankara.

Another legend says that the lovestruck Shiva was once waxing eloquent about the beauty of his consort. Inspired, he was writing in a frenzy on the walls of his abode. But when Adi Shankara visited him, he hastily erased these delirious verses, reluctant to share intimate details about his wife with an outsider. But it was too late. Adi Shankara had already seen some of it, and he was poet enough to be able to divine the rest!

~

Only when with her can he stir Śakti, she's Śiva's power
Even Śiva who's a god
only prevails
when paired with her

Then how can I
Mere I

Never did a good deed
Meritless I, how

dare I even
bow to you

even praise you
You whom even the gods Śiva Viṣṇu Brahmā

adore

*

Jingle girdle askew
Slim waist sashay

She stoops, for
bosom's heavy

like the swollen lobes of an elephant's forehead

Face like the radiant
autumn full moon

holding a bow, noose, goad and arrows in her hands

Oh the pride of
Śiva, crusher of cities

may she be
before us

                              *

I wonder if

after usurping the left half of Śiva's body

discontented

you took
the other half

It explains this look:

crimson glow all over stooping due to breasts

(and yet like Śiva)
three-eyed, crown awry moon crested in your hair

                              *

O Goddess,

the sun and moon your breasts

You are Śiva's body
I believe

your very self
is Śiva

of nine attributes flawless

As for who's primary
who secondary

your relationship stands
equal

by what you share:
transcendence, and bliss

                              *


You are mind

You are space

You are wind

You are fire whose
charioteer is wind

You are water

You are earth

There is nothing beyond
your full manifestation

You, yourself,

expression of
blissful consciousness

you assume the role
of Śiva's damsel

to become fully manifest
through the physical

universe

                              *


O daughter of
the king of mountains

Sages say the world ends
and begins

with the closing and opening
of your eyes

but I suspect

your eyes gave up
blinking

to save this whole world
from annihilation

this world that was created
by opening your eyes

*[translated by Mani Rao]*

# Chandamaharoshana Tantra:
# Goddess-speak

## [Tenth or Eleventh Century CE]

This Buddhist text in the Yoginitantra genre offers perhaps the most unique celebration of women in world sacred literature. Considered to be a 'revealed' teaching that emanated directly from the bliss body of the Buddha, it takes the form of a conversation between the deity Vajjrasattva and his consort Vajradhatvishvari. While the writer (or the channel, depending on one's perspective) remains anonymous, the text was probably authored in the Kathmandu Valley in Nepal.

Here, the goddess clearly instructs the deity on how women are to be exalted if one seeks to attain ultimate liberation through the conscious practice of sexual intercourse. We are told that it is only by experiencing, understanding and integrating the four types of bliss that arise from the sexual act that such freedom is possible.

Plucked out of its context, this can seem, like many tantric texts, disconcertingly unconventional. While it clearly belongs to another moment and a very particular worldview, the efficacy of tantra, it must also be remembered, is rooted precisely in the logic of inversion of the norm as a means to liberation: 'By passion, passion is killed,/ A conflagration is killed by fire./ One should destroy poison with poison,/ Applying the instructions,' as the text succinctly puts it. Moreover, this was clearly not a layperson's manual but an instructional text for initiates who had already mastered advanced meditative states. It was a 'secret teaching' imparted only if and when a master believed the moment was appropriate. It would also have been in a controlled atmosphere, with the precise use of mantras as well as prescribed rites and rituals.

What makes these extracts fascinating to a lay reader is their tribute to womanhood. The male god is an ardent devotee and student of this goddess. And this goddess does not merely insist that she be propitiated; she demands that such adoration be accorded to *every woman*. It is also interesting to hear the poetic voice of the goddess herself—powerful, ringing and authoritative. 'Women are the Buddha, women are the Sangha,' she says, and her consort, Vajrasattva, prostrates before her and acknowledges the truth of that utterance.

~

. . . Then the lord made full prostrations to the goddess
and said:
'How should a yogin
Perceive your form, dear?
And by what means should the goddess
Be honoured by the yogins?'

    The goddess then said:
'Whenever a female form is seen
In the world of the three abodes,
It should be regarded as my form,
Be it of low or respectable family . . .

'These and all other women
Possess my form.
They exist for the welfare of all beings,
Each identified by her own individual function . . .

'Women who are served will, for their part, instantly
grant
Accomplishment to all those seeking
To benefit living beings.
One should therefore serve women.

'Women are heaven, women are the Dharma,
And women are truly the supreme austerity.
Women are the Buddha, women are the Saṅgha,
Women are the Perfection of Wisdom . . .

'There is only one goddess, wisdom,
Abiding in five forms.
One should worship her with flowers, incense
and so forth,
Clothes, prose, poetry, body ornaments,

'Conversation, bowing,
Folding one's hands,
Beholding and touching her,
Thinking of her and talking to her,

'With kissing, embrace, and the like,
One should regularly worship Vajrayogini.
If one is able, one should honour her physically,
If not, one should do so verbally or mentally.

'Worshipped by him, pleased,
I shall grant complete attainment.
I am none other than the form
Found in every woman's body.

'Apart from worshipping women,
There can be no other worship of me.
By this propitiation, I will be satisfied
For the sake of the practitioner's accomplishment.

'Everywhere, always and invariably,
I will be within his sight.
One should make love to one's woman
Visualizing her in my complete form.

Then the goddess said, 'Is it possible, O lord, to attain
the level of Chandamaharoshana even without a
woman? Or is it not possible?'

The lord replied, 'It is not possible, O goddess.'
The goddess said, 'Is it impossible, O lord,
because bliss does not arise?'
The lord said:

'The highest awakening is not attained
Merely by the arising of bliss.
Only by the arising of a particular kind of bliss
Can it be reached, not otherwise.

'And this bliss is not felt without doing what needs
to be done—
It is produced only through the right cause.
And the cause is union with a woman;
There is no other cause, ever.

'Among all illusions,
Only the illusion of a woman is praised.
Whoever would transgress against her
Will not attain accomplishment.

'Therefore separation from women
Must never take place.
So if there should occur suffering,
Death, bondage, or fear—

'One should put up with all of this,
Rather than abandon a woman,
Since all women can cause one
To attain Buddhahood by means of the four joys . . .

'Therefore all women should be viewed
As goddesses on all occasions . . .

*[translated by the Dharmachakra Translation Committee]*

# Garba: The Womb of the Goddess

## [Pre-Fifteenth Century CE]

When one watches the star performers of Gujarati garba unleash their prowess during Navaratri in Mumbai or New York, transporting audiences to states of frenzied exultation, it is fascinating to think of how far a form can travel. And how much it can shape-shift. The ritual performance of garba has morphed into so many pan-Indian and globalized avatars—even uniting with the raas to produce that high-octane progeny, 'disco dandia'—that it is easy to forget its origins in goddess worship.

In the villages of Gujarat, the Goddess has been traditionally honoured with a unique circular dance performed by women, accompanied by song, around a perforated earthenware pot that contains a flickering lantern. The word 'garba' encompasses all three ingredients of ritual performance: the clay pot, the lyric poetry and the dance. It was performed to mark auspicious events, rites of passage and Navaratri, the nine-day festival of the goddess. While the dandia raas, with its use of sticks and rotating partners, is connected with the celebration of Krishna, the garba, with its rhythmic clapping and twirls, is associated with the Mother Goddess, although there are occasional overlaps between the two.

The very word 'garba' appears to derive from the Sanskrit *garbha*, or womb—a reminder of the form's connections with the mysteries of fertility and regeneration. The earthen pot with its lantern is representative of the womb that sustains the burning flame of life. The metaphoric association with the human body—the sacred vessel

that sustains and nurtures human aspiration and divine possibility—
is also significant.

Here, then, are village songs created mainly by women for
various goddesses. Their tone ranges from wonder and worshipful
supplication to banter and complaint. The goddess Amba is the awe-
inspiring source of creation, but she is also a mother and friend. If she
doesn't deliver on her promises, the devotee mischievously threatens
to abandon her for a rival goddess from another village. She manifests
as some of the iconic women of the great epics. But she also manifests
as the woman in every home. She is universal and local, divine and
domestic all at once. And she is indulgent with women who want to
confide, banter, let off steam about family politics.

She's been there. She knows.

~

Your energy is unknowable, Ambika!
    Your praise is sung in fourteen worlds!

You wear a new guise every moment
    leaving us all bewildered!

Each particle of the cosmos is your abode.
    Yet you reside deepest in our hearts, Ambika!

You are the mother of the whole world!
    Auspicious songs are sung for you, Ambika!

You are one, but you permeate all.
    Your radiance envelops us all, Ambika!

*

You are dark and auspicious, mother.
Wherever I turn I see you, Yogamaya!
Your glory is sung in every epoch, mother
Wherever I turn, I see you, Yogamaya!

You were known in the first epoch.
You were then the queen of Shiva!
And the destroyer of Bhasmasura, mother.
Wherever I turn, I see you, Yogamaya!

You were known in the second epoch.
You were then the queen of Harischandra.
You sold your life for truth, mother.
Wherever I turn, I see you, Yogamaya!

You were known in the third epoch.
You were then the queen of Ramachandra.
You were the one to trample Ravana, mother.
Wherever I turn, I see you, Yogamaya!

You were known in the fourth epoch.
You were then the queen of the Pandavas.
You were the destroyer of the Kaurava clan, mother.
Wherever I turn, I see you, Yogamaya!

You are known in the fifth epoch.
You are a woman in every home.
You are the light of humanity, mother.
Wherever I turn, I see you, Yogamaya!

*

With a quarter in my hand, I had gone to Pavagadh
        O goddess of Pavagadh, give me your darshan!
        Give me your darshan!
        Or give me my quarter back!

With a quarter in my hand, I had gone to Arasur!
        O goddess of Arasur, give me your darshan!
        Give me your darshan!
        Or give me my quarter back!

With a quarter in my hand, I had gone to Becharaji!
    O goddess of Becharaji, give me your darshan!
Give me your darshan!
Otherwise give me my quarter back!⁵

               *

My sickle weighs two and a quarter pounds;
    and was made by blacksmith Laliya.
But my beloved, I will go harvesting no more.

My husband earns just a quarter every day;
    and I, a full rupee and a half.
But my beloved, I will go harvesting no more.

My husband crops only five bunches;
    and I cut ten or twenty.
But my beloved, I will go harvesting no more.

My husband gets a cup of millet in wages;
    and I get a ton of wheat.
But my beloved, I will go harvesting no more.

*[translated by Neelima Shukla–Bhatt]*

---

⁵ [*The poem contains references to various goddess shrines in Gujarat, such as Pavagadh associated with Kali, Arasur associated with Ambika, Becharaji associated with Bahuchar.]

# Mei Hukum: Earth Mother

For the Khasis of the hills of the north-eastern Indian state of Meghalaya (literally, 'the abode of clouds'), it was customary to begin a story with the line, 'When man and beasts and stones and trees spoke as one . . .' This profound connection with the natural world suffuses the folklore of the community. A rich pantheon of deities, spirits and ancestors, including a fair share of goddesses, endures to this very day. While the written script of the tribe was born only with the advent of Thomas Jones, a Welsh missionary, in 1842, an oral tradition of fable, legend and verse goes back into Meghalaya's swirling white clouds of antiquity.

Poet–translator Kynpham Sing Nongkynrih writes: 'It is part of our pantheistic culture and our belief that man came to earth not to be the "crown of creation", but to be the caretaker of Mother Earth. He cannot take anything from the Earth without first asking divine permission since he owns nothing. When a woodcutter goes into the forest, for instance, he always has to pay his obeisance to God through the Mother of Divine Law . . . before he can touch a single tree.'

Perhaps it is not surprising that even the Khasi creation story speaks of human pain arising from the severance of a tree that connected earth and sky.

As for the Goddess, as the primal law of the natural world, she is, as this traditional Khasi prayer suggests, impossible to ignore. Invoking her, the woodcutter assures the tree that it will 'live again' as a part of his home, 'a part of my fields and gardens'. The Goddess, for her part, ensures that if a tree must be felled, it will be a mindful felling. Since the sacred groves of the Khasis have existed for over two thousand years, it is clear that this invocation has had a hoary history, even as it speaks to an environmentally ravaged planet today with a searing urgency.

~

## On Tree Felling

Oh, Mei Hukum, Mother of Divine Law!
You, the power of God!
You, his manifest presence on earth!
You, who reveal yourself
most closely through Mother Earth!
Look you, I am going to the forest;
look you, I have need of trees for the hearth,
for the fence, for the hut.
Accept my prayers,
*ka nguh ka dem*, 'the bow the homage,'
I'm going to the forest,
since everything must carry your sanction,
bless me, forgive me.
I will speak to my brothers, the trees,
bless me, so they listen to me,
so they cooperate,
so they don't curse me
when I take them down with an axe
or a machete.
I have need of them,
let them live through what I am doing.
Bless me, forgive me, I have spoken.
Oh, brothers! Look here,
that I have come to cut you down
is not because I detest you
or want to destroy you without cause.
I have a great need for you.
Ka Mei Hukum has given me her consent
that I may cause your fall,

so you too may have a role in my undertakings,
so you may live again,
becoming a part of my home,
a part of my fields and gardens.
Allow me, my brothers, obey me,
bend to my will,
so I may fell you with an axe
or a machete,
for even though you may fall now,
yet your fame shall rise and grow before God.
Before the spirits, it shall rise,
before kings and nobles,
before priests and elders,
before all the people from generation to generation.
So that your seeds, your branches, your trunk
may proliferate, may spread, may rise, may grow,
hey ho, I have given you my blessing,
hey ho, Ka Mei Hukum has given you her blessing,
and you too, forgive me. I have spoken.
Oh, Mei Hukum! Bless me, forgive me!

*[translated by Kynpham Sing Nongkynrih]*

# Annamacharya

## [Fifteenth Century CE]

The author of thousands of compositions (of which around 13,000 appear to have survived), Annamacharya was a celebrated Telugu poet whose work was engraved on copper plates and stored in the vault of the temple of Tirupati—an indication of how much it was prized in his own lifetime. Initiated into the Vaishnava tradition and god-intoxicated at an early age, he was honoured as a saint and devotee of Lord Venkateswara, whom he refers to in his poetry as 'the god on the hill'. Although his work was forgotten for three intervening centuries, it was revived in the nineteenth century and grew rapidly in popularity. His direct poetic address to his god is intimate, familiar and free, suggesting a relationship that was unusual even among temple poets. These musical poems are still a significant part of the classical music repertoire of south India.

Annamacharya's legacy comprises work in the spiritual (*adhyatma*) and romantic (*shringara*) mode. The former poems feature a male devotee as the speaker (one who expresses his doubts, fears and misgivings), while the latter feature a very singular female speaker: Goddess Alamelumanga, the consort of Lord Venkateswara. When goddesses become consorts, they often seem to turn into docile and decorative junior partners. This is emphatically not the case, however, with Alamelumanga. She has her own independent temple at the foot of the hill, and according to sacred lore, the god, Venkateshwara, makes a nocturnal journey of fourteen kilometres each night to visit this proud goddess in her abode.

Alamelumanga is a goddess with a high opinion of herself. As the poems indicate, she is sensual, feisty and flirtatious, capable of sparring with her lover, confident that her love is fully reciprocated. She bemoans his lack of subtlety and teases him when he is diffident or when his ardour runs high. Irony is a verbal resource that she uses masterfully: she says one thing, but almost always means something else. 'He's the master,' she declares time and again in one poem, leaving the listener in no doubt of what she *really* means.

~

When I'm done being angry,
*then* I'll make love.
Right now, you should be glad
I'm listening.

When you flash that big smile,
I smile back. It doesn't mean I'm not angry.
You keep looking at me,
so I look too. It isn't right
to ignore the boss.

*Right now you should be glad.*

You say something, and I answer.
That doesn't make it a conversation.
You call me to bed; I don't make a fuss.
But unless I want it myself,
it doesn't count as love.

*Right now you should be glad.*

You hug me, I hug you back.
You can see I'm still burning.

I can't help it, god on the hill,
if I'm engulfed in your passion.

*Right now you should be glad.*

\*

He's the master. What can I say
when he says I'm better than the others?

I don't even have to ask.
He takes whatever I say as a command.
Why should I brag?
My husband is under my thumb.

*He's the master.*

Who am I to serve him, when *he*
takes joy in serving me?
How can I tell you the thousand ways
he's with me?
He knows everything, just like god,
and *he* praises me.

*He's the master.*

I'm always in his arms.
He's always laughing with me.
He's the god on the hill
and I'm Alamelumanga.
Do I have to make a statement?
He's my slave.

*He's the master.*

\*

Why cross the boundary
when there is no village?
It's like living without a name,
like words without love.

What use is ecstasy
without the agony of separation?
Shade is nothing without the burning sun.
What is patience without fury of passion?
Why make anything—love or poetry—if two
can't be one?

*Why cross the boundary?*

What good is profit without praise?
Why speak tender words when there is no closeness?
What use is love if you can't let go?
Beauty is empty without desire.

*Why cross the boundary?*

Why have a lover you don't need to hide?
Intimacy is dull without doubt.
What fun is there in just making love,
no extras, no questions?
Bring in our god on the hill.

*Why cross the boundary?*

*

You tell him about subtlety.
If I insist, they'll say I'm too demanding.

Instead of talking back to me,
he would do better to send a messenger.

Why stare at me over and over?
He might bend his head, a little shy.

*Tell him about subtlety.*

Better than laughing so loudly,
he could be a little quiet.
Instead of pestering me to play,
let him simmer with some affection.

*Tell him about subtlety.*

Rather than tiring me by making love,
let him live quietly by my side.
I'm Alamelumanga. He's the god on the hill.
A loving touch would make all the difference.

*Tell him about subtlety.*

                        *

I'll serve you as best I can
but some things I just can't do

I can melt your heart just like that,
but I can't stop you breaking out in sweat.
I can sink my teeth deep into your lips,
but I can't help it if they leave marks.

*Some things I just can't do*

I can touch you where you are shy,
but can I stop you from feeling the thrill?
I can look you straight in the eyes,
but hey, can I keep you
from smiling?

*Some things I just can't do*

I can wear you out with hugs and kisses,
but I can't stop your sigh.
Now that you've made love to me,
god on the hill,
can I keep you from wanting more?

*Some things I just can't do*

**[translated by V. Narayana Rao and David Shulman]**

# Yellamma: 'It is You they Come to Serve'

When faithful hordes surge towards Saundatti (in Belgaum district of Karnataka in south India) in November and December, they are heading to celebrate a goddess named Renuka Yellamma. Her idol is carried out in procession at this time, and multitudes congregate at this ancient hilltop shrine by the Malaprabha River to witness this sight.

The goddess' antecedents are fascinating. Married to an irascible sage named Jamadagni, the faithful Renuka failed to come home one day after setting out to fetch water. The reason? She was briefly distracted by the sight of young male beauty. Her roving eye, or perhaps the rising temperature of her passion, melted her unbaked pot. Something shifted irrevocably within her that day. An inner awakening was underway. In terms of external circumstance, however, she was doomed: she had failed the chastity test. Her enraged husband commanded her sons to chop off her head. The only son who complied was Parashurama. (He also later revived her, but mistakenly fixed her head to the body of a non-brahmin woman.) The other two sons, who recoiled from his command, were 'cursed' to lose their masculinity and became *jogappas*.

And what of Renuka? In the fiery smithy of suffering, in the powerful alchemy of pain, yet another human turned divine. She became the Goddess Yellamma, a composite entity capable of embracing every polarity—the ascetic and the erotic, the high and the low, brahmin and non-brahmin, man and woman—and every shade in between. In short, she became a true Jagadamba, Mother of the Universe. And so, following an ancient poetic logic, a curse became a blessing for those who had the eyes to see.

In time, this strange and compelling story was to engender a unique gender-fluid subaltern community. Today's jogappas are those who say they have been possessed by Yellamma (and often plagued by incurable physical diseases until they succumb to her call). Once they surrender, however, they believe she has singled them out for membership in a special transgender community, viewed with habitual mistrust by many in the mainstream but revered by devout insiders as a direct link between the human and the divine.

The legend of Yellamma probably predates the tenth century, and the poem remains a shape-shifting legacy of the oral tradition. This song (with its own singular variations on the main story—typical of the vibrant and protean nature of folk literature), translated from Kannada, celebrates a powerful and mysterious goddess.

~

*You who were born*
*to be a goddess,*
                    *Yellamma,*
*You who were married off to Jamadagni*

*That monarch, Renuka, was your father,*
*Bhogavati your mother.*
*You were born into their womb,*
*rocked in the cradle of their love*

On her head was a serpent wreath,
a pot of sand balanced above it
She dutifully served her husband,
fetched him water from the river.

One day by the riverside
she caught sight of two fish.
As her gaze fell upon them
her pot
        fell, smashed
                to the ground

*The saint–man who sat meditating*
*grew enraged, Yellamma*
*Your husband cursed you*
*Your body was struck with disease*

Her body ravaged by leprosy
Yellamma roamed the wild forests
but when she went to the saints Yakkai and Jogya,
her life was transformed

*The grace of Shiva was upon you, Yellamma,*
*Your devotion bore you a son*
*and with the birth of Parashurama*
*you became at last a mother*

But then a wrathful Jamadagni
summoned Parashurama
'Behead that mother of yours!' he cried
and that Parashurama,
　　　her son,
　　　　　　he dutifully obeyed

*And yet, in the district of Belgaum*
*in the collectorate of Athani,*
*it is you they come to serve,*
*the people of the higher and lower towns,*
　　　*Yellamma--*

*it is you,*
*it is you*

*it is you they come to serve.*

**[translated by Shilpa Mudbi]**

# Gondhal: 'My Life's Anklet has found its Rhythm'

The Marathi word gondhal literally means 'chaos', a fascinating word to describe the realm of the Mother Goddess. Hers is a seeming arrhythmia. She catapults one from a manicured social world to a lawless playground infused by her mysterious energy. In her domain, worshipper and worshipped meet in play. When you cannot fathom her, you simply turn participant and conduit, whirling to her crazy tune, dissolving in her sacred illogic.

The Gondhal is a traditional performance art of the state of Maharashtra. It involves the dramatic narration of mythic stories as part of a ritual dance and music performance dedicated to deities like Bhavani, Amba or Yellamma. Traditionally practised by members of a community called the Gondhalis, the form was performed on auspicious occasions, such as marriages and religious festivals. A blaze of energetic movement, vibrant colour, flaming torches, narration, music and percussion, the typical Gondhal had a lead singer–narrator, the Naik, who called on the Goddess to awaken the warrior within her, descend and dispel darkness, and protect the world.

The form traces its origins to a fascinating tale around the martial sage, Parashurama. When he slaughtered the demon Betasur, the sage decided to put the carnage to creative use. He fashioned a musical instrument out of the demon's severed head and began to play upon it. He then exploded into a thunderous dance in praise of his mother, Renuka Yellamma. This primal and ecstatic performance was called the gondhal. It was later to unfold into the ritual performance that sought to

channel the divine in order to cleanse the human spirit of all corruption
and ignorance.

The following is a free translation of a folksong in the Gondhal
tradition from a Marathi film, *Jogwa* (2009), directed by Rajiv Patil
(in which the lyrics were authored by Sanjay Krushnaji Patil, music
composed by Ajay–Atul and sung by Ajay Gogavale).

~

Beyond the river lies the mountain
where our mother lives,
and atop the summit
is her sacred shrine.
Here on this summit we will keep vigil all night.

Smear my forehead with sacred turmeric
and dispel the darkness.
I have come from afar
crawling my way up the mountain.
Goddess, open the doors of your abode!

The mountain gleams in the river waters.
My heart dances to the pulse of her gaze.
My life's anklet has found its rhythm.

Smear my forehead with sacred turmeric
and dispel the darkness!
I have come from afar
crawling my way up the mountain
Goddess, open the doors of your abode!

Answer my prayer, heed my call
Heed my call, settle down in my heart,
settle down in my heart, destroy all delusion,
destroy all delusion, ferry me across.

I will make you an offering,
serve you, worship you,
make your temple my home,
and fulfill my desires.
Protect me, mother, make me your own!

This is the vigil of Yellamma Devi, this sea of devotion.
Your devotees gather to eat your tender bread
as the full moon overflows with your maternal love.
Awaken, mother, awaken this sea of devotion.

Smear my forehead with sacred turmeric
and dispel the darkness!
I have come from afar
crawling my way up the mountain
Goddess, open the doors of your abode!

~

*[translated by Lokendra Balwe]*

# Abhirami: 'Who Needs to Go Meditate?'

## Abhirami Bhattar

## [Eighteenth to Nineteenth Century CE]

Abhirami Bhattar was an ardent devotee of the Thirukadaiyur temple, on the east coast of Tamil Nadu, and the pre-eminent Tamil poet of the goddess Abhirami.

Subramania (as he was named) nursed from his childhood a deep connection with the local temple where Shiva was termed Amritaghateswar and his Goddess Consort Abhirami, or She Who is Forever Beauteous. Legend has it that the temple was the site of the ancient pot of nectar (that emerged in the primordial churning of the ocean of milk by the gods and anti-gods). It is also regarded as the site where the sage Markandeya was blessed with immortality—a boon that prevented all death on the planet for a time. It explains why the shrine is still worshipped by those seeking the blessing of longevity.

Subramania grew in devotion, and his ferocious bhakti led many to consider him mad. The story goes that he provoked the visiting King Serfoji I with his goddess-intoxicated proclamation that it was a full moon day when it was actually a new moon. The king ordered that he be beheaded if the moon did not rise that night. Abhirami Bhattar lit a large fire and erected a platform over it, tied with ropes. He sat on the platform, spontaneously singing verses in praise of Goddess Abhirami. With each verse, he cut off one rope. On completing the seventy-ninth hymn, the goddess Abhirami appeared and threw her diamond earring skyward so that it shone like the moon. Ecstatic and overwhelmed,

Subramania composed twenty-one more verses in her praise. This was the legendary genesis of the *Abhirami Antadi*, an inspired collection of 100 hymns. Each of these verses is believed to be consecrated, capable of blessing those who chant them. The chastened king bestowed the title of Abhirami Bhattar (Priest of the Goddess Abhirami) on the poet.

The poems in this selection speak of the glory of the Abhirami, the power of her breasts to scar the battle-hardened chest of Shiva; her capacity to be formless and embodied; her ability to be one, many and none at all. For her devotees, however, her form is intoxicating enough to keep them drunk for a lifetime. In a subtle jibe directed at less emotionally exuberant, more contemplative spiritual practitioners, the poet remarks scornfully, 'It's enough/ to sit alone/ and gaze at you,/ three-eyed Goddess./ Who needs to go meditate?'

~

Your waist slender,
swathed in soft vermilion silk
your breasts heavy
with streaming garlands of pearl
your dark tresses woven
with fragrant jasmine, pursued
by clouds
    of maddened bees.

It's enough
    to sit alone
    and gaze at you
three-eyed Goddess.

Who needs to go meditate?

\*

Isn't it funny
That though she's Mother of the Universe,

we warble
about her lotus bud breasts
and her eyes more limpid than a doe's?

And though she has no beginning or end
we hail her as the little girl born
to the Monarch of the Great Mountain?

Hilarious really
all the hype

when she's beyond it all—
description, explanation,

perception.

\*

And then you drenched me
with your grace,
colonized me,

Is it fair now to deny the fact?

Even if I plunge headlong
into the ocean now,
it's your call—

fish me out
or leave me to drown.

You that are One
You that are Many
You that are beyond
Form.

Your call, my Uma.

\*

Their eyes deluged
in ecstasy,

their bodies stippled
with goose flesh.

their intellects stunned
into imbecility,

like drunken bees,
incoherent, words vaporizing

on their tongues—
their madness testimony

to your worship, Great Mother,
unrivalled by any other.

                    *

Origin of rapture
        Wellspring
        of wisdom
Ambrosial, abundant
        Rim
of the rimless horizon
        Terminus
of the four Vedas—

    your feet,
Mother Abhirami

that crown the head
    of the Lord
    who whirls

through swirling forests
   of white ash.

   Your feet.

*

He used the golden bow
of Mount Meru
   to decimate
   three great cities

and he slayed the elephant
   dispatched to annihilate the world,

   then donned its hide
as his mantle.

But you
   you scarred
this warrior's body
with your breasts,

great Goddess,
   you whose golden hands
wielding a bow of sugarcane
and flower-tipped arrows

   are lodged
   forever
   in my heart.

*[translated by Arundhathi Subramaniam]*

# Kali: 'I'll Rub Kali All Over his Face!'

## Ramprasad Sen

## [Eighteenth Century CE]

She isn't the gentle benefactor of material abundance, or of that subtler acquisition—knowledge. And yet, she is regarded as a great goddess. She is naked for a reason. She is the end of veils. The end of acquisition. The end of life, as we know it. She refuses to conceal. She comes clad with no seductive status-quoist promises, no gossamer veils of just-a-little-moreness. She is emptiness. The goddess of dead ends, of darkness, of a universe bleached of all meaning. She is severe, exacting, final. She strips until one can be stripped no more.

And yet, while she is dissolution, she is also liberation. She turns dead ends into doorways. She turns chaos into consciousness, death into possibility and the relative into the absolute. For those who learn to see change as a friend rather than an adversary, she is the ideal guide. For those willing to look her fearsome visage in the eye and meet the end of all their make-believe worlds, she is the end of fear. And for those willing to fall back into the bosom of the absolute, she is nothing less than the ultimate mother.

A tribal goddess of immeasurable antiquity, she enters the Sanskrit tradition when mentioned in Vedic literature and the Mahabharata, but erupts into an electrifying presence in the *Devi Mahatmyam*. Here is Kali the way we know her: black, red-eyed with bloodlust, roaring, naked, lolling tongue, multiple arms, a girdle of human arms, a garland of skulls, a decapitated head in one hand, sometimes dancing on the corpse of her husband, Shiva. There are iconographic variations (four-armed or ten-armed, right foot forward or left foot forward, standing on Shiva or without) and multiple forms and appellations (Mahakali, Dakshinakali, Samhara Kali, Raksha Kali, Bhadra Kali and Guhya Kali, among others).

While her worship as divine mother is prominent in Bengal, Kerala and Kashmir, she is pervasive all over India and is now a symbol of growing power for feminist and New Age movements in the West. In many texts, such as the *Mahanirvana Tantra, Yogini Tantra* and *Niruttara Tantra*, among others, she is seen as the origin of existence, the source of all creation—the Ultimate.

Her stories of origin are many. She is born of the fury of Goddess Durga, springing to life to slay a demon, Raktabija. She is one of the sloughed-off skins of Parvati, a process by which the ancient goddess steps into the daytime world as Gauri, the fair consort of Shiva. But the truth is obvious: Kali precedes mythic time. She is the archetype you turn to when you're ready to be undone, made over. You don't fiddle with the instructions on the knob of this particular technology; once you step in, you're hers. She is the ultimate spin cycle that leads you out of cycles of time and space. The supreme deliverer.

The poems of Ramprasad Sen, which brought tears to the eyes of the saint Ramakrishna Paramahansa, continue to be sung in Bengal today. Indeed, he founded an entire genre of Bhakti music, the 'Ramprasadi', which integrated Baul flavours and other diverse folk elements with classical melody and intense devotional fervour. The legacy was to have an enduring impact on the Bengali Shakta literary canon and practice. And yet, for all his ecstatic devotion, Ramprasad Sen was no conventional bhakta. Not much is known of his life, although legends abound. What seems clear is that he evinced a talent for poetry and music at an early age. Initiated early into the tantric path, he seems to have developed into a committed practitioner of the esoteric path of kundalini yoga. The intensity of his spiritual journey is evident in the fascinating, if apocryphal, story of his furiously scribbling goddess poems in the margins of his ledger when he worked as an accountant in Kolkata. His employer eventually told him to follow his calling and even paid him a generous stipend to do so. In short, he was lucky enough to get fired with a golden handshake!

Ramprasad's poetry is a mix of intimacy and arcana. He is capable of scolding his goddess as well as plunging into an esoteric description of the chakras and inner yogic states. What makes the intimacy so interesting is the fact that it includes a remarkable tonal palette: rebuke, complaint, flippancy, criticism, doubt, ecstasy. When Kali becomes a mother and sometimes a little girl, a host of poetic tenors is possible. It is legitimate now to whine, throw a tantrum or two, chide her for her dangerous, whimsical ways and rebuke her for never listening to mortal needs. Wit, affection and exasperation, pun and wordplay become ways to converse with her. For she embodies ultimate love, even when her ways remain inscrutable. This is a fluid, dynamic devotion, not a passively worshipful one. Ramprasad was undeniably an original, a poet who radically extended the scope and width of the Shakta and Bhakti poetry of his time.

~

All right Kali,
Now I'm going to eat you up
(Deen Doyamoyi, going to eat you up!)
I was born at a maleficent moment
So you can blame it all on the stars!
It's the astral connection that turned me
Into a cannibal mother-eating son!
Will I eat you? Or you eat me?
Today is the day of reckoning!

I'm going to make a stir-fry
With Dakini–Jogini in it
(Witch and Worshipper both)
I'm going to snatch away
Your garland of skulls
And use it temper the broth.

I'll rub Kali on my face
I'll rub Kali on my hands
I'll rub Kali all over my body

And when Death comes
To tie me down tight
I'll rub Kali all over his face!

I keep saying
'I'll eat you up, Ma, my dear'
But not to fill my belly!
Just to sit you down in my heart
And pray to you with all my mind.

If you say eating Kali
Will make Time stretch out his hand
To get me—
Let him—that doesn't scare me!
I'll tell him who I am—Kali's son no less!
I'll thumb my nose at him
And let him know what's what
The body's fall or the prayer-call
What's meant to be will be—
It's I who will make it happen!

                    *


Death, be off, what can you do,
I've made Ma Shyama my prisoner
I've put mind-chains around her feet
And locked her inside my heart!

The heart-conceived-as-a-lotus
Is what I've made to bloom
The brain-shaped-like-a-lotus
Is my mental prayer room

I've surrendered my soul to her Shakti
Her mighty pedigree.
I've set it all up so cunningly
There's no point in breaking free.

On guard my liveried footman—
Devotion—now and evermore
While my two eyes are the watchmen
I've put on duty at the door.

I've known a mighty fever's coming—
Shiva's iron tonic is the cure,
Having drunk the essence of Guru's teaching
There's no fever I can't endure.

Says Sri Ramprasad (that's me)—
I've broken your establishment, Death!
My journey's done and now I'm resting,
Saying Kali Kali with every breath.

\*

Mind you don't know how to farm
The fallow fields of all mankind
If sown they'd have yielded gold
Mind you don't know how to farm

Put up a fence in Kali's name
No crops shall come to harm
The sturdy fence of the wild-haired one
Even Yama won't dare approach it
When the end of all words is nigh
All gains embezzled, encroach it

This time of day when my one-track mind's
On a single string—why not go all out
And bring the entire harvest in?
Mind, you don't know how to farm!

The Guru's word has sown the seed
Go water it with your bhakti

And mind, if you can't do it alone,
Take Ramprasad along for shakti

*

Mind my dear, I fall at your feet
Call Kali by her name—
She's the boat to the other shore.

The taste of honey on my tongue
Is Kali's name—
The best fruit comes from uttering it.

Mind my dear, if Kali shows her mercy
How can I fear Death?
Twice-born Ramprasad, he says,

'Say Kali, I'd like to ride your boat'
She'll take pity, that daughter—
And ferry you across this earthly water.

*

I get a kick out of you Ma
Though you're a pitiless one
You landed a kick
On your husband's chest
Oh you're a pitiless one!

You're the daughter of stone
So how can pity ever live
In your heart!
They call you Deen Doyamoyi
Oh give me a break—
To me, you're the pitiless one!

I don't see a speck of pity in you
When I see the skull-garland
Around your neck—
You wove it from the chopped-off heads
Of other mothers' sons—
To them, you're the pitiless one!

And yet I, Prasad, persist
In calling you Durga
Without giving a toss
That the more I call you Ma
The less you seem to heed me
The only prasad I eat
Oh pitiless one
Are your holy kicks—
They feed me!

*[translated by Sampurna Chattarji]*

# Kali: 'Crazy Woman, Robed With Sky'

## Kamalakanta Bhattacharya

## [Eighteenth to Nineteenth Century CE]

In that remarkable document about life around an enlightened master, *The Gospel of Sri Ramakrishna*, the poetry of Kamalakanta Bhattacharya is frequently mentioned. As these poems were sung, Sri Ramakrishna, we are told, often went into samadhi states. Who was this poet capable of transporting this mystic into such ecstasy?

Kamalakanta was born into straitened family circumstances in Bardhaman in the Bengal Presidency. Early in life, his priest father passed away, and he was raised by his mother. A bright student, he studied Sanskrit and evinced an early inclination for poetry and music. His thread ceremony marked his first spiritual initiation, and an encounter with a tantric yogi, Kenaram Bhattacharya, marked his second. He started a small school to earn his livelihood, but was soon recognized by the maharaja of Badhaman as a poet and singer of considerable talent and was appointed court adviser and the maharaja's spiritual adviser.

Inspired by the example of Ramprasad Sen, the trailblazing poet of the earlier generation, Kamalakanta was the author of several poems that address the goddess Kali, that terrifying icon of annihilation, as mother. His work explores a gamut of tones, from affection and exasperation to wry humour and profound surrender. The irreverence is particularly striking in the selected poems. 'Mother/ I beg you with folded hands:/ don't dance on top of Siva', the poet implores in one poem and in another, he glances at her naked form and enquires incredulously, 'Mother,/are you going to rescue Kamalakanta/in *this* outfit?'

The goddess was such a living presence for Kamalakanta that it is said that when he once pricked the feet of his beloved idol (to prove the point to his benefactor, the maharaja), it actually bled. The legend could be interpreted, among other things, as a tribute to the alchemy of poetry and its capacity to transform vision into visceral experience, word into flesh.

Who is this
dressed like a crazy woman,
robed with the sky?
Whom does She belong to?
She has let down Her hair,
thrown off Her clothes,
strung human hands around Her waist,
and taken a sword in Her hand.
Her face sparkles
from the reflection of Her teeth,
and Her tongue lolls out.
The smile on that moon-face drips
heaps and heaps of nectar.

Mother,
are you going to rescue Kamalakanta
In *this* outfit?

                              *


Kali
is everything You do misleading?

Look, Your beloved has thrown Himself
under Your feet! Mother
I beg you with folded hands:
don't dance on top of Siva!

I know how Tripura's enemy feels.
Beautiful Tripura, Kind Woman,
just this once, stop.
You're the murderer of Your own husband:
You're killing Your lord!
The King of Living Beings
is almost dead!

Once
hearing people criticize Siva
You got angry
and left Your body
for love.

Mother! The man You're standing on
is the same Three-Eyed One!
Calm down
Look at Him;
It's the Naked Lord!

This is what Kamalakanta wants to understand:
You know everything,
so why all these deceptions?
This time, I think,
You've gone too far.
You Whose Seat is a Corpse.

*

I know, I know, Mother:
You're a woman of stone.
You dwell inside me,
yet you hide from me.

Displaying your illusory power,
You create many bodies,

with Your three qualities
limiting the limitless.

Kind to some,
harmful to others,
You cover Your own fault
by shifting the blame to others.

Mother, I don't hope for enlightenment,
nor do I wish to live in heaven.
I just want to visualize Your feet
standing in my heart.

Oh Goddess filled with Brahman,
This is Kamalakanta's humble appeal:
why do You harass him unnecessarily?
What is Your intention?

*

How will You rescue me, Tara?
There's only one of You,
but there are so many plaintiffs
I can't even count them!
You thought that because of my devotion
You could save me
          by hook or by crook,
But the devotion of a non-devotee
is like a conch-shell marriage bracelet
on the arm of a slut. It's true
          there is nothing more important
          than the name of Brahman
but even that is a great burden for me.
My mind and my tongue think alike
only at mealtimes.

Kamalakanta's Kali!
I'll tell You how to save me:
          sit in my heart.
The only worthwhile solution
is for You to keep watch.


                    *


So, forgetful Mahadeva,
You have fallen in love!

You got Her footprints
and now there's no separating You;
staring, staring,
You worship Her.
Her heavy locks of hair,
darker than a mass of clouds,
fall disheveled over Her body.
                    Incomparably glamorous!
Who knows the greatness of either of You—
          You sky-clad sixteen-year-old,
                    And You, naked Tripurari!

There is no end
to the bliss of Madana's Bewitcher.
Lying lazily under the woman's hold,
He thirsts for the taste of love play.
Saying endearing things
He makes love to the beautiful one
          in the lotus heart of Kamalakanta

*[translated by Rachel Fell McDermott]*

# Kali, Saraswati, Devi, Ardhanarisvara: 'Breathe On'

## Sri Narayana Guru

## [Nineteenth to Twentieth Century CE]

A mystic and a voice of the marginalized, Sri Narayana Guru, played a revolutionary role in shaping the spiritual and cultural ethos of modern Kerala. Born to a family of Ayurvedic healers in the erstwhile state of Travancore, he travelled extensively through south India, during which time he met various spiritual teachers and later immersed himself in meditative practices for several years. In 1888, in the village of Aruvippuram, when he consecrated a piece of rock and proclaimed it an idol of Shiva, he scandalized the brahmin orthodoxy. What gave this common, unentitled man the right to perform consecration, they asked? His famous reply was that this was not a brahmin Shiva but an *ezhava* Shiva, or a casteless divine.

Narayana Guru proceeded to live out a life of spiritual inspiration and social reform, consecrating forty-five temples across southern India, opening shrines and schools for the underprivileged of all castes and authoring literary works in Malayalam, Tamil and Sanskrit. His genius lay in his versatile and seamless blend of contemplation and commitment to social justice, jnana and karma yoga, as it were. It was his own awareness of the non-dual inner state that seemed to inspire this vision of social equality, famously distilled in his credo: '*Oru Jaathi, Oru Matham, Oru Daivam, Manushyanu*' (One Caste, One Religion, One God for All).

In his lifetime, the Guru consecrated temples dedicated to various goddesses and often wrote poems to mark these occasions. The selections here are excerpts from poems to Kali, the auspicious dark goddess; Sharada or Saraswati, the goddess of knowledge; Devi, the Eternal Feminine; and that composite figure of perfect unity, Ardhanarisvara.

The last is a tribute to the inseparability of male and female (Shiva fused with his consort, Parvati), in which the Guru implores 'the half-woman God' to awaken a world that has turned into a nightmarish wasteland. What makes this poem striking is the fact that the panegyric mode gives way to a tone of reproach and despair. (According to translator Vinaya Chaitanya, this work was written in 1894, when a prolonged drought had assailed Aruvippuram, where the Guru had lived for many years.)

In these mystical odes, the Guru sees the Goddess as nothing less than the Absolute.

### The Black Goddess
[*Kali Natakam*]
. . . Look at you, traipsing through Mount Kailasa
triumphant, proud, resplendent in yourself, rejoicing
in the music from the veena, as your anklets
set off enchanting beats . . .
Your stride stunning, how you walk with your friends,
confident in your power, as the world surrenders at your feet.
How your exuberant grace and beauty sweeps
over everyone and everything!
How you choose to finally look at those who
wait in faith for you, and all so casually!
You know so well, sweet one, that all but those

caught in desire and earthly misery find solace
in your compassion, in your infinite love;
how they suffer, deprived of that glance of yours.
My divine one, I salute you!

*[translated by Anupama Raju]*

*

## Nine-Gemmed Bouquet for the Mother
[*Janani Nava Ratna Manjari*]

5

Veiled by the root-mind on high,
Mother, Your gently flowing dance—
water, air, fire, this loud medley of the world,
is mere sound alone. A thin, beautiful veil,
woven of the soft thread of time and such, hides
Your form,
so no one knows the real,
O One who remains beyond the scriptures!

9

No basis have they, the earth and other elements;
they are distortions mere;
created by You alone
do these elaborations of awareness here in the
world abide.
Beyond the objects of the tongue and so on,
shines Your abode of pure space;
who is there to know its glory,
O Mother, it is impossible
even to praise you!

*

## Hymn to the Goddess
[*Devistavam*]

1

O mother, Your sacred limbs precede the earth,
so say the silent sages. They are unable to say
anything else, and Your word now comes to me
as this silent state, and reverberates here.

6

This ear, this eye—all the senses— which,
turning upside down, away from You,
finally attain their peak and merge in You.
Breathe again and bless so I, rowing here
just to stay afloat, rise up to reach and rest in You.

9

In the turbulent inner ocean
waves heave and foam seethes.
Why do you fight like a mare?
Give birth to the steady, harmonic state.
Crumble all this to play in the water.
You know the waveless water
is a bower of refuge.
Breathe on.

\*

## Hymn Praising the Half-Woman God, Siva
[*Ardhanarisvara Stavam*]

4

Poverty is dire, grass and trees are all burned,
without water, sorrow has filled; don't you have a care?

We stay thinking, who is there but You to shower
ambrosial kindness, and You set this cruel fire on us;
Is it right, say, You half-woman God?

5

The three worlds all come to destruction, see;
wearing the famous waters in Your crown,
You sit still, meditating on the supreme Self, how come?
Who now will rule this earth? To whom shall these
folk complain?
Other than the shade of your sacred feet, what help
do we have,
O half-woman God?

*[translated by Vinaya Chaitanya]*

Let's be girls, Ma
and play with dolls;
          Come into my playroom.
I will take the Mother's role, so I can
teach You how.

If you make one dull or wretched,
hold him to Your bosom;
who else will ease his pain?
One who gets no jewels and gems, Ma,
at least should get his mother.

Some will be quite naughty,
others lie about inside their homes,
but all play games of hide-and-seek
          (our world here has no death, Ma),
crying as they leave at night, returning with the morning.

This little boy
    You made him cry
          You made him fear.
          Now love away his fear,
    cease to make him cry—

or casting You aside
he'll run away.

When this play is finished
lull him into sleep;
          hold him in your arms.

*[translated by Rachel Fell McDermott]*

# Kali to Hecate—and Beyond:
## 'Have You Seen My Daughter?'

## [Twentieth to Twenty-First Century]

In 1975, a popular Hindi film, *Jai Santoshi Maa*, catapulted a virtually non-existent deity into instant stardom. For her devotees, however, she is as old as time.

She is not alone. Indeed, goddesses—inherited and improvised—seem more alive than ever before. Forgotten and remembered, submerged and excavated, dreamed and invented, a torrent of goddesses seems to be re-emerging into the world.

The book closes with five vignettes—a small mosaic of recent poems by women that celebrate the Goddess' refusal to separate past from present, east from west, the secular from the sacred.

Anglophone poet Rukmini Bhaya Nair dreams her way into the loneliness of Kali—'mistress of the temporal worlds' and yet thirsty for 'bliss defined in human terms'. Kannada poet Prathibha Nandakumar offers a critique of patriarchal retellings of myth and their sly efforts to douse and manipulate female wrath. Twentieth-century American poet May Sarton approaches the Kali archetype in all its majesty and grandeur. 'Every creation 'is born out of the dark', she reminds us, and until we learn to stay 'open-eyed, in the terrible place', there is no escaping our darkest terrors. Contemporary Sri Lankan poet Aazhiyaal reminds us that goddesses can re-emerge in the unlikeliest places, wearing different faces and names. The Greek goddesses Demeter (mother and goddess of harvests) and Hecate (goddess of doorways, crossroads and magic) make their way into her moving Tamil poem on the horrors of war. The poem also reminds us that goddesses know no cultural or theological divides. My final poem is a dedication to two goddesses: Neeli Mariamman, a little-known village goddess whose jurisdiction is no larger than the universe and Linga Bhairavi, an ancient goddess consecrated as recently as 2010—a tribute to the nowness and foreverness of the sacred feminine.

Vaulting gracefully across centuries and contexts, the Goddess travels.
The Goddess listens.
The Goddess endures.

~

## Kali

A goddess chews on myth
As other women might on paan
Red juices stain her mouth.

Bored by her own powers
Immense and spectral, Kali broods
About Shiva, she is perverse.

She will not plead with him
Nor reveal Ganesha's birth
She will not ask him home.

Shiva loves her, but absences
And *apsaras* are natural to him
No god is hampered by his sins.

Kali desires a mortal, whose day
Begins with her, ends at nightfall
In her arms, a man who will die

Without her, whose love is fallible
But secure, she wants to be held
Like a warm creature, not a fable.

Loneliness drives this goddess mad
She is vagrant, her limbs askew
She begs a mate, her hair unmade.

Fickle as Shiva, memory deserts her
Chandi or Durga or Parvati, which
Is she, which of her selves weeps here?

Even Ganesha, for whom she feels
Only tenderness, excludes her, even he
Seems impatient with her flaws.

Where should such a goddess turn?
Kali, mistress of the temporal worlds
Wants bliss defined in human terms.

Staid Ganesha knows this wildness
Must be curbed, Shiva, peripatetic
Agrees, and across the wilderness

Both gift Kali a companion eagle, hurt
By no arrow, fed on nothing, it returns
Each night to its eyrie in her heart.

*[Rukmini Bhaya Nair]*

*

## Devi, the Mother

(*When no one could kill the Daruka demon, the gods requested the Devi to protect the world. After slaying the demon, the Devi could not calm down and the gods prayed to Lord Shiva to pacify her. He took the form of an infant and cried. The Devi could not ignore the infant's cry and picked up the child to put to her breasts and the infant sucked out her anger as well.* Commentary to 'Sri Lalita Sahasranama')

Pootani, the demon, once tried to feed baby Krishna
with poison-smeared breasts.
He, the Lord that he is, sucked out
her life and she died, attaining nirvana.

But this isn't the same story.

Just when the Devi is surging forward
flashing her sword and her weapon-wielding ten arms,
the infant cries, halting her in her path.
Isn't to suckle an infant the main purpose of breasts?

Never mind if it sucks out her anger as well.
They know for sure it is her weakness.
The Devi cannot be angry for long.
There is always a way to pacify her.
They know the godlike infant
with its cute mouth
keeps her calm.

But when in need, they also know
how to get her to become
a demon-slaying angry woman.

*[Prathibha Nandakumar; translated by the poet]*

## (from) The Invocation to Kali

1.

There are times when
I think only of killing
The voracious animal
Who is my perpetual shame,

The violent one
Whose raging demands
Break down peace and shelter
Like a peacock's scream.

There are times when
I think only of how to do away
With this brute power
That cannot be tamed.

I am the cage where poetry
Paces and roars. The beast
Is the god. How murder the god?
How live with the terrible god?

2.

The Kingdom of Kali

Anguish is always there, lurking at night,
Wakes us like a scourge, the creeping sweat
As rage is remembered, self-inflicted blight.
What is it in us we have not mastered yet?

What Hell have we made of the subtle weaving
Of nerve with brain, that all centres tear?
We live in a dark complex of rage and grieving.
The machine grates, grates, whatever we are.

The kingdom of Kali is within us deep.
The built-in destroyer, the savage goddess,
Wakes in the dark and takes away our sleep.
She moves through the blood to poison gentleness.

She keeps us from being what we long to be;
Tenderness withers under her iron laws.

We may hold her like a lunatic, but it is she
Held down, who bloodies with her claws.

How then to set her free or come to terms
With the volcano itself, the fierce power
Erupting injuries, shrieking alarms?
Kali among her skulls must have her hour.

It is time for the invocation, to atone
For what we fear most and have not dared to face:
Kali, the destroyer, cannot be overthrown;
We must stay, open-eyed, in the terrible place.

Every creation is born out of the dark.
Every birth is bloody. Something gets torn.
Kali is there to do her sovereign work
Or else the living child will be stillborn.

She cannot be cast out (she is here for good)
Nor battled to the end. Who wins that war?
She cannot be forgotten, jailed or killed.
Heaven must still be balanced against her.

Out of destruction she comes to wrest
The juice from the cactus its harsh spine,
And until she, the destroyer, has been blest,
There will be no child, no flower and no wine.

5

It is time for the invocation:

Kali, be with us.
Violence, destruction, receive our homage.
Help us to bring darkness into the light,
To lift out the pain, the anger,

Where it can be seen for what it is—
The balance-wheel for our vulnerable, aching love.
Put the wild hunger where it belongs,
Within the act of creation,
Crude power that forges a balance
Between hate and love.

Help us to be the always hopeful
Gardeners of the spirit
Who know that without darkness
Nothing comes to birth
As without light
Nothing flowers.

Bear the roots in mind,
You, the dark one, Kali,
Awesome power.

*[May Sarton]*

                                    *

## The Mother and the Goddess of Night

She has walked and walked
for nine long days.

All of nine days
and nine long nights
have passed by.

Weary of wandering as she is,
the mad woman mutters brokenly,
'Have you seen my daughter?
have you seen her?'
All along the paths she takes

the heavy clouds freeze—a thousand
birds fly past her in scorn
and the wind howls aloud.

No man or woman would help her
nor would the great gods come to her aid.
Wherever she walks, at the touch of her feet
all the plants burn and blacken.

No one spoke up on her behalf,
no eye shed one tear,
no living creature came forward
as witness.

She walks on, mumbling
'My daughter, my daughter.'

The earth hardens and freezes
along her path,
fields of corn, their ears ripe and milky
rot from their very roots,
flowers lose their golden pollen and wither,
honey-birds die and fall like dead leaves,
while the tall trees lose themselves
in a profound sleep.

'Wastelands of snow
wastelands of snow
only wastelands of snow
will I grant you all,'
she fumes within,
as she walks on and on.

A snowstorm flings down
a million, million needles.

The earth freezes, water freezes,
light darkens.

On the tenth day, look,
here she comes, Hecate,
heart of the dark,
with the faces of night hours.
She comes from the place where
Time's cycles meet.

'I heard your daughter scream.
but I haven't seen her,' she says
abruptly, pointing to the south.
Then the goddess of dark nights
and of all things black,
urges her hounds to run ahead,
raises her two torches on high
to light the way, as she hastens,
along with the mother.
Not a god blinks an eye,
all tongues are shocked into silence.

They travel through dense forests
of betrayals, humiliations
and falsehoods,
to find at last, the daughter tasting
sweet–sour pomegranate pearls.
With their own eyes they saw the daughter!

And then, with her, they returned home.

In her boundless joy, the mother
gave to all, with both hands,
three-times ploughed fields
of rich, red earth, and the promise
of never-ending fruitfulness.

And as all living things thrilled
into renewal, a fine rain fell
throughout the hemisphere
ushering in the spring.

*[Aazhiyaal; translated by Lakshmi Holmstrom]*

*

**Goddess**
[after Neeli Mariamman]

*'It's enough/ to sit alone/ and gaze at you/ three-eyed Goddess./ Who needs to go meditate?'*— Abhirami Bhattar (translated from Tamil)

Those who go to the great temples
of Perur and Avinashi
know nothing of her.

She isn't interested
in being the flavour
of a few thousand years.

She's been around
since the planet was a seizure

of waterness
and protoplasm.

In the great garrulity of gods
she is silent.

She'll never be the life
of the party

but she's not concerned with the party.

She is life—
twisty blue nerve fire—

life local,
life perennial,

      the goddess Neeli Mariamman.

On Tuesday afternoons
in the month of May

she erupts
into an epilepsy of form,

ballooning a small nut-brown priest
into prescience,

and as he foams and curdles,
his eyes sightless,

she prescribes remedies
to a peasant plagued
by blisters in his gum,

advises the crone to be patient
with her daughter–in-law

for women must be wooed
and fear must not spawn a new generation.

Then she turns towards you
and her eyes are craters,

her light molten jaggery
and burnt almond,

her tongue is toxic shock,
her gaze tundra.

She is the shockingly naked wire
at the centre of the world

where your future is a long burnt-out
morning star.

The universe is her hamlet,
she says,

a flystain
in her monarchy.

Her laughter is her empire.

*

**Goddess** II
[after Linga Bhairavi]

In her burning rainforest
silence is so alive
you can hear

listening.


*[Arundhathi Subramaniam]*

# Acknowledgements

This book owes a debt to the many people I've been in conversation with over the years.

My sincere gratitude to the following:

All the women questors who are in this book. And the many who aren't. I couldn't have asked for more invigorating company these past five years.

Dr Suvarnalata Rao, head of music at the National Centre for the Performing Arts, Mumbai, who graciously hosted a festival of music and poetry, 'Wild Women', that I curated in 2019; it sowed the beginnings of this book.

All those fellow adventurers ready to work on new translations without a question about publication or remuneration (listed in alphabetical order): Ahalya Ballal, Lokendra Balwe, Sampurna Chattarji, Smita and Mustansir Dalvi, Subhashini Kaligotla, Kanya Kanchana, Kala Krishnan, Prabhanjan Mishra, Shilpa Mudbi, Robin Ngangom, Jerry Pinto, Mani Rao, Anupama Raju, Dibyajyoti Sarma, Avtar Singh, Rahul Soni, K. Srilata, Neelima Shukla–Bhatt, Anand Thakore and Vanamala Viswanatha.

The anthologies—*Women in Praise of the Sacred* by Jane Hirshfield, *The Unfettered Note: Indian Women Seers and Mystics* by Subhadra Desai and *Women Writing in India*, edited by Susie Tharu and K. Lalita—for being companions on this journey, variant enough to stimulate, akin enough to guide.

Sujatha Vijayaraghavan, for her thoughtful and meticulous transcripts of verses by Avvaiyar and Andavan Picchai and her love of Tamil literature and Carnatic music.

Prateek Pattanaik, for his unstinting help, his contagious passion for the literary and musical history of Odisha, and Devdutt Pattanaik, who generously connected us.

Jasmina Kumar and Bhavnesh Desai, for their kindness in furnishing me with literature on Indira Devi and Dilip Kumar Roy.

Priya D'Souza, for research and technical support, for being an intrepid trawler of online realms, for friendship.

All those who, at various junctures, have offered suggestions, solidarity or both: Alarmel Valli, Bombay Jayashri, Andrew Schelling, Jane Hirshfield, Miranda Shaw, Maa Karpoori, Maa Janani, Lata Mani, Sanjukta Wagh, Arpana Caur, Gieve Patel, Alok Bhalla, Ranjit Hoskote, Sudeep Sen, Dileep Raj, Sreelatha Nelluli, Kamini Dandapani and Danish Husain.

Padmini Subramaniam and Raghu Sundaram, for forms of support too varied to name.

Kanishka Gupta, Vaishali Mathur, Aparajita Pant and Yash Daiv for believing in this project and for patiently midwifing it.

Sadhguru, in so many ways, the key.

# Notes on Translators and Contributors

**Kanya Kanchana** is a poet and translator. Her work has appeared in *POETRY*, *The Common*, *Asymptote* and elsewhere. Kanya is also engaged in practice, teaching, non-profit work and philological research at the intersection of tantra and yoga. She has a research MPhil in Sanskrit Studies from the University of Cambridge.

**Thanissaro Bhikkhu** is an American Buddhist monk of the Kammatthana (Thai Forest) tradition. He was ordained in 1976, and in 1991, he helped establish the Metta Forest Monastery in San Diego County, California, where he serves as an abbot. He has translated and anthologized numerous suttas and classical Buddhist texts. Much of his work can be found online at dhammatalks.org.

**Kala Krishnan** lives and works in Bengaluru; she teaches creative writing and Indian literature to BA students. She has published two books of poetry and is currently working on the second part of a fiction trilogy; her translation of Bhartrihari's poetry has appeared in print.

**Andrew Schelling**, a poet and translator, lives in the Colorado Rockies. He teaches at the Jack Kerouac School at Naropa University. Linguistics, animal tracks, Sanskrit poetry, ballads and oral tradition are among his studies. He has authored twenty-odd books published in North America. Books in India include *The Oxford Anthology of Bhakti Literature* (OUP, 2011).

**Miranda Shaw** is an American author and scholar of Vajrayana Buddhism. Her book *Passionate Enlightenment* won the James Henry Breasted Prize, the Tricycle Prize for Excellence in Buddhist Scholarship and the Critics' Choice Most Acclaimed Academic Book Award in 1995. She earned her doctorate from Harvard University and is an Emerita faculty member of the School of Arts and Sciences at the University of Richmond.

**Archana Venkatesan** is a professor of religious studies and comparative literature at the University of California, Davis. She studies text, visuality and performance in the early-medieval Tamil country. Her translations are inspired by extensive fieldwork in the temples of Tamil Nadu, where Tamil devotional poetry continues to be read, recited and relished.

**Ravi Shankar**, PhD, is a Pushcart-prize winning poet, translator, memoirist and professor. He has written and edited sixteen published as well as forthcoming books, including *Correctional* (finalist for the 2022 Connecticut Book Awards) and W.W. Norton's *Language for a New Century*. He has appeared on the BBC, PBS and the *New York Times* and teaches creative writing at Tufts University.

**Priya Sarukkai Chabria** is an award-winning poet, translator, SSF and non-fiction writer with nine books and, as editor, two poetry anthologies. She channels Sanskrit *rasa* and Tamil Sangam poetics in her work. Priya is currently translating mystic poetry from classical Tamil; as founding editor of *Poetry at Sangam*, she is also compiling an anthology of translations from its pages and can be reached at www.priyasarukkaichabria.com

**A.K. Ramanujan** (1929–1993) was a poet, translator, folklorist, philologist and professor of Dravidian studies at the University of Chicago. His translations include *Speaking of Siva* (Penguin, 1973) and *Hymns for the Drowning* (selections from Nammalvar, Penguin, 1981), as well as two collections of classical Tamil verse, *The Interior Landscape* (NYRB Poets, 1967) and *Poems of Love and War* (Columbia University Press, 1985). He received the Padma Shri in 1976.

Academic and translator **Dr Vanamala Viswanatha** has taught English studies for decades and translated Kannada writers such as Sara Aboobacker, Lankesh, Vaidehi and Ananthamurthy. *The Life of Harishchandra* (Harvard University Press, 2017), her translation of a medieval Kannada classic, is a landmark publication. Her translation of Indira Bai (with Padikkal, OUP, 2019) received the Kuvempu Bhasha Bharati award in 2020.

**Ahalya Ballal** is curious about words and the several ways in which one language can be translated into another. Her mother tongue is Kannada. Engaged professionally with the world of advertising, her other abiding passions, as practitioner and viewer, are theatre and classical dance.

**H.S. Shivaprakash** is a poet, playwright, critic and (retired) professor of theatre and performance studies at Jawaharlal Nehru University, New Delhi. Widely translated, his interests include literary history, medieval studies, comparative literature, translation and folklore. His awards include various book prizes from the Karnataka Sahitya Akademi, the Kusumagraj Kavya Puraskar and the Kuvempu Bhasha Bharati Translation Award, among others.

**Prabhanjan Mishra** is a poet, writer, critic, translator and the former editor of *Poiesis*, the literary journal of Mumbai's 'Poetry Circle', active in the 1980s and 1990s. He has authored three books of poems and has also been included in several anthologies. His latest poems have appeared in *Kavya Bharati*, *Literary Vibes*, *Spillwords* and *Our Poetry Archive* (OAP).

**Arun Kolatkar** (1932–2004) was a bilingual Mumbai-based poet who wrote in both Marathi and English. His books in English include *Jejuri* (NYRB, 1976; winner of the Commonwealth Poetry Prize), *Kala Ghoda Poems* (Pras Prakashan, 2004), *Sarpa Satra* (Pras Prakashan, 2004) and *Collected Poems in English* (Bloodaxe Books, 2010). His Marathi verse collection, *Bhijki Vahi* (Pras Prakashan, 2003), won the Sahitya Akademi Award in 2005.

**Neela Bhagwat** is a classical *khayal* singer of the Gwalior gharana. She holds master's degrees in Marathi, Sanskrit and sociology, and aims to interpret medieval saint poetry in a contemporary context. Her response to a time of communal conflict has been to sing the poetry of peace and love of Kabir, Meera, Tukaram, Chokhamela, Soyarabai, Janabai and other Bhakti mystics.

**Jerry Pinto** lives, works and writes in a city by the sea with many names. He is co-translator with Neela Bhagwat of *The Ant Who Swallowed* *the Sun: The Abhangs of the Marathi Women Saints* (Speaking Tiger, 2020). His poems in English have been collectively published as *Asylum and Other Poems* (Speaking Tiger, 2021) and *I Want a Poem and Other Poems* (Speaking Tiger, 2021).

**Shruthi Veena Vishwanath** is a singer, song-catcher, stirrer of herstories, educator and curator. Her practice celebrates mystic music traditions from South Asia and beyond, especially celebrating herstories and voices that have been sidelined. She performs and teaches around the world and translates when the words find their way to the heart.

**Dilip Chitre** (1938–2009) was a poet, translator, critic, editor, painter and documentary film-maker. He wrote in both English and Marathi and translated extensively from the Varkari literary tradition. His book of translations of *Tukaram, Says Tuka* (Penguin Classics, 1991) received wide attention. He authored several poetry collections, his last, in English, being *As Is, Where Is: Selected Poems* (Poetrywala, 2007).

**Ranjit Hoskote**'s collections of poetry include *Central Time* (Penguin, 2014), *Jonahwhale* (Penguin, 2018; in the UK as *The Atlas of Lost Beliefs*, Arc, 2020), *Hunchprose* (Wesleyan University Press, 2021) and *Icelight* (Penguin, 2023). Hoskote's acclaimed translation of a fourteenth-century Kashmiri woman mystic has appeared as *I, Lalla: The Poems of Lal Ded* (Penguin Classics, 2011).

**Neelima Shukla-Bhatt** is professor of religion and South Asia studies at Wellesley College. With a PhD from Harvard University, her work focuses on devotional literature of medieval north India, goddess traditions in Gujarat, South Asian models of religious pluralism, and Gandhi's thought and life. Her books include *Narasinha Mehta of Gujarat: A Legacy of Bhakti in Songs and Stories* (Oxford, 2015) and *Hinduism: The Basics* (Routledge, 2023), among others.

**Sumanta Banerjee** is a cultural historian and journalist who specializes in research into popular culture, particularly of the colonial period. He has been a fellow at the Indian Institute of Advanced Study, Shimla. He is the author of many books, including *The Parlour and the Streets: Elite and Popular*

*Culture in Nineteenth-Century Calcutta* and *Dangerous Outcast: The Prostitute in Nineteenth-Century Bengal,* both published by Seagull Books.

**Malini Bhattacharya** is an author, scholar, translator, playwright and activist in the women's movement. She is a retired professor of English and former director of the School of Women's Studies at Jadavpur University, Calcutta, as well as a former member of the Lok Sabha for the Communist Party of India (Marxist).

**Anjali Purohit** is a painter, writer, poet, translator and curator. She is the author of *Ragi Ragini: Chronicles from Aji's Kitchen* and *Go Talk to the River: the Ovis of Bahinabai Choudhari.* Anjali has been the founder and curator of several literary initiatives in Mumbai including The Cappuccino Readings and the Cappuccino Adda.

**B.V.L. Narayana Row** was a polyglot, Telugu scholar and professor of linguistics at the English and Foreign Languages University, Hyderabad.

**Rahul Soni** is a writer, editor and translator. His translations include a selection of Ashok Vajpeyi's poetry, *A Name for Every Leaf* (Harper Perennial, 2016), Pankaj Kapur's novella, *Dopehri* (Harper Perennial India, 2019), Shrikant Verma's Sahitya Akademi Award-winning poetry collection, *Magadh* (Eka, 2023) and International Booker Prize-winner Geetanjali Shree's novel, *The Roof beneath Their Feet* (Penguin Random House India, 2023).

**Jane Hirshfield** is an American poet, essayist and translator. A 2019 elected member of the American Academy of Arts and Sciences, her books include numerous collections of poetry, essays and translation. Widely published and translated, she is the recipient of numerous awards and has been Chancellor of the Academy of American Poets (2012–2017).

**Neerja Mattoo** is a writer and translator. She taught English at the Government College for Women in Srinagar, Kashmir, from where she retired as principal. She is chief editor of the quarterly journal *Miraas,* which is devoted to Kashmiri culture. Her work as a translator includes the book *The Mystic and the Lyric: Four Women Poets from Kashmir* (Zubaan, 2019).

Writer and editor **Dibyajyoti Sarma** has published three volumes of poetry, four books of translation and two academic titles. Born in Assam, and now based in Delhi, he runs an independent publishing venture called Red River.

**Kanchana Natarajan** specializes in classical Indian philosophy and has taught at the University of Delhi for four decades. Her book *Transgressing Boundaries: The Songs of Shenkottai Avudai Akkal* was published by Zubaan in 2012.

**Srinivas Rayaprol** (1925–1998) studied civil engineering at Stanford University and combined a career in engineering with a committed pursuit of poetry. Widely published and anthologized, he was the founder–editor of the literary journal *East and West*. His three poetry collections are *Bones and Distances* (Writers Workshop Kolkata, 1968), *Married Love and Other Poems* (Writers Workshop Kolkata, 1972) and *Selected Poems* (Writers Workshop Kolkata, 1995).

**Mani Rao** is the author of twelve books of poetry and three books in translation from Sanskrit, including *Saundarya Lahari* (HarperCollins, 2022), *Bhagavad Gita* (HarperCollins, 2023) and *Kalidasa* (Aleph, 2015). She researched mantra experience among tantrics for *Living Mantra: Mantra, Deity and Visionary Experience Today* (Palgrave Macmillan USA, 2018). She lives in Bengaluru.

**Anand Thakore** is a Mumbai-based poet and Hindustani classical vocalist. The author of four poetry collections, most recently *Seven Deaths and Four Scrolls* (Paperwall Media & Publishing Pvt. Ltd, 2017), he is the recipient of grants from the Ministry of Human Resource Development and the Charles Wallace India Trust. He divides his time between writing, performances and teaching music.

**Robin Ngangom** is a bilingual poet and translator who writes in English and Manipuri. He teaches at the North-Eastern Hill University, Shillong. He has published several books of poetry, and his poems have appeared in literary journals such as *The New Statesman, Verse, Planet: The Welsh Internationalist, The Literary Review* and *Kunapipi*.

**Subhashini Kaligotla** is a poet and art historian of early South Asia. She is the author of the poetry collection *Bird of the Indian Subcontinent* (Great Indian Poetry Collective, 2018) and has been featured in various poetry anthologies. She teaches at Columbia, and lives and writes in New York City.

**Velcheru Narayana Rao** is the Krishnadevaraya Emeritus Professor of Languages and Cultures of Asia at the University of Wisconsin–Madison. He is the author of several books on Telugu literature and south Indian history, including *The Story of Manu—Allasani Peddana,* with David Shulman (Murti Classical Library of India, 2015) and *God on the Hill: Temple Songs from Tirupati,* with David Shulman (OUP, 2005), among others. He received the Sahitya Akademi Fellowship in 2021.

**David Shulman** is an Indologist, poet, literary critic and peace activist. He gained his doctorate at the School of Oriental and African Studies, London. He is Renee Lang Professor of Humanistic Studies at the Hebrew University of Jerusalem. He is the author of over twenty books, including *Tamil: A Biography* (Harvard University Press, 2016) and *Freedom and Despair: Notes from the South Hebron Hills* (University of Chicago Press, 2018). He received the Israel Prize in 2016 for his work on the literature and culture of south India.

**Scott Kugle** is a professor of South Asian and Islamic studies at Emory University. His research languages are Arabic, Urdu and Persian, and his areas of expertise include Sufism, Islamic society in South Asia and issues of gender and sexuality. His many books include *When Sun Meets Moon: Gender, Eros and Ecstasy in Urdu Poetry* (The University of North Carolina Press, 2016) and *Hajj to the Heart: Sufi Journeys across the Indian Ocean* (UNC Press Books, 2021), among others.

**Hemang Ashwinkumar** is a bilingual poet who works in Gujarati and English. He has translated contemporary Marathi poetry into Gujarati and contemporary Gujarati poetry and short fiction into English. His Gujarati translation of Arun Kolatkar's *Kala Ghoda Poems* was published recently. He can be reached at hemangde@gmail.com.

**Smita Dalvi** teaches architecture and aesthetics in Navi Mumbai and Mumbai. She is the editor of *Tekton,* a journal of architecture, urban design and planning, and the co-author of *Panvel: Great City, Fading Heritage*. She is an avid traveller and keen photographer.

**Mustansir Dalvi** is a poet, translator and editor. His translation of Muhammad Iqbal's influential *Shikwa* and *Jawaab-e-Shikwa* from the Urdu as *Taking Issue and Allah's Answer* (India Penguin Modern Classics, 2012) has been described as 'insolent and heretical'. His latest translation is Hemant Divate's award-winning book of poems, *Paranoia*, from Marathi into English (Poetrywala, 2023).

**Neeti Singh** is a poet, translator and associate professor of English. She combines her interest in literature with bhakti, translation, cultural studies and Hindustani music. She has authored thirty research papers and four books. She holds an MPhil in aesthetics and a PhD on the Saguna and Nirguna Bhakti traditions.

**Barbara Stoler Miller** (1940–1993) was a scholar of Sanskrit, well-known for her translation of the Bhagavad Gita. She also translated works of Sanskrit drama and poetry, including the works of Jayadeva (*Love Song of the Dark Lord: Jayadeva's Gitagovinda*, Motilal Banarsidass, 1977), Bhartrihari, Bilhana and Kalidasa. She became head of the Department of Asian and Middle Eastern Cultures at Barnard College in New York in 1979.

**Vipul Rikhi** is a poet, fiction writer, translator and singer who has been immersed in the oral traditions of Kabir and other Bhakti and Sufi poets for over a decade. He is the author of a novel, *2012 Nights* (FingerPrint, 2012); a collection of poems, *Bleed* (Hawakal Publishers, 2018); and co-author of *One Palace, a Thousand Doorways* (Speaking Tiger, 2019) and *I Saw Myself: Journeys of Shah Abdul Latif Bhitai* (Penguin Random House India, 2019) with Shabnam Virmani. He lives in Goa.

**Shabnam Virmani** is a documentary film-maker, researcher, writer and artist-in-residence at the Srishti School of Art, Design and Technology, Bengaluru. As co-founder of the Drishti Media Arts and Human Rights collective, she has directed several award-winning documentaries. She initiated the Kabir Project, a series of journeys into oral folk music traditions in quest of Kabir and other mystics for our contemporary world.

**Paul E. Losensky** is a professor in the Department of Comparative Literature and an adjunct professor in the Department of Middle Eastern Languages and Cultures at Indiana University. He received his PhD from the University of Chicago. He specializes in Persian literature and literary history, and his books include *In the Bazaar of Love* (with Sunil Sharma, Penguin India, 2012) and *Farid ad-Din Attar's Memorial of God's Friends* (Paulist Press, 2009), among others.

**Sunil Sharma** is a professor of Persianate & Comparative Literature at Boston University. He received his doctorate from the University of Chicago. His areas of expertise are premodern Persian and South Asian literatures. He is the author of *Mughal Arcadia* (Harvard University Press, 2017) and co-author of *Three Centuries of Travel Writing by Muslim Women* (Indiana University Press, 2022), among other books.

**Deben Bhattacharya** (1921–2001) was an ethnomusicologist, film-maker, writer, photographer and radio producer. He produced several influential field recordings of music in Bengal, over a hundred records and twenty-odd films, besides writing extensively on folk music, poetry, dance and his travels through south and central Asia. His books include *Songs of the Qawwals of India, Songs of the Bards of Bengal* (Grove Press, 1970) and *Love Songs of Vidyapati* (Hind Pocket Books, 1967), among others. He divided his time between Kolkata and Europe.

**Edward C. Dimock Jr** (1929–2001) was an American author, linguist, scholar of Asian studies and emeritus professor at the University of Chicago whose work centred on Bengali language and literature. His scholarly publications include *The Place of the Hidden Moon: Erotic Mysticism in the Vaisnava–Sahajiya Cult of Bengali* (Motilal Banarsidass, 1966), among others. His awards include the Desikottama in 1992 for his contribution to Bengali literature. He was also an honorary fellow of the Sahitya Akademi.

**Denise Levertov** (1923–1997) was a British–American poet who authored over twenty-four volumes of poetry, including *The Freeing of the Dust* (New Directions, 1975), which won the Lenore Marshall Poetry Prize. Her three works of translation include *In Praise of Krishna: Songs from the Bengali* (with Edward C. Dimock Jr, University of Chicago Press, 1967). Her many awards include the Shelley Memorial Award, the Robert Frost Medal and the Lannan Award, among others.

**Linda Hess** is a scholar, writer, translator and lover of the devotional and mystical literature of India, especially that of Kabir. She is a senior lecturer emerita in the Department of Religious Studies at Stanford University and co-director of Stanford's Center for South Asia. Her work on north Indian Bhakti poetry and performance includes *The Bijak of Kabir* (with Sukhdev Singh, Motilal Banarsidass, 1983) and numerous articles on Kabir, Tulsidas and Ramlila performances.

**Arvind Krishna Mehrotra** is a poet, literary critic and translator. His poetry collections include *Collected Poems (1969–2014)* (Penguin India, 2014) and *Selected Poems and Translations* (NYRB Poets, 2020), among others. As a translator, his books include *The Absent Traveller: Prakrit Love Poetry from the Gathasaptasati of Satavahana Hala* (Ravi Dayal, 1991) and *Songs of Kabir* (NYRB Classics, 2011).

**Keki Daruwalla** is a Delhi-based poet and fiction writer. Widely anthologized and translated, he is the author of twelve poetry volumes, including *Landfall* (Speaking Tiger, 2023), *Naishapur and Babylon* (Speaking Tiger, 2018) and *Collected Poems (1970–2005)* (Penguin India, 2006), among others. He is the recipient of the Sahitya Akademi Award (1984), the Commonwealth Poetry Prize for Asia (1987) and the fourth-highest civilian award of the Republic of India, the Padma Shri (2014).

**Meena Desai** has been translating Gujarati poetry since the 1980s and retains a deep belief in translation as essential to human connection. Her doctoral research was about communication in drama. She worked in the telecommunications industry and continues to devote herself to cross-cultural communication in various ways. She has translated several Gujarati ghazals and spent over a decade on the work of Narsinh Mehta. She lives in the US.

**Avtar Singh** is the author of the novels *Necropolis* and *The Beauty of These Present Things.* His work is featured in anthologies of short fiction, travel writing and pilgrimage. He has written for *Foreign Policy,* the *Washington*

*Post* and *The Hindu,* among other publications. He lives and works in Germany.

Writer, poet and translator **Taufiq Rafat** (1927–1998) was educated in Dehradun, Aligarh and Lahore. He was recognized as an influential Anglophone Pakistani poet whose work explored intimate themes as well as a country's transition from pre- to post-Partition eras. He translated the works of two iconic poets of Punjabi poetry: Bulleh Shah and Qadir Yar.

**Anju Makhija** is a poet, playwright and translator. She has written three poetry collections, co-translated *Seeking the Beloved: The Poetry of Shah Abdul Latif* and co-edited three anthologies related to the Partition, women and young readers. Her awards include the Sahitya Akademi English Translation Prize (2011). Her latest book is *Mumbai Traps: Collected Plays.*

**Hari Dilgir** was a poet and scholar who edited many anthologies of poetry and received several literary prizes, including the Sahitya Akademi Award, Gaurav Puruskar, Priyadarshini Prize and the Indusind Award for Lifetime Contribution to Sindhi Language. He was on the board of several institutions devoted to preserving the lost culture of Sindh.

**Kynpham Sing Nongkynrih** is an award-winning bilingual poet and writer, in Khasi and English. His works include *The Yearning of Seeds* (HarperCollins, 2011), *Time's Barter: Haiku and Senryu* (HarperCollins, 2015) and *Funeral Nights* (Context, 2021). In 2018, he was awarded a Tagore Fellowship by the Indian Institute of Advanced Study, Shimla. He teaches literature at the North-Eastern Hill University.

**Shilpa Mudbi Kothakota** is an artist and social activist who has worked in the fields of media consultancy, documentary film-making and the performing arts. She is the co-founder of Urban Folk Project, a collective that collates folk knowledge systems of north Karnataka. Born in Bengaluru, she graduated in media arts and production from Sydney, and currently lives in Kalburgi, Karnataka.

**Lokendra Balwe** grew up in Pune. He worked as a software engineer but retained a long-standing fascination with music and poetry. After experiencing a radical transformation during a programme for inner well-being, he moved to Coimbatore in 2011, where he volunteers full-time at the Isha Yoga Center. In a bid to reach a non-English-speaking audience, much of his work has entailed translating from English into Marathi.

**Sampurna Chattarji** is a writer, translator, editor and teacher. Her twenty-one books include her short story collection about Bombay/Mumbai, *Dirty Love* (Penguin India, 2013) and eleven poetry titles, the latest being *Unmappable Moves* (Poetrywala, 2023). Her translation of Joy Goswami's prose poems *After Death Comes Water* (Harper Perennial, 2021) has been widely acclaimed.

**Rachel Fell McDermott** is professor of Asian and Middle Eastern Cultures at Barnard College. She received her PhD from Harvard University. She has published extensively on the Hindu-goddess-centred religious traditions of Bengal. Her books include *Revelry, Rivalry and Longing for the Goddesses of Bengal* (Columbia University Press, 2011) and *Encountering Kali* (University of California Press, 2003), among others.

**Anupama Raju** is a poet, novelist, literary journalist, translator and communications professional. She is the author of *C: a novel* (Aleph Book Company, 2022) and the poetry collection *Nine* (Speaking Tiger Books, 2015). Widely published, Anupama was a Charles Wallace fellow at the University of Kent, Canterbury and Writer-in-Residence at Le Centres Intermondes, La Rochelle, France.

**Vinaya Chaitanya** was born in Muvattupuzha, in the foothills of the Western Ghats, before the invasion of rubber plantations. He was accepted as a disciple by Nataraja Guru, a disciple and successor of Narayana Guru, the philosopher–poet of Kerala. His books in Malayalam, Kannada and English include a translation of Akka Mahadevi's vachanas, *Songs for Siva* (HarperCollins, 2010).

Writer, translator and academic, **K. Srilata**'s novel *Table for Four* (Penguin India, 2011) was long-listed in 2009 for the Man Asian Literary Prize. She is the co-editor of *The Rapids of a Great River: The Penguin Book of Tamil Poetry* (Penguin India, 2009). Her most recent book *This Kind of Child: The 'Disability' Story* (Westland, 2022) is a reflection on the disability experience.

**Rukmini Bhaya Nair** is a poet, fiction writer, critic and professor of linguistics and English at the Indian Institute of Technology (IIT), Delhi. Her poetry volumes include *Yellow Hibiscus: New and Selected Poems* (Penguin India, 2004), *The Ayodhya Cantos* (Penguin India, 1999) and *The Hyoid Bone* (Penguin India, 1992). She is the recipient of the J.N. Tata Scholarship and the Hornby Foundation Award, among others.

**Prathibha Nandakumar** is a Kannada poet, journalist, film-maker, columnist and translator. Her twenty-four books include poems, short stories, biographies, plays, translations, essays, an autobiography in Kannada and a forthcoming collection of poems in English, *What I Fed the Cat*. Her awards include the Infosys Foundation Award for Literature, the Bangalore Literary Festival Award and the Karnataka Sahitya Akademi Book Award, among others.

**May Sarton (1912–1995)** was a Belgian–American novelist, poet and memoirist whose works were informed by themes of love, mind–body conflict, creativity, lesbianism and the trials of age and illness. She wrote fifty-three books, including nineteen novels and seventeen books of poetry, and taught at various institutions, including Harvard University and Wellesley College.

**Aazhiyaal** is a Sri Lankan poet who now lives in Australia. She was a lecturer of English at the University of Jaffna and travelled extensively before settling down in Canberra. She has published three collections of poetry and a volume of Tamil translations of Australian Aboriginal poetry. She received the 2021 Poetry Award from the Canadian Tamil Literary Garden for her contribution to Tamil literature.

**Lakshmi Holmstrom** (1935–2016) was a writer and critic who translated short fiction, novels and poetry by major contemporary writers in Tamil (Sundara Ramaswamy, Ashokamitran, Ambai and Salma, among others) and made significant contributions to rendering classical Tamil poetry in English. She was the founder–trustee of SALIDAA (South Asian Diaspora Literature and Arts Archive). Based in the UK, she won numerous awards and was made an MBE in 2011.

# Sources

**Published**

**Section One**

**Buddhist Nuns of the Therigatha**

Bhikkhu, Thanissaro. *Poems of the Elders: An Anthology from the Theragāthā & Therīgāthā*. 1994. A selected anthology of thirty-two suttas from the Therigatha (and eighty-eight from the Theragatha) is distributed free of charge by Metta Forest Monastery. It is also available to read online and in various ebook formats at dhammatalks.org

**Vidya**

**Schelling, Andrew.** *Dropping the Bow: Poems of Ancient India,* White Pine Press, copyright 2008.

**Lakshminkara**

Shaw, Miranda. *Passionate Enlightenment: Women in Tantric Buddhism*. Princeton, NJ: Princeton University Press, 1995.

**Andal**

Venkatesan, Archana, trans. *The Secret Garland: Translations of Andal's Tiruppavai and Nacciyar Tirumoli*. UK: Oxford University Press, 2009. Republished in Subramaniam, Arundhathi, ed. *Eating God*. India: Penguin Ananda, 2014.

Chabria, Priya Sarukkai and Shankar, Ravi, trans. and ed. *Andal: The Autobiography of a Goddess*. India: Zubaan, 2015.

## Akka Mahadevi

Ramanujan, A.K., trans. *Speaking of Siva*. India: Penguin Books, 1973.

## Molige Mahadevi

Shivaprakash, H.S., trans. *I Keep Vigil of Rudra: The Vachanas*. India: Penguin Books, 2010.

## Lingamma

Shivaprakash, H.S., trans. *I Keep Vigil of Rudra: The Vachanas*. India: Penguin Books, 2010.

## Gangambike

Shivaprakash, H.S., trans. *I Keep Vigil of Rudra: The Vachanas*. India: Penguin Books, 2010.

## Muktabai

Kolatkar, Arun. *Collected Poems in English*. Edited by Arvind Krishna Mehrotra. UK: Bloodaxe Books, 2010.

Bhagwat, Neela and Pinto, Jerry, trans. *The Ant Who Swallowed the Sun: The Abhangs of Marathi Women Saints*. India: Speaking Tiger, 2020.

## Janabai

Kolatkar, Arun. *Collected Poems in English*. Edited by Arvind Krishna Mehrotra. UK: Bloodaxe Books, 2010.

Chitre, Dilip. 'Poets of Vithoba'. First published in Schelling, Andrew, ed. *The Oxford Anthology of Bhakti Literature*. UK: Oxford University Press, 2011. Republished in Subramaniam, Arundhathi, ed. *Eating God*. India: Penguin Ananda, 2014.

Bhagwat, Neela and Pinto, Jerry, trans. *The Ant Who Swallowed the Sun: The Abhangs of Marathi Women Saints*. India: Speaking Tiger, 2020.

## Soyarabai

Bhagwat, Neela and Pinto, Jerry, trans. *The Ant Who Swallowed the Sun: The Abhangs of Marathi Women Saints*. India: Speaking Tiger, 2020.

## Nirmala

Bhagwat, Neela and Pinto, Jerry, trans. *The Ant Who Swallowed the Sun: The Abhangs of Marathi Women Saints.* India: Speaking Tiger, 2020.

## Lal Ded

Hoskote, Ranjit. *I Lalla.* India: Penguin Classics, 2011.

## Kanhopatra

Bhagwat, Neela and Pinto, Jerry, trans. *The Ant Who Swallowed the Sun: The Abhangs of Marathi Women Saints.* India: Speaking Tiger, 2020.

## Rami

Tharu, Susie and Lalita, K., ed. *Women Writing in India.* India: Oxford University Press, 1991.

## Atukuri Molla

Tharu, Susie and Lalita, K., ed. *Women Writing in India.* India: Oxford University Press, 1991.

## Meerabai

Subramaniam, Arundhathi, ed. *Eating God.* India: Penguin Ananda, 2014.

'The wild woman of the forests', translation © Hirshfield, Jane, ed. *Women in Praise of the Sacred: Forty-three Centuries of Spiritual Poetry by Women,* (NY: HarperCollins, 1994); used by permission, all rights reserved.

Schelling, Andrew, trans. *For Love of the Dark One: Songs of Mirabai.* Arizona: Hohm Press, 1998.

## Habba Khatun

Mattoo, Neerja, trans. *The Mystic and the Lyric: Four Women Poets from Kashmir.* India: Zubaan, 2019.

## Rupa Bhavani

Mattoo, Neerja, trans. *The Mystic and the Lyric: Four Women Poets from Kashmir.* India: Zubaan, 2019.

## Bahinabai

Bhagwat, Neela and Pinto, Jerry, trans. *The Ant Who Swallowed the Sun: The Abhangs of Marathi Women Saints*. India: Speaking Tiger, 2020.

## Shenkottai Avudai Akkal

Natarajan, Kanchana, trans. and intro. *Transgressing Boundaries: The Songs of Shenkottai Avudai Akkal*. India: Zubaan, 2012.

## Tarigonda Venkamamba

Tharu, Susie and Lalita, K., ed. *Women Writing in India*. India: Oxford University Press, 1991.

## Muddupalani

Narayana, Rao Velcheru and Schulman, David, trans. *Classical Telugu Poetry: An Anthology*. New Delhi: Oxford University Press, 2002.

## Mah Laqa Bai Chanda

Kugle, Scott. *When Sun Meets Moon: Gender, Eros and Ecstasy in Urdu Poetry*. Chapel Hill, NC: The University of North Carolina Press, 2016; Series: Islamic civilization and Muslim Networks.

## Gangasati

Ashwinkumar, Hemang. 'Get Ready to Live like a Pauper'. The Guftagu Collection (2023), https://guftugu.in/2020/07/03/four-poems-by-ganga-sati/

## Sharika Devi

Mattoo, Neerja, ed. and trans. *Sharika Devi: A Yogini of Kashmir*. India: DK Printworld, 2013.

## Section Two

## Nammalvar

Ramanujan, A.K., trans. *Hymns for the Drowning: Poems for Visnu by Nammalvar*. India: Penguin Books, 1993.

## Basavanna

Ramanujan, A.K., trans. *Speaking of Siva.* India: Penguin Books, 1973.

## Jayadeva

Miller, Barbara Stoler. *The Gitagovinda of Jayadeva: Love Song of the Dark Lord.* India: Motilal Banarsidass; NY: Columbia University Press, 1977 (twentieth-anniversary edition).

## Amir Khusrau

Rikhi, Vipul and Virmani, Shabnam. *One Palace, A Thousand Doorways: Songlines Through Bhakti, Sufi, and Baul Oral Traditions.* New Delhi: Speaking Tiger, 2019.

Losensky, Paul E. and Sharma, Sunil, trans. *In the Bazaar of Love: The Selected Poetry of Amir Khusrau.* India: Penguin Random House, 2011.

## Vidyapati

Bhattacharya, Deben, ed. *Love Songs of Vidyapati.* New Delhi: Hind Pocket Books, 1967.

## Chandidas

Bhattacharya, Deben, trans. *Love Songs of Chandidas: The Rebel Poet–Priest of Bengal.* NY: Grove Press, 1970.

Dimock Jr, Edward C. and Levertov, Denise, trans. *In Praise of Krishna: Songs from the Bengali.* Doubleday Anchor Original, 1967.

## Kabir

Hess, Linda, trans. *Singing Emptiness: Kumar Gandharva performs the Poetry of Kabir.* Calcutta: Seagull Books, 2009.

Mehrotra, Arvind Krishna, trans. *Songs of Kabir.* India: Hachette Book Publishing India with Black Kite/Permanent Black, 2011.

## Narsinh Mehta

Subamaniam, Arundhathi, ed. *Eating God.* India: Penguin Ananda, 2014.

## Bulleh Shah

Rikhi, Vipul and Virmani, Shabnam. *One Palace, A Thousand Doorways: Songlines Through Bhakti, Sufi, and Baul Oral Traditions.* New Delhi: Speaking Tiger, 2019.

Rafat, Taufiq, trans. *Bulleh Shah: A Selection.* Lahore: Vanguard Publications, 1982.

## Shah Abdul Latif

Makhija, Anju and Dilgir, Hari. *Shah Abdul Latif: Seeking the Beloved.* New Delhi: Katha, 2005.

Rikhi, Vipul and Virmani, Shabnam. *I Saw Myself.* India: Penguin Ananda, 2019.

## Kshetrayya

Ramanujan, A.K., Rao, Velcheru Narayana and Shulman, David, ed. and trans. *When God is a Customer: Telugu Courtesan Songs by Ksetrayya and Others.* Berkeley: University of California Press, 1994.

## Uddhabadas

Bhattacharya, Deben, trans. *Songs of Krsna.* India: UNESCO Collection of Representative Works, 1978.

## Section Three

## Devi Mahatmyam

'*Namo devyai mahadevyai sivayai satata namah*'. Arunachala Archive. https://archive.arunachala.org/docs/devi-mahatmyam/

## Saundarya Lahari

Rao, Mani, trans. *Saundarya Lahari: Wave of Beauty.* India: HarperCollins, 2022.

## Chandamaharoshana Tantra

Translated by the Dharmachakra Translation Committee under the patronage and supervision of 84000: Translating the Words of the Buddha

## Garba

My sickle weighs two and a quarter pounds: *Savaa basher nu maaru daatardu lol*

'My sickle is two and a quarter pounds': Shukla–Bhatt, Neelima. 'Celebrating Materiality: *Garbo*, a Festival Image of the Goddess in Gujarat'. In *Sacred Matters: Material Religion in South Asian Traditions*, edited by Tracy Pintchman and Corinne Dempsey. pp. 89–114. Albany, NY: SUNY, 2015.

## Mei Hukum

Traditional Khasi prayer from Nongkynrih, Kynpham Singh. *Funeral Nights.* India: Context, 2021.

## Annamacharya

Rao, Velcheru Narayana and Shulman, David, trans. *God on the Hill: Temple Poems from Tirupati: Annamayya.* India: Oxford University Press, 2005.

## Abhirami Bhattar

Subamaniam, Arundhathi, ed. *Eating God.* India: Penguin Ananda, 2014.

## Kamalakanta Bhattacharya

McDermott, Rachel Fell. *Singing to the Goddess: Poems to Kali and Uma from Bengal.* USA: Oxford University Press, 2001.

## Narayana Guru

Chaitanya, Vinaya, trans. *A Cry in the Wilderness: The Works of Narayana Guru.* India: HarperCollins, 2022.

## Kazi Nazrul Islam

McDermott, Rachel Fell. *Singing to the Goddess: Poems to Kali and Uma from Bengal.* USA: Oxford University Press, 2001.

## Rukmini Bhaya Nair

Nair, Rukmini Bhaya. *Yellow Hibiscus: New and Selected Poems.* New Delhi: Penguin Books India, 2004.

## May Sarton

from allpoetry.com

## Aazhiyaal

https://wordswithoutborders.org/contributors/view/aazhiyaal/

## Arundhathi Subramaniam

Subramaniam, Arundhathi. *Love Without a Story*. India: Westland Amazon, 2019.

## Unpublished

## Section One

## Vac

Ṛigveda maṇḍala 10 anuvāka 10 sūkta 125

'I move with the Rudras and the Vasus; I, with the Ādityas and the AllGods':

*ahaṃ rudrebhirvasubhiścarāmyahamādityairuta viśvadevaiḥ*

## Bhadda Kapilani

'He is the Buddha's son and heir'—*Putto buddhassa dayado*

[unpublished translation based on renditions by Ken Norman, Hellmuth Hecker and Sister Khema]

## Karaikkal Ammaiyar

'Breasts withered': *kongkai tirangki*

'Having taken birth and practiced language': *piranthu mozhi payinra pin*

'Then too, without seeing the sacred form': *Anrum tiruvuruvam kaanaate*

'Is it out of longing': *viruppinal nee pirikayillayo*

'Sky-dwelling, he is, there are those who say': *vaanattan enbarum enka*

'It is I who is with penance': *yaane tavamutayen*

'One thing alone, I dwelt on': *ondre ninaintirunten*

## Avvaiyar

'Vinayaka Agaval' from Kandaswamy, S.N. *The Yoga of Siddha Avvai*. Quebec, Canada: Babaji's Kriya Yoga and Publications Inc., 2004.

Two excerpts from the Vinayaka Agaval:

'And now to enslave me you materialize as mother': *i-p-polud(u) ennai atkola vendi-t*

'You immerse me in the source where darkness and light mate': irulveli irandukku onr(u)idam enna

From Tani-p-padal Tirattu

'Lord of the lance, you ask me to define greatness': *Periyadhu kaetkin yerithavazh veloi*

## Akka Mahadevi

'Hear me if you will; spurn me, if you won't': *ayya, nee kelidare kelu, keladiddare manu*

'Gazing at him, I closed my eyes': *kanutta kanutta kangala muchchide nodavva*

'He laid siege to my heart!': *enna manava marugondanavva*

'Other men, they are like thorns': erada mullinante paragandarenagavva

'Hunger, wait a moment': hasive neenu nillu nillu, trisheye neenu nillu nillu

'The despairing heart has turned turtle': kalavalada manavu talekelagadudavva

'Melting, like moist soil': *ereyante karakaragi, malalante jarijaridu*

## Sule Sankavva

Original Kannada verses for Ahalya Ballal's translations from Kalburgi, Dr M.M., ed. *Basavayugada Vachana Samputa*, Vol. 1. 3rd ed. Bengaluru: Karnataka Pustaka Pradhikara, 2016.

'Having accepted my fee from one man': *Otteya hididu mattotteya hidiye*

## Molige Mahadevi

Original Kannada verses for Ahalya Ballal's translations from Kalburgi, Dr M.M., ed. *Basavayugada Vachana Samputa*, Volume 1. 3rd ed. Bengaluru: Karnataka Pustaka Pradhikara, 2016.

'Why lose precious gold in collecting coins': *Kaanige hori kadavarava neegaletakke?*

'Whatever the seed sown, roots grow into the earth': *Aava beejava bittidadoo*

'The light born along the path of vastness': *Bayala holabinalli huttida belagu*

## Lingamma

Original Kannada verses for Ahalya Ballal's translations from Kalburgi, Dr M.M., ed. *Basavayugada Vachana Samputa*, Vol. 1. 3rd ed. Bengaluru: Karnataka Pustaka Pradhikara, 2016.

'Sir, once a body burns in a blaze, does it have any distress?': *Ayyaa, kicchinolage benda kaayakke acchugavunte?*

'Like a lamp on the threshold': *Hostilolagirisida jyothiyante olage noduvanu taane*

Sir, why don't they see': *Kangala munde maanikaviddu kaanalekariyarayyaa*

## Neelambike

Original Kannada verses for Ahalya Ballal's translations from Kalburgi, Dr M.M., ed. *Basavayugada Vachana Samputa*, Vol. 1. 3rd ed. Bengaluru: Karnataka Pustaka Pradhikara, 2016.

'Basava's wisdom has become free of all support': *Basavanarivu niradharavagittu*

'No one knows me': *Nannanaaroo ariyaru, naanu swargiyalla*

'Sir, I do not entangle myself': *Aadalillavayyaa naanu hennu roopa dharisi*

## Kalavve

Original Kannada verses for Ahalya Ballal's translations from Kalburgi, Dr M.M., ed. *Basavayugada Vachana Samputa*, Vol. 1. 3rd ed. Bengaluru: Karnataka Pustaka Pradhikara, 2016.

'Those who eat mutton, poultry and fish': *Kuri koli kirimeenu timbavarigella*

'Those without dedicated work are not devotees': *Krtya kaayakavilladavaru bhaktaralla*

## Amuge Rayamma

Original Kannada verses for Ahalya Ballal's translations from Kalburgi, Dr M.M., ed. *Basavayugada Vachana Samputa*, Vol. 1. 3rd ed. Bengaluru: Karnataka Pustaka Pradhikara, 2016.

'Everyone can read the vachanas': *Ellaroo oduvudu vachanangalu*

'Can you see the footsteps': *Heerolage hodavana hejleya kambavarunte*

'If you can that can soar to the sky': *Aakarshakke haruvange kola hangetakayya?*

'Does the sun make a distinction': *Suryange alli illi emba sandehavunte*

## Nagalambike

Original Kannada verses for Ahalya Ballal's translations from Kalburgi, Dr M.M., ed. *Basavayugada Vachana Samputa*, Vol. 1. 3rd ed. Bengaluru: Karnataka Pustaka Pradhikara, 2016.

'With the guru as my parents': *Shriguruve taayitandeyaagi, lingave patiyaagi*

## Jira Dei

'The mind grows watchful': *Janu dekhe manua thai*

'It stumps the imagination': *Akalpita mana stambibhuta bai*

'A boat adrift in an ocean of time': *Kala samudre boita bhase*

'As long as the body persists': *Yavat Kaya tavat maya*

## Muktabai

'Listen, from where has this anger come?': *Aho, krodh yave kothe?*

## Toral

'Jesal, think about it': *Jesal kari le vichaar*

## Liral

'Who styled this brittle body?': *Kaci ram kone ghadi tari kaya*

## Loyan

'Lakha, a woman, Loyan, says to you': *ji re laakhaa abalaa loyan tamane em bhane re ji*

'Lakha, want to dissolve in the Ultimate?': *ji re laakhaa brahma ma bhalavu hoy to*

## Kanhopatra

'No, my god, no!': *Nako Devaraya*

'My lord, I implore you': Varm Vairiyache haati

'Nearest to my soul': Jeevache jivlage maajhe krishnaai kanhaai

'You claim the grand title': *Patit paavan hmanaavisi aadhi*

## Madhabi Dasi

'Nanda's son, the prince of Braja': *Sri nandanandano se jagabandano*

'Krishna savours the hour': *Radhamadhaba bilasai punjaka maajha*

'The young and handsome Gaur dances': *Anande naachata sange bhakta*

## Meerabai

'rana i won't live within your walls': *ranaji ab na rahungi tori hatki . . .*

'i'm dyed the colour of my master': *mha girdhar rang rati, saiyan mha . . .*

'i sit awake the world sleeps': *ri mha baithyan jagan, jagat sab sovan . . .*

'struck by beauty i was struck by your beauty': *roop dekh ataki, tero roop dekh ataki . . .*

## Padmapriya

'O mind, do not forget the Guru's words': *Guru pada nu bhulibi mon taay*

## Bahinabai

Original Marathi verses from Abbott, Justin E. *Bahinabai: A Translation of Her Autobiography and Verses*. New Delhi: Motilal Banarsidass, 1985.

Abhang 175, 'For her milk, you serve the cow': *Doodhachiye chaade gayiche sevan*

Abhang 120,' Who plants grass in a forest?': *trun aranyant peravaya jaave*

Abhang 134, 'When I wind my ten senses around Hari's feet': *Daha indiriye hee govin haripadi*

Abhang 168, 'No darkness haunts': *Suryachiye ghari ghane jayaasi*

Abhang 180, 'Words and meanings belong to the visible realm': *shabdache bolne drishya he tovari*

Abhang 190, 'Here's pride. There's ignorance of the heart's ways': *jethe puso jave tethe abhiman*

## Taj Bibi

'He's a dashing trickster': *Chhail jo chhabila, sab rang mein rangila*

## Tarigonda Venkamamba

'My dear, see, the luminosity of this Light': *Jyoti velugu cunnadammā*

'What's 'bad', what's 'good'?': *Ceḍudaṇte nemi? Mañcidi yaṇte nemi?*

'To Him who lives on the Seshachalam peak': *śrī pannagādrivara śikharāgra vāsunakū* [Mutyala Harati]

## Sahajo

Originals sourced from https://sufinama.org/poets/sahjo-bai/all and Desai, Subhadra. *The Unfettered Note: Indian Women Seers and their Songs*. New Delhi: Indira Gandhi National Centre for the Arts and Aryan Books International, 2017.

'Ram? I could perhaps abandon him': *Ram tajoon pai guru na visarun*

'Into the mirage of doership': *Hari ne karm bharm bharamayau*

'Hari ensnared me': *Hari ne kutumb jal mein gheri*

'And again Hari bound me': *Fir Hari bandh-mukti gati laye*

'Hari did his damnedest': *Hari ne mo sun ap chhipayau*

## Daya

Original verses from Aveling, Henry and Friedlander, Peter, ed. and trans. *The Songs of Daya Bai: Daya Ki Bani.* New Delhi: Prestige Books, 2005.

from 'On Courage' (dohas 4–8):

'How shrill and sudden, how full of joy': *Sunat sabd neesaan ku man mein uthat umang*

from 'On Chanting Without Chantin'g (dohas 13–19):

'I sank at first into the depths of the underworld': *Pratham pethi pataal su dhamaki chadhe aakaas*

## Shija Laiobi

'Gouranga is compassion incarnate': *Kebale karunamaya e-ii abatar*

## Gavari Bai

'Repeat 'I am That! I am That! The Ultimate Truth!': *Soham soham brahma bhajile*

## Muddupalani

Three Verses from Rādhikā Sāntvanamu

'The Definition of Bad Poets': They know how to take a book apart: RS 1.6 *'Kukavi nindanamu'— pottamuna nundu salyambu lettivaichi*

'A Manifesto for New Poetry': Can your poems stand in the field, girl: RS 1.7 *'Navya kavya nirmana karanamu'—chelugam burva satkavulu chesina kabbamulenno yundanga*

Worldly stuff and worldly ties may be given up: RS 1.74 *Sommuliyyavachchu sammandamiyyavachchu*

## Gangasati

'Let Mighty Meru Rumble and Shake': *Meru Dage*

'Neither Joy nor Woe Raises a Hiccup': *harakh ne shok ni na aave jene hedki*

'Keep it hidden': *Vastu raakho gupat*

'Abandon wandering, once the self awakes': *abhyaas jaagyaa pachhi bahu bhamvu nahi re*

## Liral

'Tell me, guruji, how do I worship': *Ha ha re guruji! Kaho bhajan kem kariye*

## Peero

All originals from Das, Sant Vijendra, ed. *Sant Kavyitree Maa Peero*. Panchkula, Haryana: Sutlej Prakasha, 2011.

'Flung in the company of foolish zealots': *Jahilan de vass pai Rabba, maru-maru ju aap pukarde nee.*

'They bring me no profit, these men': *Nafa nahi ehnaa manasan te vich sara de bann bahaiya mai.*

'My lover is casteless': *Sa-een mera ajaat hai, na Hindu Turka.*

'The lover's presence, Peero can sense': *Peero sa-een majood hai, so subnee than-een.*

'Let us go where the mendicants live, come Peero!': *Chalo nee Peero chaliye, jahaan sadhu rehte.*

## Andavan Pichhai

Originals from YouTube

https://www.youtube.com/watch?v=I_hG18vRLrE

https://www.google.com/search?q=pittan+endralum&oq=pittan+endralum&aqs=chrome..69i57j0i10i15i22i30.4781j1j7&sourceid=chrome&ie=UTF-8#fpstate=ive&vld=cid:b5433514,vid:OrSqOGYtr2k

'Mind, if you want to dance with me': *Maname inimel*

'Call him a madman. Call him a ghost': *Pittan endralum*

## Indira Devi

Originals from Devi, Indira and Roy, Dilip Kumar. *Indiranjali*, Vol. 1 and 2. Pune: Harikrishna Mandir Trust, 2000.

Unpublished translations based on renditions by Sri Dilip Kumar Roy

'My heart longs for you': Hai dil mein asha tujhe main chahun

'To what land do you belong, traveller?': Kaun desh se aaye musafir, kaun desh hai jaana?

'Tell me, friend, who enters my courtyard?': *Sakhi ri! Aangana mere kaho to kaun yeh aaya?*

'She's stormed out of her childhood home': *Babul ka ghar chhod piya ghar Meera aaj chali*

## Section Two

## Narsinh Mehta

'What merits have I earned to be born a woman?': *kon punye kari naar hun avatari?*

## Kabir

Unpublished translation [forthcoming in *Burn Down Your House: Provocations from Kabir*, Speaking Tiger, by Shabnam Virmani]

'What a match she found, that crazy girl': *Ghano Rijaayo Vo Baanwari Ne*

## Guru Arjan Dev

'My Lord's name is without limit and beyond price': *Har har naam apaar amolee*

## Section Three

## Garba

'Your energy is unknowable, Ambika!': *Shakti nahin taari kalaay re o ambikaa*

'You are dark and auspicious, mother': Tu kaali ne kalyaani re ma jyaan joy tyaan jogamaaya

'With a quarter in my hand, I had gone to Pavagadh': Paavali lai ne hu *to paavaagadh gai'ti*

## Yellamma

'You who were born to be a goddess Yellamma': *Huttiya bande Yellammanaagi*

## Gondhal

'Beyond the river lies the mountain': *Nadichya palyaad aaichaa dongur*

## Ramprasad Sen

'All right Kali, now I'm going to eat you up': *Ebar Kali tomay khabo*

'Death, be off, what can you do': Tui ja re, ki korbi shomon

'Mind you don't know how to farm': Monre krishi kaaj jano na

'Mind my dear, I fall at your feet': Monre tor choron dhori

'I get a kick out of you, Ma': *Je hoy pashaner meye*

## Naryana Guru

'. . . Look at you, traipsing through Mount Kailasa': from *Kali Natakam*

## Subramania Bharati

Prayer to Parashakti: *Parashakti Vanakkam* [from *Panchali Sabatham*]

An Appeal to Mahashakti: Mahashkthikku Vinnappam

Kannamma, My Treasure: *Chinnan Chiru Kiliye*

A Piece of Land: *Kaani Nilam*

## Prathibha Nandakumar

'Pootani, the demon, once tried to feed baby Krishna': *Vishada mole unisidare saavinallu saarthakya* [from '*Kshetrapala Samarchitaa*']

# Copyright Acknowledgements

master. What can I say'; 'Why cross the boundary'; 'You tell him about subtlety'; 'I'll serve you as best I can'.

**V. Narayana Rao**: for translations 'A Woman to Her Reluctant Lover'; 'When I'm done being angry'; 'He's the master. What can I say'; 'Why cross the boundary'; 'You tell him about subtlety'; 'I'll serve you as best I can'.

**Rachel Fell McDermott**: for translations 'Who is this/ dressed like a crazy woman'; 'Kali/ is everything You do misleading?'; 'I know, I know, Mother'; 'How will You rescue me, Tara?'; 'So, forgetful Mahadeva'; 'Oh hey, All-Destroyer'; 'Let's be girls, Ma'. Reproduced with permission of the Licensor through PLSclear.

Scan QR code to access the
Penguin Random House India website